WILL CARLING

MY AUTOBIOGRAPHY

WILL CARLING

MY AUTOBIOGRAPHY

Will Carling
with Paul Ackford

Hodder & Stoughton

First published in Great Britain in 1998
by Hodder and Stoughton
A division of Hodder Headline PLC

10 9 8 7 6 5 4 3 2 1

A CIP catalogue record for this title
is available from the British Library.

ISBN: 0 340 69658 3

Typeset by Rowland Phototypesetting Ltd, Bury St Edmunds, Suffolk
Printed and bound in Great Britain by
Clays Ltd, St Ives PLC, Bungay, Suffolk

Hodder and Stoughton Ltd
A division of Hodder Headline PLC
338 Euston Road
London NW1 3BH

CONTENTS

CONTENTS

Acknowledgements

This book arose from the bowels of the Petersham Hotel in which I spent many happy years preparing for internationals with England. Paul Ackford and I used to tuck ourselves away in the boardroom next to the wine cellars, drink endless cups of coffee and wander down memory lane. It was fun.

I am grateful to Paul for making sense of my recollections on and off the pitch, and to the Petersham's Greville Dare and Rebecca Hornor for the coffee.

Thanks also to my publisher Roddy Bloomfield for his advice and support. With over a thousand books to his name, Roddy's experience was invaluable when it came to tweaking the final version.

And, finally, a word to Mum and Dad. I haven't been the easiest son to have around, but your unconditional help through the various ups and downs has meant a lot.

Photograph Acknowledgements

The author and publisher would like to thank the following for permission to reproduce their copyright photographs: AllSport, Colorsport, Rex Features.

—1—
PROLOGUE

FIFTEEN minutes to go and you're on your own. That's when the adrenaline really kicks in. Coach, manager, physio, even the guys on the bench, have left, leaving fifteen men to do battle. Outside the England dressing room you can hear the crowd gaining in excitement. Inside, the realisation grows that this is a match England cannot afford to lose – 3 March 1991, England against France at Twickenham, the Grand Slam decider, the game that changed my life.

The time for chat is all but gone. The night before I had slipped handwritten notes under the doors of the players' rooms at the Petersham Hotel. Nothing earth-shattering, just a few words on what they meant to me as people, how much the country was behind them, how good they were as players. It was more for my own peace of mind than anything else. Dean Richards probably still hasn't read his.

By now the forwards have wandered off into the bathing area, an annex off the main room, to hit a few scrums and psych themselves up. Huge men, ponderous, controlled, but with the tension etched across their faces. Their job is to prepare for the contact, those fiery opening minutes which set the tone of the match. Take a backward step at that first line-out, that first scrum, and you may as well concede victory there and then. As I talk to the backs, to Rob Andrew, Jerry Guscott, Rory Underwood, and the rest, I can hear the thuds as the forwards slam into the scrummaging machine and the contact pads.

Brian Moore articulates the need for aggression. Until we leave the sanctity of that changing room, Mooro will chop away, goading, needling, asking if the guys are up for it. The questions are superfluous. You can see it in their eyes. What you want is an intensity, a commitment which stays one step away from madness. On the edge but not beyond it. If it isn't there, there is nothing you can do to get it back.

The atmosphere becomes more charged as the players withdraw into themselves, each rehearsing the mental and physical routines with which they're comfortable. An hour previously, as we got off the bus and walked through the corridor of fans to get to the changing room, we were guardedly relaxed. There was still time to luxuriate in the moment, to read the programme, to recognise that you are representing your country, to look round at the huge Twickenham stands, to sniff the wind, to imagine the first tackle, the first high ball. But as kick-off arrives, those images are replaced by questions. Can I cope? What if we lose? How good is my opposite number? Are we ready? But only for a moment. Then the routine takes over, collapsing any doubts.

Ten to go and the forwards have returned from their private corporate warm-up. Beads of sweat break out on Peter Winterbottom's head. Paul Ackford and Wade Dooley shuffle across together, each gaining physical and emotional support from the proximity of the other. Deano waddles forward, socks down, a massive slab of a man, the bedrock of this team.

I call the guys into a huddle, the contact, the closeness important. Now is not the time for impassioned speeches, for rhetoric of any kind. Most minds are closed at this stage, unreceptive to new information. In any case, a passionate call to arms has never been my style. My concerns are with detail, line-out signals, scrummage calls, communication, the strike moves. This is what

I do on Friday night at the team meeting. Without the instinctive reaction to signals and calls, the team will not function.

I check that there are no misunderstandings, that everyone is working from the same script, and I run through the key points. No penalties, do not kick ball away, especially to Serge Blanco the French full-back, watch France round the fringes, don't get involved if all hell breaks loose, provoke but do not retaliate. Then it's time for a few sharpeners, quick reaction sprints to make sure that people are switched on.

The hugging becomes stronger. For a time we sway, roller-coaster-like, as Jason Leonard grabs Brian Moore and pulls the circle with him. Players are chipping in with their own exhortations. Most are meaningless. 'Come on. Let's do it. We've got to win.' But it's not the comments that matter. It's the way they are said. Today is going to be OK. No one is gazing at the floor. Heads are up and players are looking away from their playing partners, which is another good sign. Mike Teague searches for, and locks eyes with, Jerry Guscott. No words are necessary.

This is the best bit, the sense of togetherness, the sense of destiny, the culmination of years of training in the wet and the mud. This is what we are all there for, the chance to bring England their first Grand Slam for eleven years with guys you care about. No one else, nothing else, matters. Just fifteen players about to be judged in the rarefied atmosphere which international sport offers. That's as stimulating as it gets. Nothing else comes close. When players talk about the buzz of international rugby this is what they mean. Fear, anticipation, fatigue, danger, drama, reward, humiliation, pain, disappointment. All are on offer and only you can affect which ones you receive.

A knock on the door and the referee shouts 'Two minutes!' The circle comes together for one last tight grasp and is broken. One or two make that last trip to the loo, too much liquid taken on board to ward off the dangers of dehydration. The place is calmer now. Jerry Guscott and Dean Richards shake hands, Paul Ackford pats Jason Leonard on the back, Simon Hodgkinson, the goal-kicker, is chorused with 'Good lucks'. The intimacy has gone. The team has adopted its public persona.

The dressing-room door opens and the light and sound smash their way in. So much space, so much noise. The tunnel is short, no more than ten metres long, not enough to allow a gradual adjustment from a private domain to a public arena. The crowd, alerted by the French team who have run onto the pitch, are desperate to make their mark on the day. The sound builds, but it is not until they see the white shirts of England that they really let rip. The roar as I step onto the field is deafening, comforting, forbidding.

And a release. The trick now is to keep composed, to channel the adrenaline rush. The anthems have yet to be played and there is no point in getting over-aroused. Usually, I'd keep an eye out for new caps, make sure that they are still on this planet, but this team is characterised by age and experience, not youth. 'Dad's Army', the tabloid headline-writers labelled us, too old, too slow, past it. And they were right. But tell that to France. Ask them if they would prefer to face callow youngsters, or battle-hardened veterans.

The national anthem begins and I sing. It's another key, another familiar ritual to make use of. Queen and country are important to me but it is more than that. Behind the words lies the feeling that 65,000 people are willing you on, imploring you to make a statement on their behalf. Their endorsement is humbling, and lurking at the back of your mind is the know-ledge that many in the stands, no matter how rich or successful, would give anything to stand in my boots, to lead their country against France in a Grand Slam decider.

It was never the same again. Either for me or the sport. That match was a watershed, catapulting rugby into the public's imagination and me, as captain of a successful national sports team, into the spotlight. Maybe the public were starved of suc-cess. Maybe it was just a quirk of history, but rugby raced ahead in the next few years. England's performance in the World Cup, staged for the first time in Britain and Ireland later that year, when they reached the final only to be beaten by Australia, cranked up the interest several notches higher.

Eighteen and a half million viewers watched that match, many of them women. Hairdressers arranged for TV sets to be installed in salons so that folk could follow the game as they enjoyed their cut and blow dry. And the lives of some of the players who played on that grey November afternoon changed irrevocably, lighting the torches for the current generation who now enjoy rewards and largesse undreamed of in those so-called amateur days. Rob Andrew, Rory Underwood, Jeremy Guscott and Dean Richards became cult figures, sportsmen of real stature, sought after by the feature writers, women's magazines, and the team who send out the invitations for BBC's Sports Personality of the Year.

And the sport could not cope. The ridiculous state of affairs by which players were generating all this enthusiasm and money for the game, yet were forbidden by amateur regulations to benefit themselves, was seen for what it was. A sham. I told the authorities that, we all did. Our experience in South Africa, where players were openly paid for playing, was reported back to Twickenham. Did they listen? Did they heck! Their backwardness in coming forward is the reason the game is in the state it is today, why for the last three years there has been a pitched battle between the players, the clubs and the Rugby Football Union.

My life changed, too. I was viewed by many within the RFU as the devil incarnate. As captain I felt compelled to take a stance, to say what I believed about the sport and the people in it. I never guessed the trouble it would cause. I have always had a problem with authority and I rebelled. The run-ins were bitter and many. I had blazing rows with many RFU committee men, especially Dudley Wood, the RFU Secretary. On one occasion, a little the worse for wear after an international against Ireland in Dublin, I grabbed a senior administrator by the throat, threatening to punch his lights out, but was eventually pulled off and restrained by Rob Andrew.

My various spats have been well documented in the media – the differences of opinion with England manager Jack Rowell, Lions boss Fran Cotton, Harlequins director of rugby Dick Best, Australian winger David Campese, the Scots. The best known was the 'old farts' affair, the time when I was sacked as England captain in May 1995 when off-camera, and I thought off-mike too, I labelled the fifty-seven-strong RFU committee old farts, only to be reinstated three days later. Until now I have never come clean about what really happened behind those closed committee room doors, in the murky corridors of power, on and off the playing field. But now is the time.

Time, too, to take stock of the impact rugby has had on my private life. The sport has given me more than I could ever dream, but it has demanded a great deal as well. Thanks to Jon Holmes, who takes care of the personal side of things, rugby has made me comparatively comfortable. By the age of twenty-two I was driving around in a top of the range Mercedes. Rugby has also enabled me to set up my own company. Insights has evolved as a business and now provides motivational and leadership seminars for managers and business executives. Then there are the invitations to film premières, tables at top restaurants and the chance to meet people like John Cleese and Hugh Laurie. All of that has been fantastic and never, for one moment, would I opt for the days when I was an impoverished young man beginning to forge a career in the army or working for an oil company. Anyone who states that the problems which notoriety can bring far outweigh the advantages is talking nonsense.

But there have been bad times. My relationship with and marriage to Julia Smith was hurtfully and publicly discussed in the tabloid newspapers for weeks at a time. Speculation over my friendship with Diana, Princess of Wales, was so intense that I was forced into hiding in a flat in London's Covent Garden. Those were dark days. My phone number was known only to two of my closest friends during that period and if I went out at all, which was rare, I always checked cars and loitering pedestrians to see if they were journalists. Never once did I take a taxi back to the front door of the apartment block, choosing instead to be dropped off to walk the last half mile and shake off any would-be pursuers.

I was so confused that I eventually sought therapy from Alice Cleese, John's wife, and she as much as any person has enabled me to understand myself, to put relationships and events into perspective. A period of happiness followed with Ali Cockayne. Our son Henry Alexander was born on 5 October 1997, but sadly Ali and I did not work out as we both had hoped and we are no longer together. And now my rugby career has finished and I am amazed at how little I have missed several aspects of what had hitherto dominated my life.

What follows is my story. I have tried to be truthful, to be fair to the people and places, the conversations, the issues and the events. I have told it as it was: turbulent, confusing, painful, rewarding and, I hope, interesting.

— 2 —
BREASTS, BULLYING AND PETER WINTERBOTTOM

RUGBY and me were an accident waiting to happen. Literally. Still in nappies, Mum took me to watch Dad play when I was eighteen months old. Curious to discover what precisely was interesting a dozen or so grown men who were leaping on top of each other in search of an object I couldn't quite make out, I wandered onto the pitch to get a closer look. Just then the ball was freed up and play swept towards me. Mum rushed onto the pitch and snatched me out of harm's way but not before she received a belt on her chin which required four stitches. Didn't worry me much, though. Apparently I thought it was hilarious. I must have found something attractive about all those people crashing about and banging into each other. Still do.

That notion informed my first attempts to play the sport itself which were captured on video when I was two and a half and Marcus, my brother, was four. The film was shot in the garden of a house in Hong Kong where we lived. The game was pretty simple. Dad kicked the ball down the garden and Marcus and I chased after it to fetch it back. But it was more than a game for me. I had to get to that ball first and if it meant shoving Marcus out of the way then that was no problem. Marcus and

I had that kind of relationship. Bumpy. Although I followed him to prep school and then on to Sedbergh, we were never very close emotionally. Marcus was a rebel at school, always up to mischief. He didn't take his work seriously and managed to attract trouble, never quite knowing when it was time to bale out. He was threatened with expulsion from Sedbergh when he was caught drinking, which didn't go down too well with our parents. He also actively disliked sport in those days. My infatuation with all things sporting must have been difficult to live with. He probably thought I was the kid brother from hell and, while he never appeared resentful or jealous, he grabbed every opportunity to show who was boss.

There were many clashes between us, most quite incidental, but occasionally our sibling rivalry careered completely out of control, invariably sparked by trivial events. One such incident happened at a friend's house as Marcus and I were getting ready for bed. I came into the bathroom to find him cleaning his teeth at the wash-basin. As I sidled up to do mine, Marcus twisted his body to prevent me getting to the sink.

'There's not room for both of us in here,' he said.

'Don't be silly. Of course there is. Move over and let me clean my teeth as well.'

Sulkily, reluctantly, Marcus slunk out of the bathroom, only to return seconds later and belt me over the head, knocking me to the ground. It took me years to pay him back, but I did. Again, a momentous incident grew out of an incongruous setting. We were on the beach during a family holiday in Italy and Marcus was annoying the hell out of me chucking sand about. I had asked him to stop but he was having none of it.

'Throw sand at me one more time, Marcus, and you're going to get it.' The warning was as clear as I could make it but Marcus wasn't getting the message. Still the sand kept coming my way, so I whacked him and this time Marcus was knocked out cold. Intolerant? Perhaps. Belligerent? Probably. Obnoxious? Definitely. The Carling character was shaping up nicely.

At home when the weather was bad I used to invent fantasy

rugby matches indoors. I would mark out pitches with a box of sticks, plonk two chairs at either end for the posts and play England against the Rest. That kept me entertained for hours. I didn't need anyone else, just the box of sticks and my own imagination. During the holidays I would make a point of searching out a quiet space so that I could get on with my series of matches on my own. If Marcus came to find me, I would up sticks for another room where I wouldn't be disturbed.

When I grew tired of rugby, which wasn't often, cricket or football would grab my attention. Dad used to say that if he ever wanted to find me he would look first in the garden, and then at another area where I loved to knock a tennis ball up against a wall. If not there, the next best bet was in front of the television where I would be devouring the latest sporting occasion on BBC's *Grandstand*. That evocative signature tune has haunted me throughout my playing career. This was in the days before satellite television, when the BBC had a monopoly of the great global sporting events, and you just knew that the tune would herald another afternoon of compelling drama. I found that magical, a trigger for a whole range of emotions. Years later I used to organise England's routine on a Saturday afternoon so that I could listen to the first five minutes of *Grandstand* in the team hotel, and watch the flashbacks from the great rugby occasions of the past before going downstairs to deliver a pep talk. It never failed to set my heart pumping.

We were always a rugby family. Dad played for Cardiff, Bath, Blackheath and Cornwall. He was good enough to be called up for an England trial but a back injury prevented him from attending. Our shared infatuation with rugby was a natural bond, but I've always admired my father for other reasons, mostly from a distance. Tours of duty as a lieutenant-colonel in the Army Air Corps meant that he was never home for long. But there were a few perks. On a couple of occasions he left the car in the garage, choosing instead to visit the school by heli-copter. The reaction of the other kids as my father strolled towards me with the blades of the helicopter still rotating made up for his occasional absences. He was very matter of fact, reluctant to make a scene or indulge in unnecessary displays of emotion. Marcus became very upset once when he was dropped off to begin his second term at boarding school. As we pulled away in the car, Marcus ran after us, screaming, begging to be taken home. But Dad would have none of it. 'Either you walk back or I'll carry you back,' he said. It wasn't as callous as it sounds. A decision had been made, one which Marcus had been a party to. There was no alternative, so it was purely a question of confirming the contract.

I could understand that attitude. I respected Dad's level-headedness and his consistency. When he told us that another indiscretion would result in us being sent to our room, he meant it. There would be no argument, no debate. Dad and I got on well with each other, any potential for trouble defused by a mutual love of sport. When he was home from the army we would often jog together and he still regularly trots round Clapham Common early in the morning. We were also on the same wavelength emotionally. He understood that I was instinctively a loner and he did not mind that I rarely asked for advice.

Mum was different. Until I went to prep school she was always around when it mattered, dishing out the meals, washing the kit, but she was never the earth mother type. She was far more volatile than that. She is a powerful, dominant character and found it difficult to accept that I was growing up. From a placid two-year-old who only ever smiled and ate, and a similarly easy-going five-year-old, I became much more independent when I went to prep school. That marked the turning point in our relationship. Afterwards we were like two magnets repelling each other, both single-minded, stubborn individuals who fought to get our own way and that did not make for a restful home life. Mum had interests other than raising a family. She worked as a personal assistant to headmasters in two different schools before turning her hand to interior design. If I inherited my stubborn streak from Mum, she also passed on her love of colour and detail.

We had few family rituals but one which was sacrosanct occurred every Saturday lunch-time when Dad would make beefburgers and we would pretend to enjoy them. Actually, that's not fair. Over the years he became a dab hand at the hamburger-making business. Other than that, the main relax-ation we took *en famille* was to set out on long walks accom-panied by various dogs. It was a pretty stable and happy environment. If my parents ever argued it was Mum who would end up apologising. There's no doubt that they were, and are, very fond of each other. Mum thinks dad is the bee's knees and he idolises her in a different way. They are good together. When it comes to the big decisions my father generally gets his way but it is invariably my mother who makes things work. If he puts his foot down that is it, but it is a fairly equal relationship.

My childhood was pretty topsy-turvy because Dad's career meant that we were always on the move, packing and unpacking. I have no memories of a particular house or location, or even of any friends. It wasn't an issue when I was young. I knew no other life and it was only after meeting and settling down with Ali Cockayne that I started to understand how dys-functional the whole process was. Ali was brought up in Leices-tershire. Her parents still live there and she can call on friends she first met when she was a little girl. I lacked that sense of place. We moved house twenty-five times, once for each year Dad remained in the army, acquiring our first family house when I was twenty and already at Durham University. But by then it was too late. I had lost the chance to set down roots and establish close relationships.

As a result, school assumed a disproportionate significance for me and I couldn't wait to go to Terra Nova prep school, aged seven. Intrigued by the size of the buildings, the colours, the newness of it all, I waltzed up the stairs to my dormitory with matron without a backwards glance at my mother. But night-time was different. Stuck in a room with eleven other boys, none of whom I knew, I realised that I wasn't going back to Mum and Dad, that this was to be my home for the foreseeable future. The brave little soldier routine began to crumble. Slowly, making as little noise as possible, I crept under the sheets to the foot of my bed and started to sob.

'You've been crying,' my neighbour said, when I eventually surfaced. 'I heard you.'

'No, I haven't,' I lied, in a vain attempt at bravado.

Terra Nova offered many salutary lessons and the most shocking lingers on to this day. I've yet to shake off the feelings of guilt which the recollection evokes. I was in the habit of bullying two other pupils. I was big for my age, able to make other people do what I wanted because of my size, and I enjoyed the feeling of power. I never resorted to physical abuse, never had to, and the bullying amounted to getting two lads to fetch and carry for me but it was still abusive and unacceptable. Except that I didn't see it like that. All I understood was that it was my first term in a new school and it was important to create an environment in which I could prosper.

Halfway through the year I became aware that this was not the way to behave and it had a massive effect on me. I had asked one of the boys to fetch my boots and was stunned by the look on his face. It was a mixture of resentment, anger and sadness. He did not need to articulate how he felt at being told to skivvy for me, his general demeanour did the job for him. It was an incredibly poignant moment. On the one hand I was disgusted with myself for exploiting my dominance but there was still part of me which despised my victim's weakness. I didn't come close to rationalising it in those terms aged seven. All I registered was a level of discomfort which persuaded me to stop the bullying. But the confusion took ages to die away.

Terra Nova was educational for other reasons. I'd like to say my interest in art was born out of a spiritual awakening to the aesthetic beauty of life. But it was more prosaic than that. My mother was very artistic and an influence of sorts but my love of painting, especially watercolours, was ignited by a pair of the most wonderful breasts in the world. Terra Nova employed an attractive young woman to teach art. She was a goddess, and the highlights of the week for me were the moments when she leaned over my desk to suggest an improvement to my painting. The smell of her scent, her warmth and vivacity and, of course, the proximity of her chest convinced an unworldly, shy eleven-year-old that the artist's life would be all the fulfilment he would ever want.

I devoted myself to art to the extent that I went to Sedbergh on an art scholarship, worth all of £45, but there my infatuation with the subject ended. A crusty mouldy old male art teacher did not quite have the same impact. That, plus his interest in oils, which I couldn't stand, stunted my artistic development. I still paint occasionally, still enjoy it, but never with the passion of the old days. She was gorgeous.

If Sedbergh killed off one avenue, it opened another. Rugby was a religion there and my arrival coincided with their celebration of a hundred years of rugby. There was plenty to shout about. Twelve Sedbergh old boys have played for England, including three who have gone on to captain their country. My illustrious predecessors in the most prestigious job which English rugby has to offer were Wavell Wakefield and John Spencer. The school is still churning out quality players. Will Greenwood, the Leicester centre who replaced me in the England side, learnt his trade there.

There was nothing fashionable about Sedbergh. Perched on the edge of the Lake District, in an idyllic rural setting on the Yorkshire Moors, the school was one of the last in the country to allow its pupils to jettison their short trousers. Black trousers, blue open-necked shirt and blazer was the dress of the day when I was there. Jeans were a no-no at all times and even outside school hours we weren't allowed to wear so-called 'home clothes'. We had to make do with gym kit in relaxed mode.

Discipline was strict, with prefects able to punish younger boys. A particular favourite was to get pupils to climb up Winder's hill before breakfast. Winder's was more of a mountain than a hill and it usually took the best part of an hour to reach the top and return. Once at the summit the miscreant had to bring back a pressing of the trigonometrical point as proof that he had completed the task. I took a more devious route when it came to my turn to be punished. A bright spark had made a cast of the trig point which I borrowed. Then it was just a matter of snoozing under a tree outside the school gates for an hour, before running the last 300 yards to reach the feet of the prefect suitably breathless and penitent.

Arriving at Sedbergh from prep school with some rugby credibility was almost a mystical experience. The new boys were taken down to the First XV pitch and told that the school hadn't lost for five years or whatever. It was surreal. There we were, a group of wide-eyed youngsters facing an empty patch of grass to which an act of obeisance was half-expected. Everything was designed to magnify the status of those who eventually represented the First XV. The whole school turned out to watch them play and the pitch itself was out of bounds to those who had not achieved that honour. There was even a different blazer awarded to the pupils who gained their First XV colours. Brown opened doors and provided privileges. Blue was Joe Average.

The symbolism surrounding rugby at Sedbergh affected me deeply. Overwhelmed, but curiously excited, I was won over on that first day and tried hard to inject that sense of reverence into playing for England. There is nothing wrong with placing sport and achievement on a pedestal. England have never quite managed that and it is one of the reasons why they have failed to fulfil potential on a world stage.

You only have to watch New Zealand and South Africa knocking seven bells out of each other to understand the cultural and social significance of the silver fern and the springbok emblems. Sport in those countries is not something to be dismissed as intellectually feeble and therefore worthless, but celebrated along with excellence in other disciplines. Mystique and pageantry are part of the induction process. Old All Blacks take time out to sit with new All Blacks for their first few games. All the old stories are trotted out, the tales of derring-do, to make them feel part of the great tradition. It's camp-fire stuff. Eventually the ingenues are totally assimilated into the group, fully aware of the responsibility and privilege of being an All Black. It has taken New Zealand many years to get to that stage but the edge it gives them in the important matches is crucial. And it all starts with believing that what you are doing has value. That was Sedbergh's way.

Yet there was also a downside to sport at Sedbergh. The perks and status associated with competence on the rugby pitch precluded the possibility of a normal existence. For the first two years I was not allowed to play with boys of my own age. Right from the start I was put in with the year above. You can imagine how that went down with my peer group. I arrive at a new school, desperate just to fit in and learn the ropes, and within the first week I am whisked away to train with boys whom I never encountered in the classroom. Not only did that alienate my classmates, the guys in the year above were also fed up with this interloper who thought he could mix it with them.

I hated it. Sport is one of the best times for getting to know a bunch of mates and I never had that chance. Then Catch 22 came into operation. Lacking common ground, I retreated into my shell, turning away from those I wanted to befriend, which exacerbated the situation. My quietness and natural reserve were interpreted as arrogance, enlarging the divide. I found it all incredibly difficult and upsetting. So upsetting that I went up to one of the masters in a bid to get reintegrated with my classmates.

'Why can't I play with my own age group?' I whined.

'Because you're talented enough to play with that lot, and it's good for you,' came the reply.

I felt like telling him it wasn't good for me at all, that it was quite the opposite, that I resented it, him and the school for putting me in that situation, but I didn't. Those are not the types of conversations you have with your teacher at thirteen. So I got on with it and when, during my third year, I eventually caught up with my age group, I found that I was enjoying the notoriety. Opinions and prejudices had been formed. There was nothing I could do to affect those and it was enjoyable being singled out as special.

Sedbergh was fun in other ways. Over the years, quite how no one knew, an illegal drinking den known as the Epicure had established itself. It was an invitation-only club and a much sought-after honour. King Epi, a pupil elected by his peers from one year to the next, would nominate a sixth-former to the club, and then the two of them would vote in a third member, and the three would agree on a fourth, and so on until about thirteen places were filled each year. We used to meet round the back of a restaurant near the school, sneak up the back stairs, drink as much as we could, put it all on the tab, and settle up at the end of the week. It was all done on trust and the consequences were hilarious. Often we staggered back to school, completely wrecked, to take evening prayers. Prefects would be swaying and belching all over the place. Some of the masters must have known what was going on but never really confronted us about it. Perhaps condoning the club was their way of allowing pupils to take responsibility for their own actions. If so, it worked because, despite the odd minor indiscretion, there were never any serious abuses. When I left there was a bar at the school and everything was above board, but it wasn't nearly so much fun.

At least drinking had its own set of rules which I knew about. Girls were not nearly so straightforward. Sedbergh was an all-boys school when I was there, isolated geographically, so the opportunities for chance meetings with them were almost non-existent. Boy-meets-girl encounters were institutionalised, part of the curriculum. Each year the Sedbergh sixth-form boys met up for a dance with their female contemporaries from Casterton, a girls' school twelve miles away. I knew nothing about girls, didn't have a clue. I had seen a few in magazines but that was about it. The dances were excruciatingly painful. The girls were almost predatory. Rugby was a currency they understood, and success at it made you a target. It seemed to me as if they careered onto the dance floor thinking, 'Let's get a rugby boy. My friends are bound to know him.' I am probably doing the Casterton girls a grave injustice but that's the way I felt. The contact was so contrived, so short-lived, that it was impossible to behave normally and it unnerved me completely.

What? Make conversation with a girl? How? What do you talk about? I was so unworldly and pathetic that I relied on an intermediary to give me confidence to meet my first girlfriend. Caroline Tucker was the sister of one of the guys in the rugby team and I asked her brother to find out whether she liked me because I did not have the guts or the social skills to do so myself. That's how wimpish I was. For a long time afterwards I found it difficult to relate to women. I used to see women as sex. Would they or wouldn't they? That's all girls were. Everyone I met, that was the dominant question, whether she was forty or sixteen. Thankfully, I have since grown up but even three or four years ago, dinner with a group of women was a chore. I would much rather have spent an evening with a few mates. Sedbergh contributed to that unease. The exclusively male environment in which we lived and were educated ensured that women remained almost alien creatures for me and when I did get to know girls at university and beyond I was still uncomfortable and unnatural in their company.

Sedbergh was where I first became interested in the notion of leadership. The First XV captain was given a captain's book in which to record the details of each game, the composition of the side and a summary. There was no set pattern to follow and it was left up to the individual to include thoughts and opinions if he wanted. The book was jealously guarded and handed down from captain to captain with a certain solemnity. No one else was allowed to read it, another example of a Sedbergh tradition which on the surface appeared unremarkable but which became something of significance to those entrusted with maintaining it.

I eventually got to read the captain's book in my last year. Oddly enough, I had already captained England Schools before leading the Sedbergh side twice in my final term. Andrew Harle, who later became my best man when Julia and I married, had custody of the book before I did. I had played under Andrew and we had enjoyed much success, going through the year unbeaten until the final game against Loretto which we lost. The defeat meant more to Andrew than a season of victories. 'Much as it would have been wonderful to have had an unbeaten season,' he wrote, 'the players learned more about themselves and developed more as people from that one match.' He was right, of course, something I experienced later when England lost important matches in Grand Slam deciders and World Cup finals but, even at the time, I remember thinking it was a pretty advanced comment from a seventeen-year-old.

I would love to report a comment of incisive brilliance when it came to my turn to write in the book. Admittedly there wasn't a great deal of scope, as my two matches resulted in defeats against the Anti-Assassins and the Luddites, both of which were men's teams, but my effort was still cringe-making. 'I owe everything to the coach and I owe everything to everyone,' were the words under my name. Not the most profound or auspicious of beginnings to a life where every utterance, every action would be dissected and debated.

Those two matches in charge pitted me against two men who would feature heavily later on in my career. Nigel Melville, now director of rugby at Wasps, and Peter Winterbottom both turned out for the Luddites against Sedbergh. I ended up playing with the pair of them for England but nothing was further from my mind that afternoon. Winters had just returned from the 1983 British Lions tour to New Zealand and I thought he was a god. It was exactly the same feeling as when we were brought down to the First XV pitch on our first day. Then the boys who were representing the school appeared huge, not just physically but in terms of achievement. Ditto with Winters. I knew he was for real, I had played against him that afternoon at school, but the contact did not destroy his mythical status. He had played for England. England. Run out in front of thousands of people, competed against the best other nations could offer, and done it all on the telly. I felt as far away from him as I did from those sixth-formers. Within four years I was his team-mate.

3

GEOFF COOKE AND THE KILLING HOUSE

MY immediate concerns on leaving Sedbergh were Durham University, a psychology degree and the army. Very soon they narrowed to the army. My rugby stagnated at Durham. I spent my first year there at full-back, the position I had played in my final season at Sedbergh, but the difference between the two experiences was enormous. Many of Durham's opponents on the circuit were men's teams. And tough ones at that. They were peppered with granite-hard characters from the small mining communities and it wasn't considered too sensible to play in haphazard fashion against them. Caution was the watchword and it was not something I was used to. Instead of running everything, as you are encouraged to do in the idealistic world of schoolboy rugby, I was coached to kick, to play safety-first rugby. It was a profoundly unsatisfactory introduction to the senior game and one which I would try to change, with little success, when I eventually graduated into the full England side.

At one stage I was depressed enough seriously to consider giving up the sport altogether. I've always kept myself fit throughout the summer in preparation for the following season but in that first summer at Durham I did nothing. Then I went

21

back to Sedbergh to play in an old boys' game and was rejuvenated. The familiar faces and surroundings brought back memories of the fun I had had there. The desire returned, as did the determination, and I resolved to give it another go. I was probably expecting too much in my first year after a decent schoolboy career, and I'm sure there was more than a touch of the little-fish-big-pond syndrome. I was very comfortable in my final year at Sedbergh, comfortable and successful, with a handle on everything and everyone. To some extent Durham was like starting again. I half planned for that and knew the transition would be awkward but I did not expect rugby to provide the early difficulties.

There were compensations, though. And meeting Donald was one of them. I arrived at Durham on an army scholarship. Marcus and my father had carved out careers in the army and I was destined to follow them into the Royal Regiment of Wales. The SAS was the ultimate fascination, to see whether I could handle myself in the toughest of environments under various constraints. I'd love to have found out how I would have reacted on some of the SAS training weeks, whether walking across the Brecon Beacons, lonely, freezing cold, dog-tired and famished, I would have said bollocks to all this and given up. I'd like to think not, that I would have risen to the challenge, but until you try you just don't know. Rugby asked testing questions but they were never as ruthless and as searching as those asked of the SAS. These days ninety-nine per cent of us live in the comfort zone, cut off and protected from exposure to risk, challenge or danger. It is difficult to break out of that cocoon, to discover what limits our potential.

That has always been around for me and Durham University took it a stage further. To be fair, it wasn't actually the university and my psychology degree which exercised my imagination in that way, but Donald. Donald was a mature student, though mature wasn't the most accurate of descriptions, and he had spent some time in the SAS. He was a shadowy figure, reluctant to provide precise details about what he had done and where he had been. I was fascinated by him and every couple of weeks Donald tried to get me to go off the rails.

With Donald that was a complete experience. We'd start in the pub, hitting it at opening time, drink our way through until closing time, and then lurch off to an off-licence for a bottle of spirits to continue the binge until the pubs opened again for the evening session, by which time I was slipping into unconsciousness. On one occasion Donald and I linked up with a couple of Marines and got so blasted that we ended up eating a curry off the Durham pavements. The three Sloane Ranger girls who daintily stepped over our prostrate figures were not amused.

In our more sober moments I used to talk to Donald for hours about what the SAS was like, what he'd been through, what qualities they were looking for. Eventually I found out for myself. In 1991 I was invited to Hereford, the SAS headquarters, to make a speech. Everything went well enough for the colonel to suggest that I bring a few of the England boys down to their Christmas party. Mike Teague jumped at the chance and he and I trekked down to Hereford later that year. It was a curious role-reversal because the soldiers were as interested in what we did as we were in them. Many of them had just returned from the Gulf war, yet they were asking Mike how it was possible to run out in Paris against the French. They considered that every bit as difficult and exacting as the experiences they had gone through. I thought they were mad even to suggest that international rugby and combat were in any way comparable, but there were some cross-overs. Both involved a shared sense of danger, a reliance on team work and a journey into the unknown.

One season I was called by the coach of 22 SAS's rugby team. They had made progress in the Army Cup and their next game was an away semi-final at a venue which was usually well supported. The guys were nervous, he said. What advice could I offer about playing in front of a crowd at a ground about which they knew little? I thought the coach was having me on, but he wasn't. I could never get my head round the fact that these soldiers would be fazed by that situation, but each to his own I suppose. The visit with Mike Teague was the start of a series of informal get-togethers involving the SAS, me and rugby. Quite a few SAS men came to my wedding and over the years they have turned up to watch England play many of their international matches. They bonded best with the forwards, same sort of mentality, and whenever the squad went down to Hereford it was always the pack who got the biggest kick out of the trip. They were kindred spirits, all slightly crazy, massively independent, yet reliant on each other to progress.

Visiting the SAS headquarters at Hereford was always a fascinating experience but the most memorable time was when we were introduced to the 'killing house', a building where they rehearse their anti-terrorist techniques. Rory Underwood and Jonathan Webb were 'volunteered' to participate in an exercise as hostages. They were seated at a table in a pitch black room with dummies either side of them, while the rest of us were asked to stand behind a rope which cordoned off a small corner of the same room. The instructions were clear. On no account should anyone move. This was a 'live exercise'. The bullets would be real.

Without warning, the darkness and silence were broken by flashes and the thud of bullets hitting something soft. The assault squad had entered the room, fired their automatic weapons and dragged Rory and Jon to safety. When the lights went up, we could all see the neat bullet holes drilled in the bodies of the dummies just feet from where the pair of them had been sitting at the table. It was a stunning demonstration of the speed and ferocity with which the SAS are expected to act and the conditions in which they are required to operate. Jon couldn't speak for minutes afterwards. His mouth had dried up completely.

Later that evening I had another taste of the SAS at work. Hereford, unsurprisingly, is pretty hot on security and it is impossible to walk from one area to the next without being challenged or confronted. But at 3 a.m. after a night out those details do not seem so important. Alex Hambly, Andrew Harle, both mates from Sedbergh, and I were weaving back to the officers' mess when we realised we had forgotten the security number to open the gate.

'Don't worry,' I told Alex. 'We can climb over the fence. No point in waking anyone up just so that we can get to bed.'

The dinner must have been better than I thought, or else Alex was just as stupid, because he began to scale the fence. Within seconds, armed police, dogs, the lot, had turned up and Alex was being bundled into the back of the van.

'Is he with you?' one of the guards asked, recognising me from the killing house demonstration earlier.

'No way. Never seen him before. Best you lock him up for the night.'

It was some time before Alex convinced them he was a legitimate guest.

Not having a crack at joining the SAS was a real regret but I did put in enough hours in the company of soldiers and officers in my short spell with the army to form some basic ideas of leadership and team-building. Some experiences were more worthwhile than others. I tended to spend time with the Regiment of Wales in the breaks from Durham and was once stuck for three hours on a small hill, chilled to the bone, while a rugby-mad Welsh sergeant interrogated the hell out of me. All he wanted to know was who would win at the Arms Park and all I wanted was a Mars Bar or two and to get into some dry warm clothes. Much more rewarding was the feedback I received in the back of a truck from a group of soldiers during a two and a half week exercise. I had joined the army on one of their officer training schemes and this exercise was to enable me to understand the life of an 'ordinary' soldier, to see the issues and problems from his perspective. What I in fact learnt was how they perceived the men who were leading them. I said nothing much for the first few days, sat in the back of that truck twiddling my thumbs, but once they had got used to me, they were more than willing to share their views on what makes a good officer.

Much of it was pretty basic but none the less valuable for that. What most soldiers wanted was to be treated honestly and fairly, and to know where they stood. They required clearly defined standards and guidelines and to be told when they stepped outside those boundaries. They wanted discipline and a commitment from the person in charge to make their platoon as good as he possibly could. The last thing they looked for was an officer who wished to be their best mate. All of which was very revealing because during that exercise I also heard the views from the other side of the fence. In the officers' mess some officers evaluated their own performance by how popular they were with the troops. The sense they had of their role and responsibilities was a mile apart from that of the men they looked after.

It is tempting to make too much of those two and a half weeks but a lot of what I saw and heard made sense to me. Provided you tell people exactly what is going on, don't hide information from them, let them know the standards you require and treat them fairly, they will be reasonably happy. I also learnt that the worst crime is to belittle a person's capabilities. Many people in positions of influence underestimate the intelligence and abilities of their employees. Most people know when they are being conned, or when information is withheld from them, and most are insulted when that happens. It pays to be completely up front with people because they will handle the truth better than a series of fudges and platitudes.

Durham also provided one more inspirational figure in my life. Geoff Cooke, whom I got to know well when he became England coach, was a selector for the North of England's divisional team. Throughout the late eighties divisional rugby was the route into the England side. They were good games to play well in, as were the county matches which fed the divisions. Geoff came to watch Durham against Lancashire in the County Championship and I had a stormer. It was one of those games where the ball seemed to follow me all over the pitch. Luck plays a massive part in the development of a sporting career

and it was with me that day. On the strength of that one performance Geoff picked me to play for the North in the Divisional
Championship. The North won the title and, from a disgruntled
nothing man going nowhere at Durham University, I moved to
the edge of international rugby in less than a month.

Geoff's faith in me was remarkable, given what happened
shortly after that Lancashire fixture. Durham's last game in that
year's County Championship was against Yorkshire. I was down
to play against John Bentley but picked up a bad dose of flu
early in the week. I should have cried off but, thinking I still
needed to impress the North's selectors, I started the match. I
played like a prize plonker, lasting fifteen minutes before leaving
the field. That's it, I thought. That's blown any chance I had of
a decent representative career, and that assessment seemed to
be confirmed by a conversation I had with Geoff after the game.
The team doctor had told me to seek out Geoff, to tell him about
the flu, just in case he put my disgraceful performance down
to ineptitude rather than illness. I wasn't used to approaching
selectors and offering excuses and it was something I have never
done before or since but I went up to this bluff, grey-haired
Yorkshireman in the bar after the game.

'It wasn't good today,' I said, forgetting the bit about excuses.

'No, it wasn't,' Geoff said.

And that was it. No other reaction from Geoff. No further
explanation from me. It was only subsequently that I learnt that
Geoff had recommended to the England selectors that they take
me to the 1987 World Cup in Australia and New Zealand. As
it happened, I wasn't selected but I'd completely misread my
first conversation with Geoff. I thought I'd blown it, he thought
otherwise and neither of us revealed our thoughts to the other.

Not making the 1987 World Cup squad was a bitter disappointment. Mike Weston, Chairman of England selectors, had
dangled that carrot in front of me earlier in the year. Mike
suggested that I find myself some club rugby to get used to the
physical side of the game and smooth down some of the rough
edges. He advised me to give Harlequins a try. Hints from

England selectors are not to be taken lightly, so for the rest of that year I made the 250-mile round trip to west London to train with Harlequins. Mike couldn't fault my commitment. I caught the midday train to London from Durham, travelled on the underground to Clapham to pick up Mum's car, drove across London to Quins for 7 p.m., trained, grabbed a bite to eat and then did the whole process in reverse, arriving back in Durham around 3 a.m. the following morning. And all that three times a week, only to be told I wasn't going to the World Cup because I was now too tired.

Mum was not impressed by all this commuting and it was nothing to do with my borrowing her car. She knew that the routine would impact on my studies at Durham and told me on several occasions that she thought I was making a big mistake. Her advice washed over me. The prospect of playing for England, however remote, was so beguiling that I decided to put rugby first and psychology second. I reckoned that I owed Durham nothing because they had conned me in the first place.

When I first went to the psychology department I deliberately asked if the psychology course was statistics-based. I was more interested in the behavioural aspects. I was intrigued to find out what made people tick and how pressure brought the best out of some individuals, while others collapsed in a heap. The Durham dons assured me that statistics would only comprise a small part of the course work. So, after three weeks of lectures devoted exclusively to numbers and abstract concepts, I opted out. I still devoured books on psychology but they were not course books, which did not put me in the strongest position when the exams came round. I didn't even turn up to the statistics exam, choosing to remain in bed nursing a hangover rather than record my inadequacies for posterity. The examiners had their revenge when they gave me a recommended pass degree at the end of the course. Anything less and I would have failed completely. The psychology department had prided itself on the fact that all its students had historically achieved a 2.2 or better, so a recommended pass was a disgrace. The only silver lining in a miserable academic three years was the thesis I wrote on dealing with stress. That was exactly the kind of work I wanted to do and the paper attracted a favourable mark. The accompanying comments were less congratulatory: 'I wonder who he copied this from,' was the head tutor's incredulous remark. I didn't blame him. I was surprised myself.

— 4 —

THE FIRST TIME

I WAS scared stupid. Petrified. Even the changing room was different, bigger than I was used to. Would I cope? Was I big enough, quick enough, clever enough? What would it be like? Playing against France is difficult enough at the best of times, playing them away at the Parc des Princes even harder. Doing both and winning my first cap into the bargain was just mind-blowing.

Nothing prepares you for your first game for your country. The books, the recollections of old players, offer a flavour but they just make matters worse. 'It's quicker than you ever thought possible,' they say. 'The hits are harder, the decisions more instinctive. After twenty minutes you will feel like you cannot run another step.' Thanks guys, nothing like a reassuring little pep talk to get me in the mood. And you have to take them on trust because rugby in those days did not offer a graduation class. Now, with European Cups and a highly competitive Premiership, the matches below international level are not so markedly different. Then the gulf was massive. All this stoked the fear as I walked into England's changing room at the Parc des Princes.

The first time I sniffed I had a chance of reaching those exalted heights was when Kevin Simms was picked to play for England against Romania. Kevin was a contemporary of mine. We had played for England Schoolboys together and I could relate to him. I knew his strengths and weaknesses, what he was like on a night on the beer. He was real, unlike the gods who played for their country. I was still reeling from the encounter with Peter Winterbottom in my last year at Sedbergh, and meeting that great England captain Bill Beaumont and Phil Bennett, Wales' mercurial outside-half, at school prize-givings. Those guys weren't human. Their achievements had set them apart but Simmsy was one of us. He unpicked the myth and also provided the motivation. If he could do it, then so could I. Maybe those blokes in the England side weren't so special after all.

My great day came about by a fluke. In the final trial which England used to have around Christmas time to determine the starting team for the Five Nations Championship, Simmsy and I were supposed to be in the junior team facing Simon Halliday of Bath and Saracens' John Buckton. Simon and John both pulled hamstrings and Kevin and myself were bumped up. The trial was nothing special. We both played reasonably well, and all we could do was wait until the team was officially published the following Monday.

I was driving Marcus down to Sandhurst and missed the team announcement which was scheduled for eleven o'clock. I wasn't too bothered. I didn't think I had much of a chance. Nevertheless, I rang up the Sportsline service to find out the news, only to discover it was out of order. It was difficult to find out anything about rugby in 1988. The interest in the sport and England teams was nothing like it is today.

About one o'clock I was in a mate's flat. He didn't have Ceefax and for some curious and inexplicable reason I began to think the unthinkable. Maybe I had sneaked in, maybe the fact that I still couldn't get hold of the team was good news. The butterflies flexed their muscles. I began to ring everyone, leaving messages all over the place. Eventually Jim Turley, a university flat-mate, called back. 'You're in,' he said. 'Congratulations.' The butterflies went berserk. There is no other feeling like it. It's like discovering your A level results, doing your first pint down in one, losing your virginity, opening your first job acceptance letter all happening simultaneously. Elation spars with apprehension, both fighting to dominate the other. Then the rush of anticipation, pride, delight, self-confidence subsides as soon as it surges, giving way to doubt and anxiety. 'My God, I'm playing,' I thought. 'The French – Philippe Sella – Paris – wonderful – shit.' That night the Carling family and friends did their best to double the profits of the French champagne houses.

Journeying to Versailles, where England still stay before internationals, was special. This was different. Rugby had always been important in my life, something I had taken seriously, but it was never this momentous. Travelling under the red rose, smartly attired in grey trousers and dark blazer in the company of Geoff Cooke and Roger Uttley, England manager and coach, made it more than recreation. It wasn't, of course. People's jobs weren't on the line, nothing disastrous would happen if it all went belly-up, but I didn't see it like that. From those very first minutes with the England side I was determined to make it as worthwhile and as significant as possible.

It may not have seemed that way to the rest of the party when I went AWOL on Friday afternoon, twenty-four hours before kick-off. Time hangs heavy during the build-up to a match with all the heavy training taking place during the earlier part of the week, which was why I approached Roger Uttley on Friday to ask for the afternoon off. I wanted to catch up with Iona, a girl I had met at Durham University who had moved to Paris. It made perfect sense to me. There was nothing planned for the team, I would be back for the evening meetings, and a coffee with an old friend would not drain the reservoir of nervous energy which was essential for the following day. The alternative was to return to the team hotel, mooch around for three to four hours and wind up the tension. Roger was gob-smacked but could see the sense in what I was saying and agreed. That Friday set a precedent. During the rest of my international career I would make time on the afternoon or evening before a big game to clear my head. Sometimes I would use flotation tanks, but more often I would take out the Walkman for a solitary stroll.

Coffee with Iona worked because I slept like a baby. A good night's kip before a match has never been a problem. Many players take bombs – sleeping pills – to get off, but I always steered clear of those because they could leave you feeling fuzzy and lethargic the next morning. It helped having Kevin Simms as a room-mate. With him around the routine was more familiar, just like playing for England Schools again. It would have been far more upsetting rooming with someone I didn't know well. In the quiet of our hotel bedroom I could kid myself that tomorrow was just another game. It was also gratifying to know that Kevin was my point of contact on the pitch. He was one of the most skilful players I've ever played with. He had great hands, soft, receptive. He wasn't necessarily into the physical stuff but in terms of acceleration and skill he was top drawer.

I awoke full of adrenaline. You can tell the new caps because they never keep still. Little movements give them away, the jigging of their legs, the drumming of their fingers. Often they don't know they are doing it. The morning of the match was a curiously unreal experience. Part of me knew what was about to occur and was preparing my body accordingly, but the other part of me refused to accept what was going on. The game was still hours away and in the tranquillity of the hotel dining room it seemed more distant than that. And it was all so normal.

Before big matches the tone is deliberately low key. A few jack the lads might wander in to breakfast noisily but the majority of the team are politely quiet. No one wants to tempt fate by appearing over-confident and there is also the desire not to do or say anything which will upset the timing. Get too excited at breakfast time and by kick-off you are past peak arousal and sliding down the other side.

Maintaining composure before an international is more diffi-cult in Paris than almost anywhere else in the world simply because of the bus ride to the ground. The journey from

Versailles to the Parc des Princes on a normal Saturday takes the best part of an hour and a half, but with a team of French police motorcyclists on escort duty to speed progress the trip takes about forty-five minutes. The ride is better than any roller-coaster, far more exciting. If the coach is in any danger of slowing down, the French police kick the blocking cars out of the way. Many's the time the England coach has left a trail of dented Renault and Peugeot side panels in its wake *en route* to the stadium. The unconventional brutality of the journey is the perfect apéritif to the match itself. France plays rugby the same way as her police officers ensure safe passage to opposition teams.

The coach journey marks another stage in the transformation from private to public. It underlines the fact that something special is about to happen, something which will transfix thousands at the game and thousands more watching television or reading their newspapers. As the coach crashes through Paris, people stare, curious to understand the cause of all the fuss. Up near the front of the bus – the old-stagers traditionally commandeer seats near the back – I am beginning to anticipate the assault on the senses when I run out onto that pitch to confront the brass bands, the cockerels and the pounding noise.

There is still one sanctuary remaining. In the bowels of the stadium the dressing room provides the final bolt hole. But not for me. The geography is new and unfamiliar and I do not know the guys I'm playing with. Before too long the hulking shapes of Wade Dooley, Paul Rendall and Peter Winterbottom will be enormously comforting, the knowledge of how they can survive crises in matches reassuring, but today they are strangers. Not that they are unwelcoming. Far from it. It's just that they know the score, know what is and will be required over the next eighty minutes, and I have yet to join that club.

I get ready in a vacuum, trying to visualise what might happen, but nothing prepares me for the shock of entry. The first match is about getting by, about survival. Later I will begin to assess and reflect during games but this is not possible today.

My senses are assaulted from all sides. I see the French forwards emerge from their dressing room covered in grease, rivulets of sweat running down their faces. Their size is intimidating. Big brutal men with misshapen faces, they exude controlled violence. The vividness of their blue shirts contrasts with the white of England. They seem more vibrant.

All this I take in as both sides line up inside the stadium before running out on to the pitch. This is my last memory. The explosion of sound which heralds the teams' arrival prevents other recollections. It's started. And then the sound disappears. Notice the noise when the game is in motion and defeat beckons, concentration shattered. Only when injuries occur, or after a score, or when the result is beyond doubt does sound intrude without damage.

The game itself flashed by, a mystery. Enjoyment didn't even come into it. The tale-tellers were right. It was miles quicker, in both thought and deed. Reactions were instinctive for the first twenty, thirty minutes, the ball a liability. And then I thought, 'Well I'm here, I may not be any good but I'm going to play.' That was the moment I became an international rugby player, the moment when I knew that I could survive. It was a fleeting, ill-formed perception and I didn't have a clue how it would translate itself into action on the pitch, but I knew I could handle and enjoy what I was experiencing. We lost 10–9, France scored right at the end to pinch the game, but I had survived.

The changing room afterwards was a morgue, the experienced players devastated. England had not got that close to France in Paris for years and it was a massive missed opportunity. I didn't see it that way. We were meant to get stuffed and we had only just lost. On top of that I had played for England and not embarrassed myself. I sat in the changing room and luxuriated in that fact. I now had the asterisk of the international alongside my name in club programmes.

I was buzzing, yet I didn't belong. It was an odd feeling. During the first few matches I felt an outsider. There were plenty of seasoned campaigners in that side, self-contained, self-confident. I was just this young kid, not quite part of it, on the outside looking in. All I wanted was approval from these guys. They were still my heroes, despite having played an international with them. But after I had played a few matches, become used to international rugby and knew I could cope, that need disappeared.

Getting confidence is a slow business. I don't think I have ever walked off a pitch feeling, yes I've cracked this, I can do this, but I played that first year and we won a few games and I started feeling more assured about the whole package. I began to relax into it, to make sure that I took in the sense of the occasion and the baggage which comes with major sporting events. I started to enjoy myself. It was still a monumental challenge but I felt I wasn't going to be exposed or make a fool of myself.

And I knew that I loved the internationals, everything to do with them: the pressure, the coverage, the crowd, the frightening physicality. That combination of disparate elements was intensely stimulating. The balance between being physical and aggressive, yet remaining mentally calm, is the crux of international rugby. I learned to love the fear, acknowledging it, anticipating it, experiencing it and then conquering it both as an individual and as a team. I loved, too, the shared sense of satisfaction when something had gone well. I am often asked to pick out my greatest moment. The questioner usually seeks a victory or a try but it was never either of those two tokens. The special memories are of changing rooms after important matches, looking around at those who had just played, relishing the experience, the knowledge that an objective had been reached. That was when the flame burned brightest. No one had to say anything on those occasions. We all knew whether we had performed and when we had the sense of silent satisfaction was enormous.

That first match against France was significant in other ways. I had tasted enough to know that I wanted as much as was decently possible. I wasn't going to let anything or anybody get between me and England, and the first casualty of that decision was a career in the army. I was due to go to Sandhurst in the August of 1988 for the officer training course, which would have eaten into part of that season. The initial arrangement was that they would accommodate my rugby ambitions but that changed when the time for me to attend Sandhurst arrived. The decision had been taken at quite a high level and I think they reckoned I would opt to put the rugby on hold and get stuck into my army career first. How wrong can you get? I saw the army as an opportunity to try for the SAS, even though a fat little runt like me would have struggled to get through the selection process. But as soon as England came along I knew that route would be closed. You can't exactly say, 'Look here, chaps, I know there's been a terrorist attack and I'm awfully sorry but I won't be able to join you because there's an international coming up.' In the end it wasn't a difficult decision. I bought myself out of the army in the August for £8,000. There was no real hassle. Dad fully accepted my reasoning, even though he had enjoyed his career in the army. It just seemed the sensible thing to do. I was hooked.

5

CAPTAIN, MY
CAPTAIN

THERE was a message at home to ring Geoff Cooke and my
brother thought I had been dropped. So did I, because when
the England manager rings before a team announcement it normally means bad news. I sat there for about ten minutes
reflecting on the games I had played, running them through in
my mind. I thought they hadn't gone that badly, not enough to
get me kicked out of the side after seven appearances. Eventually, reluctantly and very apprehensively, I rang him back.

'Will,' he said. 'I wanted you to be the first to know. You're
aware we're going to announce the side at the weekend for the
Australia match. Well, I wanted to talk to the players who have
not made the side but who played on the tour to Australia.'

'Yeessss,' I said.

And I must have sounded so profoundly anxious that he gave
up on his joke, chuckled and said, 'You're not dropped.' I was
so relieved I didn't think, well, what the hell are you calling me
for? 'I'm ringing you for something else. Would you like to
skipper the side?' My silence must have thrown him. 'I'm serious, Will,' he continued. 'Would you like to captain England?
Do you want some time to think about it?'

'It's not something you say no to, Geoff. Of course I will if
you think I can.'

'I do. This is a long-term plan up to the 1991 World Cup. I'll be around to help you and I want you to grow into the role.'

I didn't listen to much else. I put the phone down. My mother and brother were both there and I turned to them and said, 'Christ, I'm captain.' Marcus couldn't believe it. He started laughing. Then I rang my father who was away on business to tell him the news and he was as surprised as everyone else. It was just bizarre.

I knew Geoff had not settled on a captain since he had taken over as manager following the 1987 World Cup but I had no idea I was in the frame. You didn't need to be a genius to work out that a vacancy existed. Nigel Melville, Richard Harding, Mick Harrison and John Orwin had all held the post for short periods in the seven matches following my debut. Some had lost their status through injury, others through a lack of form while Orwin had had the honour taken away from him. Playing under Orwin was valuable experience. I felt that if I behaved and acted in a manner which was completely opposite to the way he carried out his duties as captain, then I would be on the right track.

Orwin had led England on the ill-fated and divisive tour of Australia in 1988 which followed my first Five Nations Championship. I missed the first half of that tour because Durham refused to allow me to put back my finals. Orwin's greeting when I eventually arrived in Australia – 'Oh, you're here, are you?' – was not the most welcoming I had ever received. The lowest moment of a disastrous tour came when he gathered the team together in the dressing room before we went out to face Australia in the Second Test in Sydney.

'I love you,' he said. 'But there's someone here who doesn't love me.' It was a pathetic attempt to get us to play for him, but instead of responding with an outpouring of desire and affection the entire team gazed at the floor trying to work out why he thought there was only *one* player who didn't get on with him. 'I'd die for you,' Orwin added. 'I wish you bloody would,' replied Brian Moore under his breath next to me. And all this five minutes before a Test match. It wasn't a particularly hard act to follow.

Geoff had rung on a Thursday with the captaincy bombshell, but I couldn't tell anyone until late on Saturday evening when the squad had gathered at the Petersham Hotel in Richmond and Geoff had told them of his decision. Those were the weirdest two days. Knowing that I had the job but being forced to keep it a secret was surreal, especially when there was so much speculation about the identity of England's new captain. On the Saturday afternoon when we were due to assemble at the Petersham, Harlequins played Richmond. In the bar after the match a feverish discussion took place about who would be made captain later that evening. Brian Moore and Simon Halliday were two players in the frame and I jokingly said, 'What about me?' I'll never forget the reaction. Everyone looked at me, laughed and said, 'Piss off. Don't be so stupid.' It wasn't the most convincing of recommendations and one I agreed with totally the moment I reached the Petersham and the significance sank in. I nearly went to Geoff to tell him I couldn't do the job. I saw a few of the boys arriving and I thought, 'No, it's just not me.'

When I was eight or nine years old I remember looking at the names England had in their side and thinking they were such good players, so why didn't they win more often? And it was the same in 1988 when I was first made captain. I gazed at Peter Winterbottom, Dean Richards, Wade Dooley and Brian Moore and felt that we were good enough to win if only we could get it right. My approach has always been to involve people, get the ideas out of them, which has the added benefit of making them feel responsible. After all, I was only twenty-two, the youngest guy in the side and the least experienced. If I had stood up in front of them and said, 'Right, this is the way we are going to do it,' they would probably have just ignored me and wandered off to the pub. I needed to involve the senior players and that's what I did. I just sat down and picked their brains.

Geoff Cooke was fantastic. Early on he did most of the work.

He played a fairly strong hand with me initially and controlled what I did but by the time he left in 1994 he had eased back a lot. He felt he had coached me into a role, which I suppose he had, but in the early days I did bugger all really.

That first announcement when Geoff told the squad that I was to be the new England captain was mind-blowing. I looked at my feet and felt this terrifying silence. I think people were in shock and I wasn't too steady in my reactions either. It was a mixture of alarm and embarrassment. In the end I was relieved at the way it was taken. I don't quite know how else the team could have reacted, a mass revolt perhaps, but I wasn't fooled that silence meant unconditional acceptance.

Years later Brian Moore came up to me and admitted that at the time he was thinking, 'What the hell's going on? Who is this Carling bloke? What about me?' And I don't think he ever really got over that. He would have loved to have captained England more than anything. Just for one game. I'm sure the forwards believed that after a couple of matches I would be history because that's what had happened previously to other England captains. They probably reckoned that I wasn't going to inconvenience them and they would be able to carry on doing what they had always done.

Apprehension characterised those early moments. When I stood up for the first time to talk to the team before the match against Australia I was petrified. A few boys were talking openly at the back but I was determined to wait for silence before I began. It was make or break for me. I wasn't going to change the world with what I had to say but I needed to be taken seriously. If I didn't start with that I would have nothing. There were still a few rumblings at the back of the room so I waited some more. And waited and waited. I was churning up inside but eventually the room quietened down and I had their undivided attention.

And the first hurdle had been negotiated. I have no idea what I said. I did plan the speech, I know that, but the content wasn't important. There were so many conflicting thoughts and emotions fighting for space. I was entirely preoccupied with getting through the ordeal, shutting all the irrelevancies out. It's an ability I have. I can focus very easily and rid myself of any extraneous detail and it can come in very handy. It was crucial in that first speech to show the rest of the team that I cared, that I wasn't going to be mucked about, that I was in for the duration.

England beat Australia 28–19 in a match which was later seen as a watershed, the beginning of the most successful period in the history of English rugby. Not that I saw it like that at the time. I wasn't in a state to see anything much. I had been carted off semi-conscious to the dressing room before the end of the game after a heavy tackle. The minute I groggily stepped into the changing room I burst into tears. It was such a relief that the ordeal was over. I had never allowed myself to acknowledge what it all meant.

Yet underneath the emotion and the anxiety I suppose I was fairly philosophical about the whole business. My instinct was to give it a go. If it worked for one game, two games, whatever, at least I'd captained my country. That was precisely the attitude I took to my debut match against France. I reckoned that I might only get one go, so I might as well enjoy it. I never really thought it would last until the 1991 World Cup, let alone the same competition four years later. Part of me dreamed that would happen but that was all it was. Just a dream.

Nevertheless I began to evolve a style of captaincy. I established a routine of ringing team-mates regularly, trying to listen, not only about rugby, but just to listen. I made attempts to find out the birthdays of wives and girlfriends and I would send flowers. I thought that was part of the job. When I first played, the England captain was around only when you met for international duty and I reasoned that, if we were going to be successful, then we had to feel that we were together all of the time. I wanted England to act like a squad who occasionally went off to play club rugby against other countries. That identity, the sense of belonging, was important. I tried to treat players as human beings, to understand what was happening in their lives.

This was before the game went professional, when people still had jobs. If someone had problems at work or had just split up with his girlfriend, I thought I should know about it because it might affect his concentration and ultimately his performance.

I pushed individual notes under the doors of the players' hotel rooms on the night before the match against France when England clinched the 1991 Grand Slam, the first Grand Slam since Bill Beaumont's side in 1980. I'm sure it didn't work for every player but if it worked for one or two it was worth doing. I was concerned to let them know how much it meant to me and how much their contribution meant to England's success. And if Jeff Probyn or Dean Richards thought what a load of bollocks, fine. To me that was part of the job. If you're going to have the honour of leading people, then you have to try to look after them. I eventually packed in the captaincy eight years later when I noticed I was taking short cuts, not devoting the same care and attention to certain members of the side. I became lazy. I didn't put in the effort and I wasn't ringing people nearly as much. These were standards I had set myself and I wasn't adhering to them any more.

Captaincy also had an inevitable distancing effect on my relationships with team-mates. I have always been a natural loner but the job did impose certain limitations on me. In my third match in charge we went to Dublin and beat Ireland and I got absolutely wrecked with the rest of the team at the post-match dinner. It was my first Five Nations away game as captain, my first championship victory, and I was keen to let my hair down. Before the dinner I met up with Paul Dean and Michael Kiernan, my opponents earlier that afternoon. They were pumping triple gin and tonics into me with the express purpose of getting me drunk and, like a prize pillock, I went along for the ride. As the gins slid down I became progressively incapacitated until it was all I could do to lean against the bar. Anything else was beyond my capabilities.

By the time we sat down to eat I was a complete mess. The knowledge that I had to make a speech in front of three hundred or so of the great and good of English and Irish rugby sobered me up a little but I wasn't in a fit state to deliver anything intelligible. Sure enough, when I stood up to offer thanks to Ireland for the game and make a few comments about the match no one understood a thing I said. Realising this, I sat down halfway through my pitiful effort, only to get up again to continue when Phil Matthews, Ireland's captain, was in the middle of his speech. My one consolation was that Michael Kiernan, who had started the gin session, had been carried out of the dinner comatose twenty minutes before I spoke. Looking back, my behaviour was a disgrace and that's what Rob Andrew told me when we met up for the next international the following week.

'I've been talking to a few of the senior players,' Rob said. 'You were pretty drunk after Ireland.'

'Yeah, I know. It was great. What a fantastic night.'

'Will, you're captain now. You can't do it. You have to set an example. People expect it of you. You were letting yourself and England down. It's not on.' Rob was right. I may have been twenty-two, playing an amateur sport for fun, but the job carried certain responsibilities. I never lost it in public again. If I wanted to cut loose I would do so in private and for the rest of my captaincy I was condemned to countless dinners on the top table, sober as the proverbial judge and surrounded by sixty-year-old administrators with whom I had very little in common.

Without the advice and support of Rob Andrew I wouldn't have lasted two minutes in the job. He was my touchstone and his support and loyalty were remarkable, given that he was high on Geoff Cooke's list of choices to captain England himself. In the end Geoff decided against Rob because he felt he had not settled into his game with sufficient confidence and that to ask him to lead the side as well as dictate play was too much. If Rob was disappointed, he never showed it. Jealousy and resentment were not in his vocabulary.

It was Rob Andrew again who collared me early on for another important lesson. He pointed out that I hadn't sat next to any of the reserves at dinner. Mistakes like that get picked up incredibly quickly in a team. Before too long you get accused of favouritism, cliques develop, and the integrity of the group begins to erode. Usually it is the informal occasions which matter most. On the training pitch everyone accepts that the team is the priority but away from the work there is no reason to focus exclusively on the successful men. Unless you are very careful, an international side can begin to lose its own identity and revert back to a collection of players from different clubs. When a team is finding its feet a decent meal together where everyone is having a good time is far more important than a slick training session. If moves break down in a match remedies can be found, but if the spirit goes there is no way back.

My task was to hit the right balance, to get inside the psyche of the team to understand how it worked, yet still retain sufficient objectivity and distance to make judgements unencumbered by sentiment. That was quite a hard thing to do, especially the effort of weeding out the emotion and trying to treat the whole team equally. It was the same when listening to what players had to say. Naturally I leant towards players I liked and respected and fed their ideas back to Geoff Cooke. It was bloody hard work taking advice from the players I didn't get on particularly well with, especially if they came up with a good idea! It was all so tiring. Sometimes I found myself thinking I'm knackered, there's a game in two days and I can't be bothered, I want to look after myself. Those are the personal issues which, as captain, are hardest to resolve. I have been criticised by players and journalists for appearing aloof, for not being one of the boys, but I don't accept that. You can't be one of the boys. Whatever people say, you just can't. You can be, should be, very relaxed with the team but there has to be a distance, a gap which sets you apart for the occasions when you have to tell a mate he is dropped, or when you lay down the law after a poor team performance. A captain has to be setting standards and pushing people to meet those standards. That is part of your job. Sure, great captaincy involves persuading others to take on responsibility but you are the ultimate role model.

Not that I was too interested in amateur psychology as England and Australia sat down to dinner in London's Guildhall. The first game had gone well and I had survived both as a captain and as a player. I had had worse days.

— 6 —
GETTING TO KNOW YOU

Iɴ fact Australia was the best and worst of starts. England had shown they were a team to be reckoned with, that they could compete on a world stage, but the victory also jacked up the expectation. According to the media and an optimistic public, Grand Slams and Triple Crowns were on the cards, milestones last achieved by England in 1980 under Bill Beaumont. It is easy now to play down the significance of Grand Slams. England acquired three in five years at the start of the nineties and now measure their progress against benchmarks set by the southern hemisphere nations. But in 1989 wins over Scotland, Ireland and Wales, let alone France, would have been cause for riotous celebrations.

The 1988/89 season was hard going. If we were flying high after Australia, we were brought down to earth three months later when we played Scotland at Twickenham in the opening round of the Five Nations Championship. It was old England again, a dour, unrelenting forward battle which was tedious to play in and boring to watch. The flights of fancy, the risk-taking, which characterised the Australia match, were history. We ground out a 12–12 draw which won us no friends. I wasn't too bothered. I was still learning the ropes, becoming steadily more comfortable with my role.

Victories against Ireland and France followed the draw with Scotland. The French match was particularly sweet. Pay-back time for the one point defeat in my first game and I also crept over for my first international try, profiting from a poorly executed planned move. Chris Oti was supposed to be the strike runner. A quiet but powerful wing, he had attracted headlines when he scored three tries in the match against Ireland the previous season. The idea was to get Chris to come in off his wing, take an inside pass from me and head for the posts. That was how we usually worked it on the training pitch. But the ball was too slow, Chris over-ran me and, with the French defence still paying him the utmost respect, I retained the ball and sprinted over in the corner.

It was great to break my duck, great to beat France who were unbeaten coming into that game, but our rugby was still very one-dimensional. Grunt and grind, lash and bash, and then release the ball for the backs. That was the way England played that season. It wasn't pretty, but we were the best in Europe at it, or so we thought.

Wales in Cardiff put paid to that theory. England hadn't won at the Arms Park for twenty-six years but this time would be different. The forwards had flexed their muscles effectively against France, the victory in Dublin had proved that we could win away from home, the team was settled and beginning to bond. Whichever way I looked at it, we were going to overturn that record. Cardiff would be the match where we confirmed our progress as a side.

Some progress. A 12–9 defeat made almost as much of an impression on me as the infamous England/Scotland match the following year. Far from being the finished article, we hadn't even begun to understand ourselves or work out how we should be playing. The forwards were turned over physically and psychologically against Wales and there was no plan B. Mike Teague's injury in the first few minutes of the match and the absence of Jeff Probyn disrupted our line-out and scrummage but those were not mitigating factors. Successful sides do not rely on the contributions of a select group of players. The truth was simple and it hurt. We talked big and played small and were nowhere near tough enough to get through close matches. On top of that we lacked the character and wit to change tack in the middle of games.

I was appalled. The season had ended on a dismal note for the team and had exposed my own shortcomings. It may have said captain on the team-sheet and in the match programme but I wasn't delivering what I believed I could. I had vague notions of leadership and the direction in which I wanted the team to go but was not sufficiently confident or resolute to put them into practice. I coveted Grand Slams and Triple Crowns as much as the next man and now I knew they did not come about by accident, that they were won with a settled team confident in their pattern of play, confident with each other, and confident in their ability to survive the inevitable periods in matches when misfortune strikes. To reach that stage I had to get to know the players, to get under their skin, and I started with the big boys.

Forwards are different animals, products of a ferociously harsh, competitive environment. It was impossible for me to understand what they got up to without having a go myself and that wasn't an option. Each position is shrouded in mystery, defined by a strange set of rules and governed by a separate code of ethics. You only have to look at the position of hooker to see what I mean. He is suspended between two props with his arms wrapped round their shoulders, completely powerless and vulnerable, and then he is slammed into the scrum. If you wandered up to somebody in the street, who had never watched or played rugby, and explained the hooker's job in that way he would think you were completely barmy. But that's the reality.

I was at a disadvantage amongst the forwards on two counts. All of them were older and more experienced than I was and I was in total awe of them – and still am – which made laying down the law extremely difficult. The players whom I respect most now were the forwards I started out with: Dean Richards, Brian Moore, Mike Teague, Peter Winterbottom and Wade

Dooley. These were guys I watched on TV, they were my heroes. I thought these guys were untouchable. To a man they were non-judgemental. Very few were prima donnas. Their peer group pressure, governed by mickey-taking, wouldn't allow egotistical outbursts. Most were very straight, loyal to their own standards, and very private. I also admired their collective strength. They knew that individual brilliance was useless, that unless the various units performed together, fed off each other, no one would function.

The more I got to know them the more I became aware that they would be the key to England's success. An old rugby truism is that forwards win matches but it was more than that. They were a team within a team. Getting them on side, winning their confidence, forcing them to think about the way they performed as individuals and as a unit would be crucial. I could cope with the backs. I knew how they felt and thought. I was one of them myself, for God's sake. But the forwards were something else. Winning them over was vital and it wasn't going to be particularly easy.

There were exceptions, of course. Peter Winterbottom was my ideal identikit rugby man. First capped against Australia in 1982, he had been a regular in England's back row virtually ever since. His abilities were admired the world over, not least in New Zealand which he toured with the 1983 British Lions, winning plaudits from all the important and knowledgeable rugby men in that country. There were no airs and graces with Winters. He was just there to do his job. He was so straight. He didn't like people mucking about and wasn't into bitching or politics. All he cared about was getting the job done. He also admired the same qualities as I do: loyalty, being focused and performing when the pressure was on. I was certain that if a match ever degenerated into a brawl he would be first in the queue to sort it out.

Winters wasn't a push-over but I knew he would not undermine my team-building plans as long as he had faith in me and my ideas. Yet there were influential forwards whom I wasn't so sure about and Brian Moore was one of those. I've always had a problem with Mooro. Everyone now knows that he was nicknamed the Pit Bull and the bright spark who came up with that sobriquet had Brian spot on. He is an immensely committed, single-minded character who will never back off from challenge or confrontation. For many people he articulated the desire which England eventually found during the early nineties and that, coupled with his intelligence, made him a formidable presence within the squad. Everyone took the mick out of Mooreo for his aggressive stance and willingness to say what he thought but, under the surface, there was a massive amount of respect for what he achieved as a player and as pack leader.

It was probably because he was such a strong presence that I found him difficult to deal with. It was an open secret between us that he wanted my job and thought he could do it, if not better, at least as well. It made sense for me to have him on my side and I tried to involve him as much as possible. We went out for dinner two or three times, outside of club and country commitments, to talk about England, where we should be going, the priorities, what we needed to do to be successful. But it never really worked. He was always reserved when we met, although that is the way he is sometimes, and the occasions were invariably uncomfortable. Needling away at Brian was the silver spoon syndrome which would dog me throughout my career. He thought I had had it too easy, everything presented on a plate, whereas he had come up the hard way, fighting for every step up the representative ladder and battling against the view held by some that he was not powerful enough for an international hooker. Brian thought, with some justification, that my route to the top had been a doddle by comparison.

Dean Richards was another influential bloke I found difficult to handle, another threat. I didn't understand Deano to begin with. Without doing anything he had this quality where people just waited to see which way he would jump. Players looked to him for a lead. Brian demanded attention because he was verbose and proactive, whereas Dean just slumped along at the back of team meetings or at the back of the bus. He would rarely take the initiative and voice an opinion, although he had clear ideas of the game he thought England should play. Dean was a maverick. His dislike of training was legendary and one of his more celebrated warm-up routines in the dressing room was to pat his stomach and see how long it would take for the wobbles to subside. While the rest of the team were stretching or jogging to loosen up, Dean would sit in the corner reading the match programme. There was nothing malevolent about the man. He was simply a one-off, a survivor despite the fact that he broke all the rules. That was why he was so popular. He never made an issue out of his non-conformism but his ability to prosper within a team without genuflecting to what was considered the norm made him almost heroic in the eyes of most rugby followers and many of his fellow players.

I never appreciated what a hell of a guy he was until my last two or three years. I just didn't understand what made him tick early on. I should have talked to him more but I was scared of him, I suppose. I felt that the immense respect that he had within the team was potentially threatening for me, not that he would deliberately undermine anyone. But he was such a powerful figure within the side that he could cause you problems if he didn't agree with what you were doing.

Jeff Probyn was another forward I did not understand but I was not alone in that regard. Even his fellow forwards thought Jeff was a bit odd. The way he played the game and his opinions off the pitch were iconoclastic. You knew the man was an odd-ball the minute you saw him warm up before an international. Jeff used to do a headstand against the changing room wall and then push himself up off the floor with his hands, a kind of vertical press-up. I always knew props were weird but Jeff was way out on his own. His hotel room was an electrician's delight. He would sit in his room surrounded by appliances and noise. The TV, the clock radio, the electric kettle would all be on and Jeff would be immersed in a computer game of some description. But if someone moved to turn the TV down Jeff would say, 'I'm watching that.' Turn the radio off and he would say, 'I'm listening to that.' And this would be happening at 1 a.m. on the night before an international. Then Jeff would put his game down, turn over and be asleep within seconds, while his room-mate was wide-eyed and assaulted by noise and lights of every description.

The way he played was unique. His scrummaging was a law unto itself. He would tuck himself into a ball, rest his belly on his right knee with his nose six inches off the floor and be happy to stay in that contorted position for ever and a day. For a man who never did any weights he was phenomenally strong and when he was playing you could guarantee that the England scrum would never be pushed backwards. He was world-class in his own particular arena but he was odd. What thirty-five-year-old does dog and phone impressions in the hotel dining room and finds it funny after the fifteenth time?

Jeff and I had a number of public run-ins. He was another player who saw me as a young upstart, the man who had it made, a bloke who had been given the captaincy without having to earn it, a bloke who had been guaranteed a place in the side by Geoff Cooke. I was everything he was not, I suppose, and no matter how often I tried to convince him otherwise he never believed me.

Those first couple of seasons as captain were awkward for me. I was terribly insecure with some of the pack. If anyone was laughing in a meeting or during a discussion, I felt they were laughing at me. I now know that wasn't the case but at twenty-two it is impossible not to feel exposed when you are dealing with men who are older and more experienced. There were many occasions, after a training session or a meeting during which I explained a particular course of action that was greeted by a stony silence, when I used to creep back to my room reflecting that dealing with these men was a complete waste of time.

But I did have some allies. If the forwards were going to be difficult nuts to crack, at least I had a few mates amongst the backs.

I had encountered Simon Halliday for the first time in 1988 when we played together against Scotland. It was an unnerving experience. I knew the guy was different from the usual rugger-bugger stereotype. He had been to Oxford University, gained a good classics degree and talked posh but I still wasn't fully prepared for the sight that greeted me as I entered the hotel room. Simon was stretched out on the bed, listening to music, reading the *Financial Times*. Then the phone rang. It was his wife. 'Suzanne, darling, how are you, tiddly-bum?' Time may have distorted my recollection of his nickname for her but it was something like that. The two of them were always calling each other names. I stood there, surveying this classic pukka Englishman whom I was due to partner against a bunch of marauding Scots, and wondered what the hell I had let myself in for.

'Nice music,' was the phrase I came up with after a long pause. 'What is it?'

'The Carpenters, dear boy. Want some tea?' And that was the start of a beautiful relationship which saw us teamed for club and country until Jeremy Guscott arrived on the scene, whereupon Simon was shunted out to the wing for a spell.

Simon's educated gentle persona was not the whole story. It couldn't have been, otherwise he would never have become a respected and commanding figure within the squad. There was steel beneath the cultured facade. In 1991 England toured Australia and Simon played in the fixture against Australia A. During that game he was stamped on in the face. Jerry, who knew him well from their spell at Bath, saw Simon clutch at his face, nudged me in the ribs as we both sat on the bench, and said, 'Watch this.'

At first Simon waggled his finger at the referee to signal his disapproval. Then, when it became apparent that he was not going to get any satisfaction or justice from that quarter, he went absolutely, completely, irrevocably berserk. For the next five minutes the ball was irrelevant as Simon careered round the pitch on a mission. He clattered into the rucks and mauls, pushing aside the England forwards to get stuck into the Aussies.

He did not know the identity of the culprit, so he decided to try to get to as many of the opposition as possible in the hope that among them he would get lucky and obtain his revenge. His finest moment came when he pole-axed the Australian full-back under the pretext of chasing a high kick when the ball was at least fifteen metres away. Jerry and I looked on with a mixture of amazement and admiration and giggled throughout.

Jonathan Webb was another man whose loyalty I could bank on. He was also a good sounding board. We had first crossed swords in the UAU final when he was reading medicine at Bristol University and I was at Durham. Jon later graduated into the England side and played full-back in the 1987 World Cup. When I joined him the following year we hit it off straightaway. He had an extraordinarily dry sense of humour and a wry, cynical outlook on life, common to most in the medical profession. He also refused to let rugby dominate his life and I found that combination immensely attractive. Jon had the knack of being able to part the gathering storm clouds when they threatened to close in over me and I often sought out his company.

The final piece of the jigsaw in my support mechanism was Rory Underwood, although our relationship was quite complex. Rory was supportive and helpful but he needed some warmth in return. I half-knew Rory from my time in the North's divisional side. I found him quiet, nondescript almost, which was unusual for a player who had already broken into the England side in 1984. He rarely contributed to tactical or strategic discussions. Able to spend more time with him in the build-up to internationals, I discovered that his reticence stemmed from a lack of confidence. Rory needed reassurance, stroking. He would dwell on the few mistakes he had made, agonising over them for hours, rather than concentrating on his match-winning abilities.

For a winger he was deceptively powerful, pound for pound the most explosive member of the side. That fact was proved in a strength-measuring test when he hurled a 16lb shot further

than any other squad member. He was quick, but not devastat-
ingly so. The combination of pace and power was his weapon.
Unless you hit Rory full on in the tackle he would brush by.
He also had the killer instinct given to the truly great strikers.
Give him half a chance in the dying seconds to rescue a match
and he would rarely let you down. I would be grateful for that
knack before too long.

— 7 —

A CRISIS OF CONFIDENCE

THE finish was disastrous but the start wasn't much to write home about either. The 1989/90 season would be remembered for *that* match, for the score line which read Scotland 13, England 7, for the Grand Slam humiliation, for David Sole's slow, majestic, tub-thumping walk onto the Murrayfield pitch, for another major occasion when England failed to deliver. But I had more pressing concerns. I had lost the captaincy and a certain Mr Jeremy Guscott was about to make his England debut.

The match against Romania was the first occasion I had missed an England game through injury. General wear and tear, too much non-stop rugby over the years with not enough rest, meant that I developed a stress fracture of the shin and I travelled to Bucharest to watch the game rather than participate in it. The problem with the leg had also caused me to miss out on a trip to Australia with the 1989 British Lions but I wasn't overly concerned about that. I've always placed England above the Lions in my personal pecking order.

I hated every minute of the Romania trip, especially as Jerry made a blistering start to his international career with three glorious tries. Jerry has always been in the limelight, attracting attention and envy in equal measure. It is unusual for anyone to make such an impact in top-level sport. As you climb through the ranks towards the international stage you find that the disparity between players narrows until everyone plays pretty much off a level playing field. The forwards would be similarly strong, the backs similarly quick. Matches would be won by the side which maximised its collective talents rather than relying on one or two outstanding individuals.

But Jerry was always that little bit different. He had confidence, he had speed and he had vision. And it was the vision which set him apart. He could be running flat out, surrounded by defenders, yet would somehow have this ability to know what was on offer. A flick of the wrists, a miss-pass, and someone would be crashing over in the corner for the try and all the while you were thinking how the hell did he see that? Jerry's change of pace was also exceptional. Injuries and age have taken the edge off it in recent seasons but early in his career he was super-quick. He was such a smooth runner that many people did not realise that he was moving into over-drive. Again, with Jerry you only appreciated what he could do when he had just done it. Even his defence was sound. He has had to live with the reputation of being a poor defender for a while now, but he tackled as well as the next man.

All this I pieced together as Jerry and I developed our record-breaking partnership of forty-five games as England's centre pairing. We eventually became good friends but when we first met our relationship was somewhat strained. One of the reasons was that we came from such different backgrounds. When you see Jerry doing his media work these days, strutting his stuff as a front man for various TV game-shows, it is easy to forget that when he came into the England side he was working as a builder. That meant more to him than it did to me but there was no doubt that he saw me as part of the privileged public-school brigade. Early on we didn't know each other and we probably didn't work hard enough at getting to know each other.

That was brought home to me at an international dinner when

I met Jane, Jerry's wife, for the first time. In the old days international dinners used to be dinner-jacketed affairs and Jane was commenting on my bow tie. It must have been a particularly garish example for her to remark on it and she wanted to know why I didn't choose another of the dozens I must have had at home. I told her it was the only one I had but she wasn't convinced. I was perceived as the dilettante glamour boy and that was a real barrier between Jerry and myself.

Jerry was also a free spirit, whereas I was shackled by the responsibility of captaincy. In the lead-up to a game Jerry would go out and have a few beers and then train the next day as if nothing was the matter. His talent enabled him to get away with murder but it was not particularly helpful when I was insisting on certain standards, trying to build a team. Jerry would take the piss during meetings and out on the pitch and whenever I attempted to upbraid him he would just smirk and make some facetious remark. He could be extraordinarily bolshy. Because the meetings or training sessions weren't important to him personally, he could not see that they were relevant to others and, as such, were legitimate as far as the team was concerned.

Romania confirmed Jerry's arrival on the international stage and proved that his exploits with the Lions against Australia that summer, when he turned the series in the Second Test, were no fluke. But I didn't feel much like celebrating. The presence of a world-class England centre had obvious implications for me. Rob Andrew was captain for the Romania match and later that evening, as the team were partying, I had a crisis of confidence. I had only been in the job for five games and wondered if I would ever get back into the side, let alone retrieve the captaincy. Jerry had been a star, Rob had handled the team well, England had won 58–3 away in blistering heat. These were not the circumstances which would have everyone starting a Bring Back Carling campaign. And to make a bad day immeasurably worse, I knew that if I was reinstated it would have to be in place of Simon Halliday who had partnered Jerry in the centre.

Hallers and I went back a long way. I enjoyed playing with him. We were good together and I didn't fancy starting afresh with a new partner.

I behaved ridiculously in the selection meeting following the Romania match.

'Jerry has to play, Will,' Geoff Cooke said. 'He has too much talent. He offers the team such a lot.'

I knew Geoff was right. There was no way he was going to leave out Jerry after his remarkable debut but because I had known Simon for such a long time and was so close to him as a player and as a friend, I tried to argue for his inclusion at Jerry's expense.

'You can't do that, Geoff. He's my mate,' I started. It sounds pathetic now and it was pathetic then and I didn't pursue the point for long, but it was the first time I realised that being involved in picking international teams meant hard decisions, that friendship was a commodity which you did not carry into selection meetings. My only excuse was that I was young and new to the business but it was a hard lesson all the same.

Geoff was great, though. He just smiled indulgently throughout. It must have been like having a temperamental child in the room but he had the good grace to see my reaction for what it was – an outburst of staggering immaturity. I was getting to know Geoff by now. A lot has been made of our relationship, on how dependent we were on each other, how we were too close, not objective enough in our dealings with players and issues. I am not best placed to comment on that theory. All I can say is that there were many occasions when Geoff and I would disagree completely and it would be Geoff who would get his way.

The selection meeting before the Romania match had been especially argumentative. I had sat in on selection ever since I was appointed captain and I thought we should take a running full-back to Romania. It was a game England should win, there was no pressure and it would be a wonderful opportunity to freshen our back play. My preferred candidate was Mark Bailey, a winger with Wasps, who had been around since 1984 but who never enjoyed a protracted run in the England side. I thought Mark would make a great full-back and Romania would be the ideal opponents to try him out. Geoff disagreed. He wanted Simon Hodgkinson to play full-back, arguing that his goal-kicking was essential at international level and that he had the necessary vision to bring the best out of other players. I was not impressed. 'Geoff, that's ridiculous,' I insisted. 'Hodgy might be a half-decent goal-kicker but he has no pace. How can you play a full-back who will struggle to hit the line with any force, who will be hard pressed to get on the outside of an overlap?' I saw Simon as an individual, not as a team member, and judged him as such.

'Will, look. Simon is not the quickest player in the world but he has other attributes which more than make up for his deficiencies in that area. He sees space early, reads situations well. Those qualities will enable him to be where he wants to be when he wants to be there. And his goal-kicking is priceless.'

My dummy rebounded round the room a few more times before we moved on to the next debate, but Geoff was right. A year later it would be Hodgkinson who kicked the penalties to win in Cardiff and Hodgkinson who would lay on the try-scoring pass for Rory Underwood to clinch the Triple Crown in Dublin. Geoff had looked at the bigger picture. He knew that no player is perfect and that the art of team-building is to camouflage one player's weakness with the strength of another. That was typical of Geoff. He always played it straight down the line. He wasn't the most sociable of men, never one to share his innermost thoughts and feelings, but he was dead straight.

I had had an early taste of his direct approach before the final trial which preceded my debut. There was a one-hour gap between Simon Halliday and John Buckton pulling out of the probables side to allow Kevin Simms and myself to be promoted. Halliday cried off first and Geoff told me I was moving up from the possibles to replace him. Stupidly, I asked to remain with Kevin because of our previous experience together with England

Schoolboys. It was that need for comfort again. Geoff cut me dead with a withering look followed by the question, 'Do you *want* to play for England?'

Geoff had faith in his own ability, a rare commodity in the England set-up. He lost his first two games in charge but refused to change tack. He also inherited many of the players who had under-performed with England during the mid-eighties. Wade Dooley, Mike Teague, Peter Winterbottom, Rob Andrew and Rory Underwood had all been on the scene before Geoff, but it was only under his influence that they grew into formidable rugby men. He believed in stability and organisation to build confidence. And he gave players time to develop and the permission to fail. One poor performance was excusable, even two were just about acceptable, provided the explanation was convincing. He was never soft on players, demanding the highest standards at all times, but once he had faith in a player he gave him every chance to produce the goods. England, like most other countries in the rest of the rugby world, do not have a bottomless pool of talent. The trick is to make the best use of the available resources and Geoff did that.

Romania was also the game where Rob Andrew came of age. Rob was another England player castrated by the mix-and-match selections of the previous regimes. He was first capped in 1985 when at Cambridge University but had never blossomed into a commanding and convincing outside-half. It was hardly his fault. He often had no idea who his playing partners were from one match to the next and he was part of a safety-first culture which England engendered. The emphasis was on getting through matches without making howlers rather than exploring potential and taking risks. Rob under Geoff Cooke became a much more settled and self-confident character.

I first came across Rob when I played divisional rugby for the North in 1987. He had already played for England and was working as a chartered surveyor in London's West End. Travelling to a practice session with the North's divisional side, I have a clear memory of sitting on a train with Rob and Kevin Simms and thinking, 'I'm on a train with two England players, I hope someone sees me'. I have any amount of time for Rob. He is such a steady guy and a fantastic team man. He was the one individual whom I could count on to place the team performance above his own, and in a highly competitive environment when everyone is gunning for everyone else's shirts that is a huge compliment. Rob was a great believer in the work ethic. If there was a weakness in his game he would move heaven and earth to remedy it. When he first made the side he was not a particularly effective kicker but come the end he was one of the most destructive kickers in the northern hemisphere, both from his hand and when taking pot shots at goal.

Rob and Jerry's form was a major plus at the beginning of the 1989/90 season, as was the improvement in the forwards. Mike Teague, Paul Ackford, Dean Richards, Wade Dooley and Brian Moore had all made the Lions' Test pack against Australia, with Teague picking up the Man of the Series award. All three Tests were bloody and bitter affairs and England's quintet did not back off one bit. That tour developed their camaraderie and their trust in each other. It hardened them up. The down side was that the Lions had won the series by playing unadventurous ten-man rugby, confirming the forwards' long-held prejudices that it was they who won matches, the backs useful only as window-dressing. No matter. Their confidence was so high that they steamrollered all before them and we blitzed the first three matches in the Five Nations Championship following the Lions tour. Ireland and Wales at home, France away and a total of 83 points for and only 13 against was an indication of the quality of the rugby we were offering. England had never played three matches of that extravagance on the bounce in their history. It was Australia revisited. Tries were run in from all parts of the pitch, forwards and backs combined in a riot of free expression and critics and supporters could not come up with the superlatives quick enough.

Then we travelled north to face Scotland. To call it an important game is the biggest misrepresentation of the century. It was massive. Both sides were going for the Grand Slam, a pair of £14 tickets was sold for £3,000 and we were 1 to 4 on with the bookies. The hype was huge, media interest at its most voracious. For the first time a rugby match was attracting the attention reserved for important football occasions.

I look back occasionally and wonder if we were too relaxed. But even now I just don't know. The last training session before that game was one of the best I've been involved with. Everything was really slick. There was no farting about, everyone was organised, not a pass was dropped, and as we came off the training pitch Bill McLaren, the BBC's voice of rugby, remarked that he had never seen a session like it.

There's a fine line between confidence and over-confidence. Who knows if we were too cocky but we were rattled as soon as the match started and we never really recovered. Jerry scored a wonderful try from halfway but we were always playing catch-up. And the skeletons poured out of the closet. Towards the end of the first half we were awarded a sequence of penalties. Brian Moore and the forwards thought they could score a push-over try which would have got us right back in the match. I backed his call, the scrums collapsed, no penalty try was awarded and Scotland escaped.

My mistake was to go to Brian in the heat of the battle. He was too close to the action, too enveloped in the red mist to make a considered decision. No self-respecting front-row forward turns down the chance of a push-over. A smarter move would have been to consult Peter Winterbottom or another of the back row. It was a crucial and expensive example of me not knowing my players well enough. I was still partly under their spell. I don't blame Brian. He played it as he saw it. Big matches hinge on small factors. But for the second year running we had blown the one game which really mattered.

Ultimately, that defeat worked against Scotland. The rampant nationalism surrounding the match, the shock of losing, the anti-English feeling in and around Edinburgh that weekend provided England with a trigger. For a couple of years just the mention of Murrayfield '90 was enough to stiffen sinews and resolve. The losses stay with you far longer than the victories and that game hurt more than any other game I've played in. It went far beyond a rugby match. It became personal. Every time England played Scotland subsequently the Scottish press had a pop at me. They seemed to channel their hatred of the English through me. Instead of Will Carling I became Edward I, Butcher Cumberland and Margaret Thatcher rolled into one.

In 1996 when England went to play Scotland at Murrayfield there were three choices in an Edinburgh wine bar. You could pee on Margaret Thatcher, you could pee on Saddam Hussein or you could pee on Will Carling. And I was the top choice by a mile. It actually hurt a lot, principally because what they said about me, my beliefs and my Englishness, was complete rubbish. But that's the power of the media for you. Many people only get an impression of me through the newspapers and when they are as vitriolic and off-beam as some of the Scottish media were that opinion is bound to be distorted. I personalised it. I thought if you are going to give me a hard time, I will do anything to beat you. I have got a lot of good friends in Scotland and I love the countryside, but after Murrayfield I worked as hard as I could to see the team won and we never lost to Scotland again after 1990. Jim Telfer, Scotland's coach, made a significant remark on the night of Scotland's emotional triumph. 'This could be one of the biggest mistakes ever made by a Scotland team,' he said, only half-joking. 'The England lads who played today will probably never forget the experience.' We didn't. I didn't.

My obsession with that defeat ultimately became stupid. In 1994 when I was giving the team talk before the Scotland match I brought up 1990. About to use it as a rallying cry, I realised there were only four or five players left who had played in that match. The rest were looking a bit bewildered. 'This doesn't mean anything to us,' they said. 'It's not relevant.' 'What do you mean?' I exploded. 'This is history. England's success has been forged on the back of that result. Never forget that.' But the moment had passed. While the memory was still cruelly vivid for me, it meant nothing to the majority of the team. To drag it up four years later was to exaggerate it out of all proportion for the new generation. But I learned something about myself from my reaction to it. I tend not to start anything, but if anyone has a go at me, I don't lie down, I'll have a real go back.

Rugby in 1990 had not quite finished kicking me in the teeth. That summer England toured Argentina. It was a lonely trip. Even in those days the pressure of relentless rugby was taking its toll and, with the World Cup seventeen months away, Rory Underwood, Dean Richards, Jeremy Guscott, Paul Rendall, Paul Ackford and Mike Teague decided they needed a break to recharge the batteries. I would have liked to have done the same but, having blotted my copy book at Murrayfield, I needed to recharge my own career. A rest was out of the question.

I knew that Argentina was a hostile country to tour at the best of times. The last country to win a two-Test series had been France in 1974. There had also been the little matter of a spat between Britain and Argentina over who owned the Falkland Islands to add spice to the trip. But I was still staggered to see the Union Jack being burned in the stand and Alsatians patrolling the boundaries of the stadium as we ran out for our first match against Banco Nacion.

The intimidating atmosphere did not excuse our lacklustre display. We went down with barely a whimper. I had never played in an England team which had been so effete. I was aware that the party was untried, that players like Gavin Thompson, Tony Underwood, Paul Hull, David Pears and Tim Rodber were wet behind the ears, but there is a huge difference between inexperience and gutlessness. Towards the end of the game I called the side into the huddle. 'Don't ever forget this,' I screamed. 'This has been an absolute disgrace.' The comments were inappropriate and unhelpful but I did not know how else to express my disappointment. It took Richard Hill, a volatile character himself, to bring me to my senses. 'For heaven's sake, Will, calm down.'

Argentina also strained my relationship with Roger Uttley. Roger was one of English rugby's war heroes. A member of Bill Beaumont's 1980 Grand Slam-winning side and a successful tourist with the 1974 British Lions, he exuded credibility. You only had to glance at his craggy, battle-scarred face to appreciate what he had been through on behalf of his country. I respected all that but wondered how relevant that experience was a decade or so later. It seemed to me that Roger was trapped in a time warp. He believed that what was good for the team he played in would work equally well for the team he coached. That was not my way. I was into experimenting, trying out new ideas.

Our first clash occurred before my third cap against Scotland. We were getting off the team bus before a training session. There was no difference in content or emphasis between training on a Thursday and a Friday and I queried this with Roger. 'Why don't we concentrate on the opposition on Thursday and our-selves on Friday? It would lend shape to the build-up and make a natural transition from the training pitch into the match.'

The comment was not meant as a criticism but Roger took it as such. 'How many caps have you got?' he barked.

'Two.'

'Do you want more?'

'Yes. Of course I do.'

'Well, you let me do my job and concentrate on your own.'

I accept it was impudent to question training routines and aspects of preparation after merely dipping my toe into inter-national waters but my view has always been that you only know whether an idea is a good one by trying it out. At that stage I had played two and lost two for England. It wasn't as if everything was working smoothly.

Roger and I formed an uneasy alliance for the next couple of seasons until the tour to Argentina, when we again hit turbulent water. On that tour it became clear that the inexperienced England party needed detailed technical input rather than the general stuff which Roger offered. Dick Best, Harlequins' coach, was following the tour in his capacity as an employee for a rugby travel company and several of the experienced forwards, including Wade Dooley and Peter Winterbottom, asked me to approach Geoff Cooke to see if we could involve Dick. Geoff agreed, and from that point my relationship with Roger deteriorated. The inclusion of Dick upset him greatly. Dick was actually a great help to the forwards on that tour, and hence to Roger as well. But Roger did not see it like that, and because I got on well with Dick, my club coach, Roger was suspicious of my and probably Dick's motives. They were quite simple: to provide the best possible coaching for the England players, regardless of personnel and egos.

Dick was unable to head off defeat in the Second Test. We had won the First Test 25–12 and were up by a point with three minutes remaining in the second when Jeff Probyn threw the game away. Jeff had been whacked in the scrum by his opposite number. No one likes getting punched but Jeff with all his years of first-class rugby behind him should have known better than to seek revenge at the next scrum, which was on the 22-metre line, smack in front of our posts. The referee spotted Jeff's retaliation, awarded Argentina the penalty and we lost the game 15–13 when we could have sneaked it.

I was livid with Jeff. The lessons of Murrayfield where we gave away two early penalties for indiscipline were fresh in my mind but obviously not in Jeff's. 'That punch cost us the game, Jeff,' I fumed afterwards. But I was wasting my breath.

'You don't understand, Will. You can never let your opposite number think he has got one over on you. I had to hit him.'

I could have told Jeff that the game was all but over when he threw that punch, that personal battles had to be put aside in the interests of the team, that if he had to belt someone not to do it within easy kicking distance, but I didn't. The incident seemed to sum up a season where I was swimming against the tide. Exhausted and thoroughly despondent, I slumped in the shower and wept.

— 8 —

MEDIA, MONEY
AND ME

It was time to find a proper job. After my disagreement with the army, I ventured into the commercial world and found employment flogging oil. Mobil employed me as a salesman to do the rounds of BMW and Mercedes garages trying to persuade the dealerships and servicing outlets to buy their products. I wasn't bad at the selling game, putting together various deals to encourage the garages to use Mobil oil, but it wasn't really me. Although I lasted two years, I soon realised that I was spending half of my day on the phone talking about or planning rugby and that commitment meant that I was doing justice neither to myself nor my employer.

So, aged twenty-four, and frighteningly inexperienced in the world of big business, I set up Inspirational Horizons, my first company. It was a way of taking rugby seriously, doing it professionally, when the sport was still amateur. That side of it was successful, a stroke of genius. I was able to concentrate on rugby without feeling guilty that I was wasting my employer's time but the venture was not exactly lucrative. There would be times in that first year when I would look at my bank balance to discover that I had £300 left in the world with no prospect of any more cash coming in.

It was hardly surprising. The business of Inspirational

Horizons was to give talks on leadership and motivation and here I was, conspicuously young, a captain of a national sports team which no one outside of a few public schools cared about, a team which had lost in 1989 and lost again in 1990. It was not the success story big business was desperate to hear and I wasn't exactly inundated with offers. In one of my first ventures I put together a package for Red Star who, at the time, were Harlequins' sponsors. A couple of months later they quit the club. Coincidence? Possibly. But it was clear that I hadn't convinced them to maintain their association.

I have been accused of ruthlessly making money off the back of the game and I do not deny now that I am financially far better off, but those early days were different, the original wing and a prayer job. I started the business because I am an eternal optimist and because I wanted to be free to take rugby seriously. I was sure something would come up though I didn't quite know what. I've never been obsessive about money and that attitude allowed me to take what was then a huge risk. I know there will be certain members of the RFU committee who think that I was always raking in the filthy lucre and that my early penury was a load of old twaddle, but it is true. The only thing which excited the bank manager was a book called *The Captain's Diary* which was literally that, a recording of mine and the team's thoughts and actions through an international season. That was worth around £15,000 and that money just about kept me going for those difficult two years. The irony is that those were some of the best years of my life. Everything was blissfully clear and simple. I was living not quite a hand-to-mouth existence but almost, doing what I loved, building a team which I believed in. They were fun days.

Some of the misconceptions about me and money were of my own making. One day at a dinner I met a guy called John Ross who worked for a garage. 'We'd like to sponsor a car for you,' John said. 'Here's my card. Give me a ring some time if you're interested.' Interested? I had a little Peugeot at the time and was definitely interested. I met up with John, taking Brian Moore along for some moral support, and was amazed to discover that the car he was talking about was a top of the range, £80,000 Mercedes convertible. In return they wanted a few tickets in order to take their clients to the internationals. Brian and I jumped at the chance and within a few days I was driving around in a car which was worth more than my flat. I should have slept in the car. It was more comfortable and had a better stereo.

Accepting the car was a naive move because it set me apart from the team and created a false impression. People would say, 'Look at that bastard Carling, he's earning a fortune.' But at twenty-four, when the alternative is a clapped out old banger or a push-bike, what would you do if someone loaned you a brand spanking new sports car? I was seduced by the glamour and the fun of running around in a swanky motor. It was my first example of the pulling power of the England captaincy and, quite frankly, I loved it. I told myself that if anyone was jealous of me in that car they would probably be jealous of anything I did but that was more for my own conscience than anything else. Me in a Mercedes. Nice. Very nice.

Inspirational Horizons evolved into Insights in 1992 and slowly the company began to be more profitable. The 1991 Grand Slam helped. That raised rugby's profile and people began to take me and the sport more seriously. The response to our marketing material improved dramatically. England had not won a Grand Slam in ten years. I was portrayed as one of the reasons for the turnaround. It was all good for business.

My attitude changed, too. I began to take more of an interest in the company as the pressures of captaincy eased and I felt more secure and confident in the job. It was blatantly obvious that a few words from me about leadership and motivation were not enough to bring in the punters. Credibility came in the form of a colleague, Jim Foley, who was an expert in his field and who provided a legitimate theoretical context to what I was trying to deliver. Jim would outline the essential ingredients of leadership and I would describe how I used them in relation to the England side. Clients would receive information which they could relate to an environment which was, I hoped, relevant and intriguing. It may look pretty basic now but in 1992 organisations did not seem terribly interested in team-building and getting the best from their employees.

The spin-offs were obvious. What I picked up from Jim in our work with Insights, I fed back into the England set-up. Geoff Cooke was already on-side because it dovetailed with his philosophy of coaching and management. Geoff had given presentations on Insights days and I had pinched much of his stuff when we discussed the importance of detailed preparation in achieving success. Together, over the years, Geoff and I introduced more personal and organisational practices to the England team.

In 1993 when an influx of new players entered the squad, they were asked to complete upward appraisals and get involved in small-group work. In the past England had been dominated by the opinions and voices of four or five vociferous individuals and the aim, building towards the 1995 World Cup, was to tap into the thoughts and experience of the entire squad. It took a while before it was taken seriously. The older players laughed themselves silly in some of the early group sessions and in one of the first upward appraisals, where players were asked what I could do better for them, Jason Leonard wrote, 'Let me earn as much money as you.' But, gradually, as the personnel changed, and the old gave way to the new, our preparation for internationals involved more of this type of work and it became an accepted and welcome part of the build-up.

Not so welcome, following the Murrayfield '90 débâcle, was the increased attention from the media, which was getting out of hand. I am the first to acknowledge the paradox, to admit that it is ludicrously hypocritical of me to complain about press hassle yet encourage media involvement when it suits to promote my business interests. I'll also admit it is more than slightly disingenuous to criticise the activities of certain journalists when I was well paid for writing a regular column in the *Mail on*

Sunday. All I will say is that there must be a legitimate balance somewhere whereby all parties can have their pound of flesh without going overboard, and I have not found it.

Everyone I meet has an image of me. It is inevitable, given my relationship with the media over the years, but how accurately the press reflect the real me is debatable. I appreciate I'm getting into a dangerous area here because opinions, by definition, are subjective and the process by which information and opinion get out into the public arena is a complicated one. Every interviewer, every feature writer will have an agenda dictated by the publication he or she represents, his or her own preconceived notions and the picture he or she wants to convey. Every interviewer will also have their judgement shaped by those who went before.

It is impossible to reflect a forty-minute conversation faithfully in a thousand-word article. Huge chunks have to be left out. Refining the piece to make it interesting, readable, necessitates selection. The writer will want to make his point, just as I am doing in this book. But why is it that throughout my life people I meet for the first time constantly say, 'You're different from what I expected'? Probably because very rarely have I been portrayed as the person I really am. I don't mean some sanitised, Goody Two Shoes character. That would be equally unrealistic, but only occasionally has the real me come across. That may have much to do with me finding it difficult to trust people enough to pour my heart out to them at a first meeting but it is also because the media is a voracious beast with an agenda all of its own.

Mind you, I made many mistakes myself early on. Soon after I had been handed the captaincy I agreed to do the old beefcake pose for a Sunday magazine. There I was splashed all over a glossy magazine, stripped to the waist trying desperately to pump up my chest muscles for the photographer. That was stupid and that one error did more to form opinions than any number of other less sensational encounters. Make one mistake and you never live it down.

I didn't get off on the right foot with the media, but now I have someone to smooth my passage and that is Jon Holmes, who can loosely be described as my agent. Jon also looks after Gary Lineker, David Gower, Michael Atherton, Alan Hansen, John Motson and John Barnes, among others. We first met in 1990 at about the time when demand for interviews and personal appearances was on the increase. I was having to handle that side of things by myself. The RFU did not have the system in place which they do now with press officers and directors of communication to relieve the hassle. And, to be honest, it was all beginning to get overwhelming. I was introduced to Jon by Colin Frewin, a mate from Harlequins, who had lent me some office space. Jon and I went out for dinner and he asked me what I wanted out of life long-term. I liked that approach. No one had ever asked me that question before. People I had spoken to had usually waded in with inflated claims of how much money they could make me. Jon was different. He listened as I outlined where I saw rugby going and where I fitted into the picture. He was also sensitive to the fact that the time I had to devote to the commercial side was limited, as I was going to concentrate on doing all that I could to make England successful.

Jon said that he would concentrate on getting my profile right, which might take the best part of two years during which he could not promise me much income at all. But if that went well and England and rugby continued to grow I could earn a decent amount of money in the future. I thought that made sense, and I also reasoned that he must be doing something right if he could persuade Gower and Lineker to stay with him for as long as they had. I would love to say that I signed on the dotted line there and then but our relationship is not like that. We do not even have a contract, although Jon takes care of most of my business affairs.

Over the years Jon has vetted most of my work. He has held firm to his belief that only the 'right' TV appearances or endorsement contracts are worth bothering about. Jon turns down around ninety per cent of the requests he receives, including recently a five-figure sum to appear on Mrs Merton's TV chat show which tested our friendship. We have only had one major argument, when he wanted me to appear on *They Think It's All Over* and I refused. That dispute was concluded in my favour on the third tee of Hanbury Manor golf course much to the amusement of Jon's business partner, Peter, but otherwise our time together has been sickeningly trouble-free.

Jon takes a percentage for negotiating the deals but that percentage varies and he does not take a cut from everything. For instance, he negotiated my £150,000 salary with Harlequins when rugby went professional but did not take a percentage because that was my job and not something he had organised or instigated. He charged a fee for his time but nothing like the twenty per cent which many other agents demand when the players they represent enter into contractual arrangements with clubs. However, if he arranges an advert or a book he will get a percentage of the total deal. He is incredibly honest about it which is why we get on so well. Although I get the accounts checked by an auditor I leave an awful lot to him. I've never been too bothered by the figures. When people say I'm only in it for the money they should talk to Jon and he will confirm that I have not got a clue what is happening financially most of the time. I have enough to do what I want but I am not massively rich.

I have always been an eternal optimist where money's concerned. I could earn more if I wanted to and I do turn an awful lot of work away but I'm not that materialistic. As long as I can afford a nice house, a decent car and can go on exotic holidays now and then I'll be happy. I'm lucky enough to have all that within my compass but the thought of having two or three houses dotted around the world just doesn't appeal at all.

9

THE GRANDEST OF SLAMS

T HEY say you never forget your first time and they are right. The first Grand Slam remains one of my dearest memories. The stink of the 1990 Scotland defeat lingered on into the 1991 season and World Cup year. It had eaten into us. All talk of Fancy Dan rugby had gone out of the window. All that mattered was the scoreboard at the end of a match. If England were so much as a point ahead, then life was sweet. After two years of chasing the championship, and with the team creaking towards its dotage, we knew that time was running out. If we didn't win something this year we wouldn't survive as a squad.

Wales were the first hurdle, the team who had frustrated our championship chances two years earlier. The bogey was still in operation. It was now twenty-eight years since England had last won in Cardiff and we were stretched tight with tension. We had gathered in the team room of the Crest Hotel in Cardiff for the final meeting. I wanted the senior players to set the tone and asked Dean Richards, Richard Hill, Peter Winterbottom and Rob Andrew to outline what they thought would be important the following afternoon. Rob and Dean went first and unloaded the usual stuff. Keep mistakes to a minimum, maintain control of the ball, maintain composure. Then Richard Hill spoke. Hilly had been around since 1984 and was familiar with Cardiff. In

1987 he had captained England against Wales and was one of four English players disciplined after violence and thuggery marred the match. I wasn't in the side that day but players who were shivered whenever they recalled Hilly's changing-room call to arms.

Four years on, Hilly began in composed and analytical fashion. Invariably astute and well prepared, he was always worth listening to.

'It starts up front,' he said. 'We need a steady scrummage so Rob and I can box kick. No taps from the line-out. The side who controls the ball, controls the game. They do not have our firepower in the forwards. The only way they can win this match is if they feed off our mistakes.'

The room was pin-drop quiet as he spoke. It was clear that he was absolutely intent on what he was saying. The Friday meeting was always the beginning of the count-down, the moment when the game became real, and Hilly, coming after Dean and Rob, was painting a dramatic and vibrant picture. I was absolutely delighted. This was exactly right. Hilly had everyone focused without tapping into the adrenaline. Perfect.

'And when you get hold of one of those bastards,' he continued, his voice noticeably louder and several octaves higher, 'let him have it, rip his head off, squeeze his bollocks. We are not going to lose this match. We cannot lose this . . .'

Hilly had flipped. The red mist had descended. He had half-risen out of his chair as he began to rant and was looking straight at me. I didn't know what to do. The rest of the team were still with him – his passion intensely compelling – but they wouldn't be for long. Soon the spell would be broken and the laughter would rise and where would that leave Hilly and our build-up?

But before I could say or do anything, Wade Dooley clamped a hand on Hilly's shoulder and shoved him down into his seat. 'Plenty of time for that tomorrow,' Wade said, and the moment passed. That is what Murrayfield '90 had engendered. It was in all of us. Only with Richard it bubbled a little closer to the surface than most.

The match itself was a picnic. Seven penalties from Simon Hodgkinson and a try from Mike Teague ensured a 25–6 victory. I was trapped in a ruck when we were awarded the penalty which would take us to 9–0. 'Brilliant,' said Hill. 'That's 3–0.'

'What are you talking about, Richard? If Hodgy kicks this we will go 9–0 in front.'

'One was a right hook, two was where I trod on his foot and three was where I elbowed him in the ribs.' Hill was back in his own special world again, locked in a personal battle with Robert Jones, Wales's scrum-half and Richard's opposite number.

Scotland were next up at Twickenham. No razzle-dazzle this time, no emotional high-octane shoot-out with both sides going for the Grand Slam. This was more like the Five Nations matches with Scotland we were used to. Scotland never reached the passionate heights of the previous year, constrained by a loyal and supportive Twickenham, and we turned in a controlled, powerful performance to notch another solid 21–12 win.

We were less convincing in Dublin, reined in by a committed Irish pack and a horribly wet afternoon. Dublin was always difficult. The night before the squad had gathered to watch Arnold Schwarzenegger in *Predator*. The forwards had chosen the film and it was a three-line whip. While we backs sat cross-legged on the floor, the forwards grunted their approval as Arnie dealt with his opponents. They became very excited when Arnie, after one particularly bloody act of revenge, whispered, 'Pay-back time,' and later, when he sustained an injury, hissed, 'Ain't got time to bleed.'

Thirty minutes into the match the next day, in the middle of a flat patch for England, Mike Teague suffered a knock to the head and lay motionless and stunned on the pitch. It was a significant moment because Teague was one of the core players of that side. He had scored the try against Wales in the previous match and his will power and determination in the face of adversity was the cornerstone of our effort. I rushed over to see blood pouring from a cut on the side of his head.

'Teaguey, are you OK? Can you carry on?'

He looked up, blinked twice. 'Ain't got time to bleed,' he said. Then he rose groggily to his feet, stared at the Irish forwards who were huddled together and muttered, 'Pay-back time.'

Dean Richards and the forwards took control, Rory Underwood scored the game's crucial try and the crisis was averted. Essentially, the script never changed all season: focused, intense, single-minded England plodding on towards their Grand Slam decider with France.

It's over. We've done it. England 21, France 19. England's first Grand Slam success for eleven years and the memory of that appalling defeat by Scotland can be pushed to one side, if not forgotten. Right at the end this fear that we might actually lose the match cascaded over me. I was in a maul with Mike Teague and a French forward was trying to rip the ball from both of us. He could have pulled out a pair of pliers and crushed my testicles for all the difference it would have made. Nothing and no one was going to hijack this victory. Then the whistle went and I screamed in satisfaction. The rest of the team followed suit. We were nearly-men no longer. Even the been-there-done-that boys went crazy. Peter Winterbottom – low key, self-effacing, understated, the man who was so dejected in Paris three years earlier – threw his head back and thrust his arms in the air. It was the way we all felt, especially after the previous year when we had come so close. It wasn't a pretty game and the French scored probably the try of the decade, but we'd won a Grand Slam.

Relief floods in. Back in the changing room confusion reigns. Geoff Cooke and Roger Uttley are wreathed in smiles. The bench have returned, back-slapping with the best of them, but oddly distant. The replacements are integral, important members of the squad but sitting in the stand is not the same as playing. They have no bumps or bruises, haven't broken sweat. A victory means they are unlikely to be selected for the next match but there is still that sense of belonging. Many will be drunk before too long, victims of the five before five club, a tradition that dictates that replacements pickle their emotions in alcohol.

Those that played can savour their win, eke it out over the long evening ahead, into the even longer night. The moment of victory parallels the time in that circle, ninety minutes earlier, when questions were asked amidst the macho male bonding. Now the answers are known and there is time to enjoy. No one rushes to get changed. Players sit in bloodstained, mud-drenched shirts, quietly reflecting on what has been achieved. The noise, the whooping and the hollering, comes from the back-room boys.

This is special. No one really knows what went on, who did what out there today except the players who contributed. No matter how intrusive the television camera has become, it cannot penetrate the darkest maul. Nor can the microphones pick up the sound of battle, the insults as players taunt each other, the wheezing as forwards crash into the scrummage, too tired to push.

That is why I played rugby. For occasions like this, when the challenges have been laid down and picked up. There were no hiding places today. Pretend to a team-mate you did something you didn't and any credibility you have as an individual is lost forever. This is what this time is for, players slumped on benches, acknowledging each other's efforts.

But the moment is short-lived. Duty beckons and chores, chores, chores. I try to get round every player, a pat on the back here, a quiet word there. They probably don't realise I've done it but some sort of acknowledgement is important, if only for me. There are no set-piece speeches. That kind of formality would be out of place in this changing room. Instead I check the casualty list and count the stitches to see what injuries we have picked up. Although the championship is over and a few weeks' rest lie ahead, we still have a tour to Australia and Fiji in the summer and then the World Cup. Those trips are in the back of my mind even now.

Geoff Cooke is telling me to get a move on. The formalities

of the rest of the day await and the timetable is tight, but I've got something for him. Sheepishly, I hand him my shirt. 'I'd like you to have this, Geoff.' I want to say more, to say that this win was down to him, his strength of character, his organisational talents, his faith in the players. I want to tell him how grateful I am that he chose me as captain, how much he has helped me develop, but I don't. Geoff is non-plussed. 'Don't be silly,' he says. 'I can't take it.' The moment is becoming awkward, even embarrassing. 'Please, Geoff,' I quip. 'I'd like to stay in the side.' He smiles, accepts the shirt, and moves away.

I slip into the bath and luxuriate in the buzz of voices next door. This is the private world which no one sees. Soon the demands of the media and the bureaucracy which accompany international matches will intrude but for the next five minutes the team is still together. Already the tales are growing taller and more outrageous. Paul Ackford and Wade Dooley are asking whether France won any line-out ball at all, Jeff Probyn is telling anyone who wants to listen and many who don't that he has never played against such a lifeless French front row. Some of the guys have still to get their England kit off, others are buck naked as I head out of the changing room and into the press conference.

I hate this bit. It is a ritual I go through after every England match. The journalists know that I will play it straight down the middle and avoid controversy and I know that the journos will not risk their best questions in front of their colleagues. The result is impasse. We bore the pants off each other but it has to be done. Image is everything. Ask Mike Atherton, the former England cricket captain. He refused to play the media game and was pilloried for it throughout his career. At least I learned that lesson early. I smile and switch into automatic pilot. 'Yes, we were good but we'll have to improve if we want to take on the southern hemisphere sides in the summer . . . It is a tremendous privilege to lead a team of this quality.' The answers would fit the pattern of almost any of the matches I've ever played in.

Then it's off again, to another ritual – tea in Twickenham's

Rose Room to meet family and friends. I'll normally have a few clients or business acquaintances along as well. What should be a few intimate moments with people I care about is the complete opposite. Already late because of the press conference, I get about five yards into the room before the autograph-hunters descend. Balls, programmes, posters, match tickets, jerseys are thrust at me from all sides requiring a signature. For half a second I flare with anger. The Rose Room is a ticket-only function. Most of these people are rugby folk, relations of the players who played. They above all others should appreciate the need for a bit of space. But the resentment dies away. Why rant and rave when there is no alternative? And what about the hypocrisy? Without their interest, English rugby would not have such an avid and appreciative following.

In later years, having learned the ropes, I will bypass the Rose Room altogether, don a baseball cap and a coat and meet some friends round the Range Rover in Twickenham's West car park, just to get some peace and quiet. But not today. Today I'm still anxious to please, keen to fulfil all my obligations. I grab a cup of tea with Mum and Dad, exchange a few pleasantries because there is no time for anything else, and head for the team bus and the journey to London's Hilton Hotel for the post-match dinner.

The size of my suite is the first indication that we have achieved something important. It must be the best the Hilton has to offer. As captain I'm normally well looked after by the Rugby Football Union but this is out of this world. I've got four bedrooms, jacuzzis, too many TVs to count, bars, conference tables, a phone next to the loo, the works. And no one to share it with. Girlfriendless, I had invited Andrew Harle to join in the fun.

The pace is still frantic. I was supposed to be at the pre-dinner reception, suitably kitted out in black tie, five minutes ago but I make time for one important routine. After any match, win or lose, I invariably go out on to the hotel balcony to look over Hyde Park and the lights of London, to take time out and reflect.

It allows me to make sense of what has happened and to put rugby and my life into context. The match may have been important to many, and absolutely crucial to me and the team, but for millions of others international rugby means nothing at all.

The dinner itself is hard work. I want to be down with the team talking about the game, swapping stories, reacquainting myself with old mates, but instead I am alone on the top table surrounded by dignitaries. This night will get better, though, because Ian Botham is in town and has sent out an open invitation for the team to adjourn to his hotel for a glass or three. It's strange how these things work out. Botham is sponsored by Nike, so is the England rugby team, and Jim Pearson, Nike's Mr Fixit, has organised a meet.

I slip out of the Hilton and taxi it the short distance to the Inn on the Park, Botham's hotel. Mickey Skinner and Andrew Harle are with me, as well as a few other England boys. Botham is a rugby nut. He has loved the game for years and his interest has been fanned by his friendship with Bill Beaumont during their stint as captains on the BBC's *A Question of Sport*. He is in the bar with Mike Teague and Paul Rendall when we arrive around 11 p.m. Within minutes the party is in full swing. Botham has gone nuts ordering case after case of champagne on his room bill and we are doing our best to make him poor. Skinner is in top form. Full of energy from his day on the replacements' bench, he is loud, theatrical and irreverent. So loud in fact that he has cleared the bar, apart from our party and a middle-aged German couple who are enjoying a quiet drink in the corner, or trying to. Upset by the noise, the man asks Skinner if he would mind toning down the celebrations a little, then disappears off to the toilet.

I look at the rest of the England lads who know exactly what I'm thinking. We wait for the fun. The man is away only a couple of minutes before returning to his girlfriend but it is more than enough time for Skinner to organise his response. He creeps round behind the couple and empties an ice bucket full of freezing water over the man. The man stands up to remonstrate but at 5ft 6ins his options are limited. Skinner towers over him and the situation is salvaged by a hotel employee who placates the couple. I am out of it by this time but go with Andrew to Botham's hotel room to continue the session. Around 3 a.m. I throw up out of the window. Andrew decides it is time to go, carries me into a cab and we slink back to the Hilton.

So much for having the best room in the house. I spend what is left of the night next to the loo, before crawling into bed to get a couple of hours' sleep. But the occasion has one spark of humour left. The next morning Andrew, who had enjoyed a more comfortable night in one of the suite's other bedrooms, decided that I needed a proper cooked breakfast to restore me to health. The waiter arrives, complete with silver salver, to find the England captain naked and flat out on his bed with another man wearing a dressing gown sitting at the foot of the same bed. 'Very good, sir,' says the waiter and flees.

— 10 —

ABSENT FRIENDS
AND BRUTALITY

I T was the week that changed my life. Nothing was ever
quite as intense again, a combination of success and
experience blunting the edge. The quarter-final of the 1991
World Cup against France in Paris was potentially the end
of the road for me. Geoff Cooke had said I would remain
as captain up to and including the World Cup. And this was
it. The first of the knock-out matches. Lose this one and I was
out, another mediocre captain of another mediocre England
team.

In the quiet moments, first thing in the morning, on the bus
to training, I caught myself countenancing the possibility of
defeat. It was an unfamiliar feeling for me. Usually I am bullish
before big matches, confident in the team's ability to survive the
challenge. If the doubts remain, I tend to rationalise them out
of my system. What's the worst-case scenario? Will it affect my
relations with family and friends? What will it be like arriving
home, having led England to an early exit from the World Cup?
Stripped to those dimensions, able to visualise and deal with
the consequences of defeat, the match usually looms less large,
but this one was different. I couldn't shake loose the foreboding,
couldn't share the burden. Two days before the match Jonathan
Webb, Rob Andrew and I had a coffee in a café a hundred yards

from the team hotel. Out of nothing Webby said, 'This is huge.' I knew exactly what he was thinking.

It was as if the game had appeared from nowhere. After the group matches against New Zealand, Italy and the United States, the squad had travelled to the Atlantic Hotel in Jersey for a break. Wives and girlfriends were bussed in and rugby was forgotten. No tackle bags, no scrummaging machines. We maintained the aerobic fitness with a few light work-outs, but that was the extent of our training. Pure bliss.

That first evening Simon Halliday, Jonathan Webb, Rob Andrew and I, plus partners, went out for dinner at a local pub. I was going out with Victoria Jackson. We had met in March at a sports dinner at London University where she was reading economics. Most of my girlfriends were friends of a friend of a friend and knew about rugby but Victoria was different. The first time she saw a collection of Five Nations shirts which I wore for training she asked whether I had played for all those teams. But, once into the rugby scene, she mucked in and got on well with the rugby wives and girlfriends, particularly Amanda Webb, Sara Andrew, Suzie Ackford and Suzanne Halliday.

Jersey was do as you please. A few of the guys who had not invited their other halves hit the local nightspots, while others played golf or lounged around the hotel games room. Some, though, opted for more traditional rugby entertainment. Peter Winterbottom, Mike Teague, Wade Dooley and Brian Moore headed for the bar. Po-faced professionals can talk all they like about diet and denial and the 450 different training methods to get you to peak condition – and I am the last person to knock the importance of those factors – but we got more from that one evening as a side than a week of solid practice.

It was carnage when we returned from the pub around midnight. Brian had taken advantage of the RFU tab and organised an impromptu wine-tasting of the most expensive wines and champagne that the hotel could lay their hands on. The food and drink bill that night came to £4,000 and half the squad had eaten out. Peter Winterbottom was the worst affected. With a bottle of wine at forty-five degrees to his lips, he was standing in the bar, legs apart, leaning forwards from the hips. I half-expected him to fall over at any minute but somehow he remained upright.

I had never seen Winters in such a state. The quietest, most composed, even withdrawn, of men was displaying another facet of his personality. 'I love you, Will. I think you're great,' he said, as I went to get a drink at the bar.

'Cheers, Wints. Thanks very much.'

'No, don't be like that. I really do.'

Then he followed me back to where we were sitting, grabbed Suzanne Halliday and bent her over the table.

'Steady on, old chap. That's not on,' remonstrated Simon as Suzanne giggled uncontrollably.

But Wints wasn't finished. 'We've got to have children together,' he told Lorraine Teague. Mike wasn't particularly concerned. In that condition Wints wouldn't even have been able to get undressed.

We never saw him the next day. He refused to leave his hotel room. No doubt the hangover wasn't great but it was the embarrassment factor which kept him inside. And did we let him forget the incident? Did we agree not to mention it again for the rest of our lives? I don't think so. Dewi Morris had recorded Wints' indiscretions on video and for the rest of our stay in Jersey we ran the tape as often as we could. France did not stand a chance. The bonds between the players as we arrived in Paris could not have been tighter.

It was just as well because this was the week that Geoff Cooke, Roger Uttley and I had left England's colossus out of the side. Dean Richards had been dropped. It wasn't the most popular of decisions.

'Suicide,' said Brian Moore.

'Absolute rubbish.' Wade Dooley was equally forthright.

Only Peter Winterbottom acknowledged the dilemma. Purged of any traces of alcohol, he was typically matter of fact. 'Do what you have to do, there are pros and cons on both sides,' he said.

Richards had been a feature of the team since 1986 when he scored two tries and contributed to a penalty try on his debut against Ireland. He was the forwards' best friend because his bear-like strength and uncanny ability to be in the right place at the right time ensured that he was always in the thick of the action controlling events. His gentle, understated personality was equally endearing. Deano, in many ways, was the heart of the team.

The selection meeting was long and tense. I normally chip in when backs are the subjects of discussion because I feel I know something about them. But that is not the case with the forwards. Then my role is to canvass opinion amongst the squad and feed it back to Geoff and Roger. This decision was not going to get the squad's unqualified support. Geoff and Roger were adamant. Deano was immense, but his influence tended to be felt close to the set-pieces. The wider you asked him to stray from scrum and line-out the less he liked it. We were also worried about how he would cope with the pace of the French back row and half-backs. No matter how often or how long Geoff Cooke and I talked to Dean following the summer tour to Australia, when the problem first surfaced, there was nothing we could say or do to persuade him to change his style of play. I found his intransigence infuriating and took the view that the team was more important than the individual. I wanted to develop the side, Deano did not fit in with the plans and I thought if he won't change for the team, then the team comes first.

I suppose that was pretty callous but that's how it was. Even if we were big mates and I had sat down and begged him to tweak his approach he would have said, 'Look, Will, this is the way I am. This is the way I play.' But I flunked out when it came to telling him. Geoff had already passed on the news and when it came to my turn for a heart to heart I couldn't face him. Usually players unload when I get to them but Dean said nothing. I can cope with the ranting and raving but it was the

My fir
look o
must l

The beginning and the end – two tries which span a career. The first against France,
It's no 18 March 1989, the last against Scotland, 1 February 1997.

I would never have met these guys without rugby. Rory Bremner, Hugh Laurie and John Cleese have been as good a bunch of friends as anyone could wish for.

silence which threw me. His passive acceptance made me squirm. I blurted out a few platitudes and left. It was a pretty undistinguished performance.

The shock of Dean's omission was palpable. A tremor ran through the squad and the practice session on the morning after the announcement was edgy and truculent. So edgy in fact that a dust-up occurred between Brian and Dean when Dean entered into his role as a defender a mite too enthusiastically, clubbing Mooro with a tackle bag. I was delighted. In all the time I had been with this side we had never had an incident on the training pitch. It meant that we were up for it: snappy, hard-headed, ruthless.

Even the significant matches blur into obscurity after a while but I remember that match with the utmost clarity. It was the most brutal and exhilarating game of rugby I had played in up to that point and nothing subsequently has removed that tag. The savagery continued after the final whistle when Daniel Dubroca, France's coach, swung a punch at the referee in the tunnel.

As a centre, I have two main concerns: marking my man and marshalling the drift defence to prevent the opposition working an overlap. But on that day the workload quadrupled. France were rampant, running with an intensity which only they can manage. Not even the great All Black sides have the capacity to rip into you in the way that France can. Within the first few seconds I had tackled Laurent Cabannes as the French flanker hurtled through the midfield. Moments later Philippe Sella exploded down the blind side. This was rugby on the edge, our flat-out response a matter of reacting as quickly and effectively as possible. Fingers-in-the-dam rugby, filling holes, patching cracks. In moments like these tactics and strategy go out of the window to be replaced by character and guts. Only players who have been through that experience know the demands it makes on you physically and mentally. All you can hear is your own breathing as you thunder in support of a break or cover across to stifle an attack. Ordinarily I would check with Webby, Rors, Brian, Rob and Wints to see what they had picked up, whether we needed to rest the big men, spread it wide, attack a certain opposition player, but there was no information coming back. The guys were too intent on their own jobs and responsibilities to notice anything else. They were playing to survive.

I've never seen a French team as committed. Some had stepped into madness. Serge Blanco reacted to a late tackle from Nigel Heslop by belting Sloppy with a haymaker. Eric Champ, Cabannes' partner, also whacked Heslop. David Bishop, the New Zealand referee, called both captains together to ask us to calm down the troops. No more than a yard from Blanco, I studied his eyes and saw that he had gone. That was the point when I knew that we had them. We still had a semblance of control. They had none so early in the game. While they were playing all the rugby, we managed to kick a few penalties, including one following Blanco's assault. It was the beginning of the end for France. Rory scored after a break by Jerry, following a miss-pass from me, and we turned round 10–6 ahead. It was then that I made the finest, most prophetic half-time speech of my career. Addressing the circle, I said with massive prescience: 'The next score wins this one lads.'

Peter Winterbottom and Mike Teague will probably mention this at my funeral because it was France who scored at the start of the second period. I could feel their combined gaze burning into the back of my neck as I huddled behind the posts for the second time within ten minutes trying desperately to think of something intelligent to say which would sound credible and invigorating. That try was crucial, not in the way I had antici-pated, but because it signalled the end of France's efforts. They expected us to creak after that score and when we didn't, the fire left their eyes. Webby kicked another penalty and a try in the final minute clinched the victory at 19–10.

And to cap a memorable week I was in at the death. Richard Hill, as he had done all afternoon, put up a box kick which landed just short of France's goal-line. Heslop and I chased after it and when Lafond, the French wing, caught the ball, I hurled myself at him, frantic to grab a piece of him to prevent a counter-attack. I wasn't too fussy what I grabbed as long as he was unable to run. Then the juggernaut arrived. The pack came pounding up and Lafond, deciding that keeping the ball from a half-crazed England team was not the most sensible act on a Saturday afternoon at the Parc des Princes, let go. The pile of bodies crashed over the goal-line with me at the bottom holding on to the ball. Mick Skinner was lying next to me yelling his head off and Brian Moore was bouncing up and down pointing to the ball over the goal-line. But it was the referee's confirmation which I wanted. Bishop raised his arm to award the try and England had won. Those worst-case scenarios would have to wait.

But Paris had one more test up its sleeve. As the coach swept towards a rendezvous at a pre-booked nightspot, Wade Dooley decided it was time to stamp his mark on the proceedings. Wade was one of the old-timers, a player who had seen more than his fair share of the rough days in the eighties, and he was enjoying his time in the sunshine. In fact, he was so chuffed with the victory, so full of goodwill towards his fellow men that he wanted to kiss the entire coach. I was seated in the middle of the bus and knew trouble was on its way as soon as I heard the commotion around the back seat as Wade commenced his journey of love. You didn't argue with Wade. At 6ft 8ins tall and a shade over eighteen stone he tended to get what he wanted.

By the time he got to me, he had perfected his technique. Grab, hug, kiss and then on to the next victim. But I wasn't to be let off so lightly. 'I've got something special for you,' he leered. 'Tongues.' And just to let me know that he wasn't joking, he licked his lips and rolled his tongue around the inside of his mouth. Brute force wasn't an option in defence against that monster so I tried another tack.

'Wade, you can't. I'm not that easy on a first date.'

Seconds later, he had me pinned against the side of the coach and was deep-throating me.

Two forwards declaring undying love for me, a brutal match, a famous win, and I still had a job. It was some trip.

— 11 —
NOT QUITE GOOD ENOUGH

V ERY few sportsmen get the opportunity to contest a World Cup final, even fewer end up on the winning side. I'm still firmly ensconced in the first category. Should England have beaten Australia to win the 1991 World Cup? Some say we should have done, but not me. Australia were the most complete side in the tournament. Their stunning last-minute try against Ireland in the quarter-final proved their durability and their comprehensive demolition of New Zealand in the semi-final proved their class. They were undeniably the best team in the world at the time and their record over the next three seasons up until the 1995 World Cup speaks for itself. During that period Australia won Test series against South Africa and New Zealand, as well as beating those two countries in one-off games and thrashing France, Argentina, Scotland, Ireland and Wales. In three seasons of continuous rugby, in which they played twenty-five Tests, Australia lost four matches. England could not have done that. We lacked the all-round firepower which Australia had and we lacked their strength in depth.

It is possible to argue that England were lucky to make the final. Victories over the United States, Italy, France and Scotland were hardly out of the ordinary, especially given the fact that we had beaten France and Scotland seven months earlier *en route* to a Grand Slam. The unpalatable truth is that we blew the two matches which were not part of our regular, familiar, comfortable routine. We froze against New Zealand, according them too much respect, and we did not have the all-round game to put Australia away in the final.

The All Blacks are a familiar part of the international scene in this country now but in 1991 they were men from a different planet. England had last played them in 1985, many of the players were encountering them for the first time, and we treated them like gods rather than the talented but mortal rugby players they actually were. The silence on the team bus as it carried us from the Hampshire hotel to Twickenham to play the opening match of the 1991 World Cup tournament was indicative of the reverence in which we held New Zealand rather than our steely determination. I was as much to blame as anyone. Early in the game I let Craig Innes, my opposite number, run at me before tackling him. Ordinarily I would have gone to meet him, to knock him back over the gain line, but I was too keen to see what he was capable of to impose myself on him. The rest of the team fared no better. We failed to dominate in any phase and a flat performance on a flat afternoon ended in an 18–12 defeat.

Scotland wasn't much of an improvement in the semi-final. The nationalistic excesses of Murrayfield '90 had subsided. Our victory against France had dispelled self-doubt. Against Scotland, we ground out a win. Gavin Hastings, Scotland's full-back and captain, missed a kick in front of the posts when the scores were tied at 6–6 but I honestly don't think it would have made a difference. I was standing next to Jerry Guscott as Gavin shaped to kick. 'If this goes over, we've got to get our asses into gear,' I said. Jerry nodded, but there was no panic. We knew that we had enough in reserve to manufacture a win. That night Rob and I met up with Gavin at Boroughmuir Rugby Club who threw a party for both teams. Gavin was inconsolable and Rob and I spent some time trying to persuade him that he was not responsible, that he shouldn't blame himself for Scotland's exit from the World Cup. Rugby had turned full circle again. A year previously the bottom had fallen out of my world when Scotland had pinched a Grand Slam and here I was helping Gavin come to terms with a defeat of similar proportions.

The attention and expectation had cranked up another notch now that we had made the final. Back in London at the Petersham Hotel we were flooded with congratulatory faxes and cards from well-wishers. Hundreds arrived each day, including one signed by all the family, Mum included. Rugby was coming out of the closet, capturing the public's imagination in a way it had never done previously. The attention was unnerving and a prelude to things to come. I had always received letters from fans but never in this quantity. Some of it got out of hand. Every now and then I would receive in the post photographs of naked or near-naked girls asking for a date or a memento they could keep. The odd pair of knickers arrived. It was all very strange, amusing to recall now, but at the time I couldn't help wondering if women were prepared to go to those lengths to get some feedback, what wouldn't they do?

The fuss did not let up, even after the final. Victoria, my girlfriend, wore stockings to the players' wives and girlfriends dinner after the match. As the girls sat down for their group photograph Victoria's dress rode up to reveal the stocking tops. The sight interested the tabloids enough for them to run the picture across their front pages. Paparazzi, rugby correspondents, gossip columnists and feature writers dogged our every move. We were easy meat. Because the tournament was played in England and everyone knew where we were staying, we were accessible and copy was cheap. I have never experienced anything subsequently in a rugby context which came close to matching it. The competition four years later in South Africa was a journalist-free zone for England players compared to '91. That tournament elevated my profile to the point where taxidrivers who had never seen or heard about rugby recognised my face and wanted to start up a conversation. A quiet drink was out of the question. I wasn't sure I liked it. I hate to think what it would have been like if we had won, but we didn't. Australia sneaked it 12–6 and the inquests started.

Should we have tried to tighten it up against Australia in the final? Before that match we reached a collective decision that we had been stuffed by Australia on tour in the summer up front and our only chance of success was to move the ball wide and recycle it. Because we happened to lose the game certain individuals climbed on the bandwagon and proclaimed we should have played a different way. Hindsight is a marvellous invention, but I still believe they were talking crap. When you look at the statistics of that match it is clear that we won as much first-phase possession as they did. We also won second-, third- and fourth-phase ball, which we wouldn't have done if we had kicked it off the pitch, as was our usual way in the lead-up matches against France and Scotland. We played as well as we could play against Australia. We made chances to win, and didn't take them. They had two chances and took one. That was the story of the match.

And I don't believe in the lead-up to the game the forwards always wanted to play it one way and the backs wanted to play it another. I just don't remember it that way. Without being funny, if the forwards had wanted to play it one way they would have done so. They received the ball first and there were enough strong characters in that pack to say to me, 'Sorry, Will, we think it's going to happen like this.'

The attacks on my captaincy hurt, especially as they came from members of my own team. Jeff Probyn was the most vociferous. He had piled in after the 1990 Scotland game and here was another opportunity to have a go. Come judgement day, I accept that defeats were my responsibility but the team must share some of the blame, too. Singling me out for criticism is ridiculous. If Jeff's logic is right, that I was uniquely responsible for the well-being of the team, then I won forty-four games and lost fourteen as captain, which is a pretty decent record. But that argument is rubbish. A captain is only as good as the players around him. The media also have this obsession with leaders.

They demand a figurehead. If you win, you're the best captain in the world, but if you lose, you're the worst. It takes some getting used to.

Maybe there are captains out there with the ability to change a game halfway through a match, but I've never come across one and I'm certainly not one myself. You've got fifteen guys out there making decisions. How can one guy transform fourteen others? I just don't think it happens. When you play against the best the amount of talk going on from everyone is incredible but even that is not guaranteed to work. You can have all the input in the world, all the right decisions, but if players knock on, lose the scrum or the line-out, it counts for nothing. Some matches have a life of their own. There were games which we won, when I said, 'Guys, do this or do that,' and nobody did it. A captain on his own isn't that influential.

I have thought about this issue a lot and I think Australia and New Zealand have got it right. Nick Farr-Jones, who led Australia in that final, is always trotted out as the wonder captain but I have talked to a number of influential people in the Aussie side who put forward an alternative viewpoint. Nick was an outstanding captain but for much of the time he benefited from Michael Lynagh at outside-half and Tim Gavin at No. 8, both of whom were very very good decision-makers. It wasn't Nick saying, 'Listen guys, change this, change that.' There were several voices exploring options, making suggestions. The All Blacks hold a similar view. Their culture encourages players to take on responsibility. Sean Fitzpatrick is a very inspirational leader, partly because the New Zealand coaches don't go on the pitch. The players have to think for themselves. Fitzpatrick is a great player, a great captain, but New Zealand profit from a general level of awareness. You can't tell me that at hooker Fitzpatrick sees a hell of a lot of the game, and makes great tactical decisions. He relies on four or five guys in the side to help him. And that's the way it should be.

For the last five or ten years England haven't had decision-makers of that quality. It comes from the whole way we approach the game which, ironically, is getting much worse in the professional era. In New Zealand the coaches don't run the sessions, the players do. When it comes to the game the players have got to know what's going on, so it makes sense to prepare in that vein. It's a process of education. In Britain the coach tells you what to do and you go on the field and do it, and when it goes wrong you have to wait for half-time for the coach to come on and tell you what to do next. We don't possess the number of players New Zealand have who just understand the game. And that goes for the backs as well as the forwards. In '91 England had accumulated a number of individuals with the skills and mental toughness to beat anyone in one-off games but we still did not understand the game.

Jeff Probyn was not the only well-known critic to have a pop at me during that World Cup. David Campese also took great delight in sticking the knife in as deep and as often as possible. Campo has been the bane of my life. If ever a journalist wanted a line about crappy England or crappy Will Carling, Campo was sure to provide it. Even when he had finished playing, or Australia were not up against England, Campo was happy to dish the dirt. Initially I was puzzled by his dislike of England's style and his criticism of me, especially since we had been team-mates in a Barbarians match and had got on well. I even gave him a lift to the airport after the game and nothing in our conversation on that journey hinted at the England-baiter he would become.

The invective reached a climax in 1991. Every paper you picked up had a picture of Campo slagging off England, criticising their tactics and their personnel. In the end I asked Nick Farr-Jones and Michael Lynagh to explain what Campo's motives were to help me understand what was going on. They had been around Campo for years and knew him as well as they knew each other.

'Don't worry,' Lynagh said. 'He's always mouthing off. He does it to me and he does it to Nick. We've just learned to ignore it.' Farr-Jones took it a stage further.

'Look, Will, Campo is cheesed off because he thinks he is the best player in the world and he is not getting enough headlines because you and the England team are receiving all the attention. We tried to explain to him that the tournament is being played in England and that the English newspapers are honour bound to concentrate on their team but he doesn't seem to understand.'

It sort of made sense. Campo was mad because the England team was pinching his space in the paper, but he loved all the attention. Once when he was surrounded by a group of tabloid journalists who were hanging on his every word, I asked him what he was saying. 'Don't worry, mate, it's just a bit of fun with the media. It's just a bit of fun, that's all.' Sure enough, the next day there was another Carling-bashing article in the tabloids. But when someone had a pop at him he would go ballistic. In the 1995 World Cup Jack Rowell often asked me how I was going to respond to Campo's gibes. My tack was not to retaliate, not to dignify the original insult with a retort of any kind. If the rest of the Australian team were slightly embarrassed by his antics then why should I get all hot and bothered? But it did not stop him. He was an impossible man to gag.

But what a talent. At his best he was awesome and more than justified his tag as the best player in the world. He saw things on a rugby pitch way before anyone else and, in his early days, had the pace to exploit that advantage. Some of the tricks he pulled were just unbelievable, light years ahead of his time. He appeared everywhere, the complete attacker with astonishing vision. His change of pace was phenomenal, his angles shrewd and he had this uncanny knack of being able to anticipate events. I think he was exceptional and he also had a tremendous attitude to rugby. It was an open secret that he was a professional rugby player when the sport was still strictly amateur, which was part of the reason why he was such an accomplished player. The other reason was natural talent. Loads of it.

He did not have it all his own way though. During the 1991 final Campo went for an interception which did not quite come off. As he recovered the ball, he was up-ended by Mick Skinner who floored him with a crushing tackle. I was right behind Skins and I could hear Campo expel a blast of air as he lay on the ground temporarily winded. It was the chance I had been waiting for for months. I came straight in and stood on his bollocks. The strangled cry he gave as I sauntered off to rejoin play was immensely satisfying.

— 12 —
SILENCE OF THE LAMBS

MY relationship with the rugby authorities, particularly the Rugby Football Union, has been at best ambivalent, at worst bloody impossible. It goes back to when I was first appointed as captain. I'm sure they all thought, young, won't want to rock the boat, ex-army, university-educated, bloody marvellous, he'll toe the line. Indulge him for a couple of years and then we'll get rid of him before he gets too big for his boots.

Well, if that was their hope, it can't have lasted too long. The RFU and I were on a collision course from day one. It was inevitable that we clashed because we were coming at issues from opposite viewpoints. As captain, I felt I was responsible for representing the England team on a range of matters and my thoughts were guaranteed to contradict theirs.

Money was only part of it. There was a massive inconsistency between what was happening in the rest of the rugby world, specifically in South Africa and New Zealand, and what was going on in England. Before rugby went professional in August 1995, it was an open secret that the top Springboks were earning small fortunes out of playing and the loot was paid directly to them. South Africa did not bother with deals which bent the letter of the amateur regulations. They chose to hand over the cash in a blatant way which smashed them completely.

That rankled inside the squad but it was the attitude of certain officials in charge of English rugby which hurt most. They were so supercilious. They believed that the RFU controlled world rugby, set the moral tone, whereas the truth was that all the big decisions were being taken by the southern hemisphere countries. New Zealand, South Africa and Australia were dictating the shape of the game on the pitch with law changes and forcing the rest of the world to face up to other issues off the pitch. I felt that England's committee in general were not behind the side, were not supportive of our efforts in public and in private, and that was the basis of my disputes with them.

I'm the first to admit I was a loose cannon at times. After my last game as captain in my first year I overheard Derek Morgan complaining about some aspect of the team's and my performance. I didn't get on with Morgan. He was in charge of student rugby when I was at Durham and he never selected me. I was drunk, as was usual in the early days, and I turned to Morgan and said, 'Christ, what the hell do you know about selection? You never picked me as a student, even though I was playing for England. Explain the logic of that to me. I was good enough to play for the senior England side but you never picked me for the students.' I had him by the throat up against the wall. Roger Uttley had to pull me off. All very embarrassing now but symptomatic of my relationship with most rugby alickadoos.

I also made bad judgement calls. The most notorious occurred after the Welsh match in 1991. We decided to boycott the press conference, even though it was the first time England had won in Cardiff for twenty-eight years. It was portrayed as a dispute over money, the original cash for questions affair. Journalists said we were demanding money before we would speak to them but I don't remember it like that. The truth was that we were getting rung up day and night by the media and the players wanted someone or something to take the heat off. This was at a time when journalists had the players' home numbers and there was no media liaison officer to deal with most of the crap. Before that Welsh match guys who were taking the field the following day were called in the hotel at 9.30 p.m. One player was even woken up later that night. There was no system in place to organise the media attention. Most of the squad were happy to agree to interviews. Relations between the players and the specialist rugby journalists had always been cordial. All we wanted was a proper structure in place.

Other factors added to the sense of unease which was gripping the team. Cardiff as always was a difficult venue for England and English players. The crowd were invariably hostile and the atmosphere forbidding. Not winning there for twenty-eight years added to the tension. Two years previously we had arrived at the ground by coach in the pouring rain to be greeted by a mass of red and white bobble hats and a sea of two fingers. As we went for our customary stroll on the pitch several of the forwards were spat at by some of the Welsh supporters who had arrived early to get the best viewing platforms. The forwards only found out when they removed their England blazers in the dressing room prior to getting changed and saw that the backs of the jackets were covered in spit. So spooked were we about Wales and Welsh rugby in 1989 that we stayed at the St Pierre Golf and Country Club just over the Severn Bridge in Chepstow rather than venturing further into the country.

All this atmosphere was still around in 1991, so the hassle from the journalists became the last straw. On the morning of the match the matter of the late-night calls was raised and it was decided that we would make a statement by boycotting the press conference, whether we won or lost. We wanted to make a point, to say, as much to the RFU as to the journalists, that we had had enough. We wanted the RFU to understand that the monthly press conferences they organised to spread the news about dull administrative issues which satisfied the specialist journalists were not indicative of the interest now being shown in the sport as far as players and personalities were concerned. The decision, once taken, did not seem a particularly big deal. I thought nothing of it at the time. There were other more pressing subjects on my mind, not least the game itself.

Afterwards, when we had beaten Wales 25–6 and created a little piece of history, I confirmed with Geoff Cooke and Roger Uttley, that we were not going to the press conference. 'No, we're not,' they said. Instead, we walked out of the stadium back to our team hotel which, this year, was adjacent to the ground. Delighted at the victory, we had no idea of the storm which was about to break. Denied their usual fodder from the press conference, the journalists were at a loss. No quotes from an England team which had ended a twenty-eight-year dry spell became a bigger story than the watershed result itself. The Sunday papers wanted a reaction and they also wanted to know why we were refusing to talk.

That was the moment when we should have come clean, communicated our dissatisfaction with the level of media intrusion and talked about the victory. But we didn't. Why should we care about a bunch of journalists with acres of space to fill and deadlines to meet? We had done our bit and beaten Wales. Writing about it was their job. They had seen the game. Let them get on with it. In any case, we had some serious celebrating to do. So we kept quiet and made our way to the dinner via the hotel kitchens to avoid the journalists waiting in the reception area. By that time most of them had rung players as they were getting changed in their hotel rooms to get the reaction they needed for their newspapers, but the damage had been done. An organised collective news blackout from an England side had to be explained and during that night and over the next few days various conspiracy theories emerged, most with the same theme. We were portrayed as greedy England, no money, no talk. It was true that the squad had engaged Bob Willis, the former England cricket captain, and his brother David to explore money-making opportunities within the regulations laid down by the International Rugby Board, and that Bob and David were researching the possibility of asking for payment for interviews as one of a number of schemes to generate revenue, but it was never as simple as pay up or we shut up. Those facts didn't stop the media, though. They thought they had found the reasons for our stand and filled their newspapers accordingly.

If that was a PR disaster, some good did come out of Cardiff '91. Soon afterwards Colin Herridge took on the post of England's media liaison officer. Colin was Secretary of Harlequins at the time and he also represented Surrey on the RFU committee. His appointment was a godsend and he and I forged an understanding and a friendship which remains to this day. Without his advice and support I am not sure I would have survived the emotional pummelling from the media which followed the revelations of my friendship with Diana, Princess of Wales.

Colin immediately became the buffer between the squad and the media. He introduced a routine where all requests had to be filtered through him, rather than the journalists going direct to the players, and he established set days and times when players and myself were on offer to newspapers, TV and radio. Colin allowed us to have a semblance of control. We were able to fulfil our obligations without them impacting adversely on our preparations before matches. But the price had been heavy. If the squad had an ally in Colin following Cardiff, we had also given our detractors within the RFU plenty of ammunition to have a pop at us.

And top of that list was Dudley Wood, Secretary of the Rugby Football Union 1986–96. Dudley was a charming bloke, a great raconteur, very clever, but a staunch defender of amateurism. Deep down, I think, he was appalled at the way rugby was going, incensed that the players were becoming important figures within the sport. He never denied that this was his stance but he was such an influential figure within European rugby administration that he inevitably became hostile to the direction in which the team and I wished to travel, that was to embrace professionalism and give England the opportunity of competing against the best teams in the world on an equal footing.

Our paths first crossed publicly in 1990 when I was hauled up in front of him because the media had alleged that I had been paid £500 for opening a sports complex. In those days that was a serious no-no. Mike Pearey, the RFU President, called me at home. 'Listen,' he said, 'they're going to investigate this payment.' Mike was unlike other senior RFU figures. He saw things from the players' point of view, as well as protecting the interests of his committee. I could do business with Mike and if there were more like him on the RFU committee when the sport was deciding its future it might not have got itself into the mess it did.

So I turned up at Twickenham to answer the charges. The money had in fact not gone anywhere near my bank account but had been paid to the Trinity Hospice, which was a charity I supported. I took a receipt from Trinity Hospice to the meeting as proof and it was fine with everyone except Dudley. It became abundantly clear that he did not believe me and afterwards he confronted me in the corridor outside the room and produced a single sheet of paper that he wanted me to sign. It was exactly like being back at school with an angry headmaster haranguing a boy he felt was lying. On the paper was a declaration? telling the world exactly what I had verbally told the meeting earlier.

'Sign here,' Dudley said.

'Why?' I replied. 'I showed you the receipt. What's the point of this declaration. Don't you trust me?'

'Sign here,' repeated Dudley.

And in the end I did but from that moment the little trust there was between us evaporated completely. Here I was, England captain, and I was being treated as an errant schoolboy. It was ridiculous.

There was another typical Dudley moment during the 1991 World Cup. The tournament was covered by ITV, with the bigger matches going live to forty countries, and it was attracting huge viewing figures. It was the first time that rugby began to come close to matching soccer in terms of spectator interest. The England squad had struck up a relationship with Jim Rosenthal, ITV's front man, and Ian O'Donoghue, their cameraman. They were people we could trust, who knew when and when not to film, and because of that we had given them access to aspects of international rugby which hadn't been seen before. They were allowed into the changing room and into private receptions after the games because we felt that, if rugby wanted to develop new fans, a knowledge of what went on would be beneficial.

Dudley didn't agree. He felt that the Twickenham changing rooms were hallowed areas and pictures of England preparing for a World Cup final should not be broadcast. Although ITV were closely involved in filming much of the preparations for the quarter-final against France in Paris and the semi-final against Scotland at Edinburgh, Dudley decreed they were not to be allowed into Twickenham. So we smuggled the equipment in via the kit bags and were rewarded with some of the best PR footage England had ever received. The pictures showed just exactly what it had meant to the players to lose the biggest match of their lives, the exhaustion, the tears, the physical toll which rugby at that level can exact. There were even shots of John Major, the Prime Minister, who came into the dressing room after the match to commiserate.

When he found out, at the end of the World Cup dinner, Dudley went ballistic. 'That's the end of you,' he told Geoff Cooke. 'Where's Carling? I'll tell him the same.'

'I wouldn't, if I were you,' Cooke said. 'He's just lost the World Cup final. It's not a good time.'

But Dudley didn't care. He just wanted to tell me, I'm going to have you. It's lucky he didn't because I don't know what I would have done to him. That's the kind of bloke I was dealing with.

And he had the gall to request favours. He used to sit at the end of the top table at black-tie dinners after international matches and ask me to join him. He knew I didn't like him, but used to say, 'Will, you stand next to me and talk to me. It's good for my image for people to see you talking to me.' His behaviour smacked of double standards to me. If the England team or I could do something for him he was sweet as pie but when we asked him for a favour, or some latitude in money matters, he shut up shop.

In 1994 Dudley vetoed an advertisement in the match programme for the Romania game. For the past two years a company called the Hospital Savings Association had bought space from the RFU to advertise their services and the RFU had taken their money without a murmur. This time their request was refused. And the reason? They had changed their advert to include a picture of me in suit and tie extolling the virtues of their company, for which I was to be paid. It was all perfectly legal and above board, condoned and approved by the International Rugby Board. But Dudley knocked it back, arguing that because the advert was appearing in a match programme it was rugby-related and therefore outside the regulations. It seemed as though he would do anything to frustrate me or the other players.

There is always going to be tension between players and officials. Nothing wrong with that. It is important that each provides checks and balances on the other but there was never a sense of give and take with certain RFU officials. They were dismissive of the players as a body, scared witless of player-power. They thought that we had no idea of what was good for the game, that we were inherently selfish when we had put years and years into rugby for no financial reward whatsoever. I was told on two or three occasions that I took winning too seriously. 'We are England,' they said. 'It's about playing the game.' I couldn't believe they were telling me this.

— 13 —

PIPE AND SLIPPERS RUGBY

GRAND SLAM number two was a breeze, our total of 118 points a new championship record. Confidence was sky high after the World Cup and we blasted through the Five Nations campaign with 18 points the narrowest margin of victory. In the context of previous campaigns, it was a walk-over. The side was running on automatic pilot. Martin Bayfield came in for Paul Ackford who had decided to hang up his boots, Dewi Morris replaced Richard Hill and Tim Rodber kicked off his career that season but elsewhere it was business as usual.

Martin Bayfield quickly earned the nickname the Captain's Parrot. An immensely tall likeable guy, with a fantastic sense of humour, he camouflaged his newness by repeating what I had said five minutes after I had said it. It was like meeting my echo. Discussing how to play against Ireland, I would suggest that not losing ball in contact was the key to the game. Other players would chip in with their own thoughts on important areas and when we eventually got round to Bayf he would mirror my point. The fact that we all noticed and turned it into a joke was indicative of how familiar the squad had become with itself. Everyone knew everyone else, knew what they were thinking, how they would react. Reassuring and immensely helpful in some ways, it was also a massive burden.

We had become too set in our ways, unreceptive to change. We didn't need training kit that season, a pipe, slippers and a comfortable old cardigan would have sufficed for the forwards. The side had stopped evolving. It did not matter too much on the domestic front because we were far and away the best side in Europe, but in terms of our dream of respectability on the world stage we were making no progress whatsoever.

The build-up to the 1992 England/Scotland match convinced me that it was time to wave goodbye to the pack I most admired. I had always sought to involve the forwards as much as possible, to ask their opinion. The backs were open and receptive to new ideas and, naively, I thought the forwards would react in similar fashion if I could present a convincing argument for change. But it was like trying to infiltrate a Masonic lodge. Unless you were one of them you had no chance.

I wanted to kick off right against Scotland. We had watched hours of video tape and worked out that Craig Chalmers, Scotland's outside-half, was far more effective playing down the right-hand side of the pitch. So if we kicked off to the right he would be tight to the left touch line and therefore disadvantaged. If that sounds simple and straightforward to you it didn't to the pack.

At the end of the team meeting I asked the forwards to stay behind to talk it through with them. 'Listen guys,' I said, 'we've had a look at it and tactically we think it would be a good idea if we kicked off to our right, because we could put pressure on Chalmers by playing on that side of the pitch. Anyone got a problem with that? Do you think it's a good idea?'

Silence. Just a sea of blank faces. Then someone piped up. 'Yes, actually it is a problem.'

'What's that then?' I queried.

'We always start to the left.'

'I know that, but just this once, do you think it would be possible to start to the right?'

'Why can't we start to the left?'

'I've been through that. It can't be that hard to start to the right, can it?' By this time I thought I was winning the argument until they dropped their bombshell.

'Have you ever won a restart?'

'Er, no, actually, I haven't.'

'Well, there you are then. We kick off to the left.'

Would they change tack? Not bloody likely. After about half an hour of trying to persuade them, with no luck at all, I left the room seething. And as I disappeared through the door I could hear loads of chuckling and someone said, 'Let's run out backwards, that'll really throw them.' I can laugh about it now but it was so exasperating at the time. I've never come across such a stubborn bunch as the forwards who played in the late eighties, early nineties.

There were occasions, though, when I was grateful for their intransigence. After four successive wins, including the dramatic and brutal World Cup quarter-final, the French match was turning into a war. France were a mess, their selection policy chaotic. Players were picked out of position and then binned when, quite understandably, they failed to deliver. Instead of tapping into their heritage, turning to flair and virtuosity which had always characterised their most successful periods, they opted to out-gun England.

So we played on it. Brian Moore was at his peak around this time, as both a player and amateur psychologist, and before every French match he would stoke the fire, deliberately and provocatively finding something to say which he knew would upset the French. One of his more famous verbal attacks was to liken the French side to a team of Eric Cantonas: temperamental, volatile, unstable. The tabloid newspapers would splash Brian's comments across the top of the back pages. They would be translated and fed back to France who would in turn get more incensed, more out of control and more vulnerable to the moments of indiscretion which would cost them the match.

We banked on being able to destabilise France. We would push them as hard as we possibly could, playing on the edge of the laws, sometimes over-stepping those boundaries. Early on a high ball would go up on the French full-back and the forwards would trample all over him. Line-outs would be caught and driven. Our entire game plan was to force France into a confrontation. We would never kick cross field to give them space to run the ball back. All the tactical kicking would be high hanging kicks, tight to the touch line, where the chasers would either hold the catcher for the forwards to do their stuff, or force him into touch where we usually claimed the ensuing line-out. And all the time I would be looking at key players, wondering and waiting to see when they would start to wobble.

In that 1992 game I did not even have to wait for the match to begin. As the anthems started I stared across at the French line-up to see their front row in tears. It was a weird feeling. On the one hand I knew that the plans had worked, that there was every chance that France would lose control, allowing us to clinch win number five, but there was also the fear that the cost in physical terms would be too great, that some day soon someone was going to get badly hurt.

That man was very nearly Martin Bayfield. Towards the end of the match Gregoire Lascube, one of the props who was so emotional before the anthems, stamped on Martin's head and was sent off. Minutes later Vincent Moscato, France's hooker, also went for punching at a scrum after the referee had issued another warning. Bayfield was not badly injured and we ended 31–13 winners, so I suppose the end justified the means yet again but that match and the game in Paris the preceding year were the nearest I came to rugby as legalised warfare.

But it was not always deadly serious in France. Those matches did have their lighter moments. The 1992 game confirmed the re-emergence of Dewi Morris who had been preferred to Richard Hill that season because Dewi offered more of a threat round the base of the scrum. I liked and respected both men but was particularly pleased for Dewi because he and David Pears had been the only two players not to have played a match in the 1991 World Cup campaign. Neither gave so much as a hint of a grumble, although both would have given anything to play. Dewi was very popular and very excitable. He had kissed Andy Robinson on his debut against Australia in 1988 after the Bath flanker had charged down an attempted clearance kick to allow Dewi to score. Nicknamed Monkey after the creature in the Peter Sellers *Pink Panther* films, Dewi over the years had developed a reputation for non-sequiturs. 'It's no fun being up front behind you bastards' was a particular favourite of mine.

France was Dewi's third match back in England colours and he was at his enthusiastic best. In the first five minutes a couple of French forwards dived over the top of the ruck to kill hard won ball and Dewi thought it particularly appropriate to draw the referee's attention to their indiscretions in case he had missed them. Summoning his best schoolboy French, with suitably dramatic arm-waving as accompaniment, Dewi shouted, 'Monsieur referee, regardez. Les Français players sont diving sur le ballon.'

'Thank you, Dewi. I am aware of it,' replied Stephen Hilditch, the Irish referee.

Hitting the balance between maintaining the mental and physical hardness to keep France at bay, while developing a style to challenge the better southern hemisphere sides, was my main concern over the next few years. We had to discover players who would lift England out of the static, one-dimensional rut and transform them into a more varied, fluid outfit. It was clear that we were not going to find the finished article. The trick was to select outstanding athletes and graft on the necessary hardness, and Tim Rodber was perfect raw material.

Tim was the prototype of the modern forward. He was big, mobile, powerful, quick, intelligent and competitive, able to play in more than one position, but it had all come too easy. Because he hadn't struggled with England, experiencing the lean times and the disappointments, he lacked that edge which turning a losing side into a winning outfit provides. Tim was never comfortable playing alongside Peter Winterbottom because he could not understand Winterbottom's approach. What I knew as single-minded intensity in Peter, Tim saw as taciturn rudeness. Tim was setting out on his international career, Wints was close to finishing his, and there was a big difference in the way they approached their rugby.

When Tim first represented England, like most debutants (myself included), he probably talked a better game than he played. During the Ireland game in 1992, his second in an England shirt, he was getting bumped and banged about at the back of the line-out. After the third time Tim turned to his opponent and said, 'That's your last warning mate. Next time I'll punch you.' The threat had no effect and the pushing and shoving continued until, after another ten minutes, Tim said, 'Right, I've had enough. That's your final, final warning.' At which point an exasperated Winterbottom ordered, 'Either hit him or shut up but whatever you decide to do, do it quick.'

Tim was very impressionable and easy to wind up. His nickname was Captain Marmite because of his army background and the fact that he was always impeccably turned out and well mannered. He enjoyed shooting and often turned up for training with an immaculate tweed shooting jacket and plus fours in the back of his car, which made him a natural target for pranksters. On one occasion Peter Winterbottom, Mike Teague and Tim were at a post-match party together with eight SAS friends of mine who had come down to watch the international. Tim was the only person who didn't know who these guys were or where they were from and it was decided to make the most of this fact because Tim was always talking about the army.

'You're Tim Rodber, aren't you?' said one of the SAS soldiers.

'Yes,' said Tim.

'In the army, are you?'

'Yes.'

'What's more important to you, then? The army or your rugby?'

'I suppose it must be my rugby,' said Tim, which was just the reply the SAS were looking for.

'In that case why are you mucking around with the army?'

And so it went on with the SAS questioning Tim's integrity and commitment to his career as a soldier as he grew increasingly irritated. Eventually he snapped. 'Who the fucking hell are you?' he blasted.

'We work for the post office.'

'Well, what right have you got to wind me up? Don't you have a go at me. I serve my country . . .' And on he went with several more seriously crass lines until he stormed off to the bar to get a drink. I followed him anxious to make sure that nothing too dramatic happened.

'Who are these blokes, Will? What are they doing here?'

'Just calm down, Tim. They're friends, people we know.'

'But the post office. What have you got to do with the post office?' It was then that he twigged. 'That's not the Hereford post office?' he said. I nodded. 'Oh Christ,' he murmured, before going back to the table to enjoy everyone laughing at his expense.

Making something out of Rodber and Bayfield wasn't the only problem that season. We had to bed down a new coach in Dick Best. My relationship with Roger Uttley remained uneasy. He was wary of me after our run-in in Argentina and we hadn't communicated as fully as we should have done. It had become apparent that Roger had not changed his coaching style, which didn't seem to me to be on the cutting edge. Sessions tended to be repetitive and he did not seem to take into account who we were playing or what we wanted to do as a side. I had been up to Harrow School where Roger worked to talk the matter over with him, but there was little improvement.

This issue was voiced strongly by others in the side and I was not too surprised when Brian Moore, Dean Richards and Wade Dooley amongst others asked me to speak to Geoff Cooke with a view to easing Roger aside. Geoff said he would think about it but decided against such dramatic action. He said Roger had always been loyal to him, had supported him throughout some difficult and turbulent years and had provided the rugby credibility which he lacked. It was a typically magnanimous gesture and it allowed Roger to depart after the 1991 World Cup with his dignity and reputation very much intact.

His replacement, Dick Best, was a breath of fresh air. He was a disciple of New Zealand rugby and spent hours talking on the phone to Earl Kirton, a famous All Black player and coach, which meant that his sessions were up-to-date and relevant. His sense of humour also helped. Dick could be a bully when he was coaching club men but at international level his wonderfully sarcastic and caustic wit stopped short of humiliating players. It was exactly what the forwards needed. Here was a man who knew what he was doing and was not averse to giving them a rollicking when required.

Dick's appointment relieved the burden which was falling on Geoff's shoulders. The two made a good team. Dick enabled Geoff to withdraw from coaching duties, though he was still heavily involved with the backs, while Geoff curbed Dick's wilder excesses, providing the overview which Dick sometimes found hard to achieve. In selection Dick could be extremely volatile, basing his opinion on the evidence of one bad match, whereas Geoff inclined to a broader view. It made for some lively selection meetings, but Geoff invariably prevailed.

My year ended memorably when I played against Danie Gerber, a boyhood hero of mine, when South Africa came to Twickenham in one of their first matches after their isolation from world rugby had ended. I had watched Gerber play for the Springboks against England in Port Elizabeth in 1984. He had everything, wonderful balance, great pace, phenomenal strength and wicked acceleration. Eight years later, aged thirty-four, he was still a hugely powerful and skilled centre. I felt like a kid that afternoon and never took my eyes off him all game. We won 33–16 and afterwards I approached Gerber to get his shirt and to tell him what a great honour it had been for me to be on the same pitch as him. 'Yeah,' he said, and walked off. It was obviously time to rethink the boyhood heroes bit.

— 14 —
RORY GOES WALKABOUT

THE pressure was on. It always was. Not even the great Welsh sides of the seventies had won three Grand Slams on the bounce but that was our target after sweeping the board in 1991 and 1992. I love that about sport. Wherever you are on the wheel of fortune the challenges are still there. Our task was the hardest of them all. To remain competitive, to continue to subdue the Celtic nations and not to relax our iron grip on France.

Staying ahead of the pack is never easy. With no one to tilt at, you have to set your own goals. But the fixture list had done us a favour. Home matches at fortress Twickenham against France and Scotland, the two toughest sides in the championship, was a big plus. Wales and Ireland away were no push-overs but both were struggling and therefore vulnerable. And there was an added bonus. For the first time there actually was a Five Nations trophy. Previously the greatest prize in European rugby was mythical. Now a lump of silverware would adorn the trophy cabinet of the winning nation. It was a good championship to win.

It was also the championship when I first met Diana, Princess of Wales. Diana was the official guest of the Welsh Rugby Union when England played Wales in Cardiff and it was my job to introduce her to the England team. To be honest, the whole business was a pain in the backside. Waiting in line on a chilly February day to press the flesh of several dignitaries isn't at the top of most rugby players' list minutes before the start of an international. It is one of those experiences relished in retrospect. During my career I have introduced various VIPs to different England teams and, while it has always been an honour and a privilege, it is difficult to observe more than the most basic courtesies with the match so close. Diana was charming as we went down the line but I can't remember a thing about it. A few months later we met again at a Help the Aged charity function at the Hilton Hotel. I was presenting an award to a remarkable man who was playing rugby well into his eighties. Again, Diana was the guest of honour and again our contact amounted to a 'Hi, how are you?' and a handshake.

Our third meeting took place at Buckingham Palace in November. The All Blacks and the 1993 British Lions had been invited to meet members of the royal family following the Lions tour to New Zealand earlier that summer. Princess Diana was part of the royal reception party, together with the Queen and Prince Edward. The gathering took place three days before England were playing the All Blacks and there wasn't a great deal of fraternising going on. The English Lions stood at one end of the room, the New Zealanders at the other, with the royal family, assorted officials and guests and the non-English Lions milling around the middle. I didn't say a word to Diana. Three meetings in 1993 and not a single splash in the newspapers? What was the world coming to?

That year we prepared as usual for the Five Nations Championship. Geoff Cooke had abandoned the Christmas trial matches long ago, arguing that any coach or selector who had to rely on a single clash to determine England's starting line-up wasn't doing his job properly. Instead the squad adjourned for some warm-weather training at Club La Santa in Lanzarote. England were the first country to head for the sun in the middle of winter. Many on the RFU committee queried the development, unable or unwilling to acknowledge the benefits of preparing in shorts and tee-shirt. They rather liked the old system when teams prepared in the wind and the rain of an English winter. That way was cheaper, too.

Lanzarote was an extension of Geoff's radicalism which had given England the edge throughout his reign. He had focused on fitness and diet long before it became fashionable to do so. It took a while to persuade the forwards that skinless chicken, baked potatoes, fruit salad and the occasional glass of white wine were better than steak, chips and a gallon of Guinness, but eventually they were won over. Geoff introduced fat and fitness tests and proficiency in those areas was a prerequisite for selection. Dip below the required standard and it was goodnight nurse. The benefits were soon apparent. Men like Wade Dooley were slowly transformed from lumbering giants, good for about sixty minutes of sustained activity, into athletes who could last the distance. Tiredness did not obliterate skill levels and England evolved into a side with the capacity to pound teams in the last twenty minutes with as much venom and ferocity as the first twenty.

Geoff did have his fair share of wacky ideas, though. Before touring Argentina in 1990 he introduced Len Heppell, a movement consultant, to the squad. Len had the impossible task of teaching cumbersome forwards to move with grace and balance. Watching Paul Rendall and Wade Dooley loosen and stretch to avoid contact when their instincts were to search for an opponent, tense up and smash him into the back of beyond was priceless. No amount of persuasion from Len was going to get that pair tiptoeing round the rugby field.

Lanzarote was also good for the soul. There was an edge to many of the work-outs with Five Nations places up for grabs, but there was always time to relax afterwards. It was a chance for the squad to gel and for the characters in the party to weave their spells. Merlene Ottey, the Jamaican sprinter, was unlucky enough to book into Lanzarote at the same time as the England party; unluckier still to find that her room was across a rooftop balcony from that shared by John Olver and Mark Linnett, two of England's more inventive and mischievous squad members. Merlene will probably always wonder why the fluorescent green training leotard that she hung out to dry on the balcony one evening did not fit quite so well the next morning. Maybe it had something to do with the fact that the leotard adorned the not-so-shapely figure of the seventeen-stone Linnett for much of the night.

Whenever we were in Lanzarote Mick Skinner and Mike Teague always seemed to be locked in a personal battle over the blind-side flanker's role for the opening game and the training would be punctuated by the sight and sound of Mick and Mike busting a gut to impress Geoff. Every activity would see them side by side straining to get what they considered the all-important edge, first on the ground for the loose ball, highest in the air at the back of the line-out, competing to make the biggest tackle, to have the slimmest body, to post the fastest sprint times. In the evening they would nurse small glasses of orange juice, sipping slowly, before heading off to their rooms for the earliest of nights – until the decision was made and Geoff announced the side at the final afternoon's practice. That was the signal for the mayhem to begin and the pair would set out on the binge to end all binges, each congratulating or sympathising with the other until after an orgy of alcoholic excess they both passed out.

Lanzarote seemed to have worked its magic when we put France away by a single point. It wasn't a vintage England performance but, as the championship habitually went to the winner of that contest, we set off for Cardiff in good heart. The third Grand Slam, if not in the bank, was still a distinct possibility until Ieuan Evans turned the game. Wales's crucial try came from the most innocuous of beginnings. Emyr Lewis, the Welsh flanker, prodded a speculative kick down the right-hand touch line for Ieuan Evans to chase. It was a situation Rory had faced hundreds of times in his career. All that was required was for him to scuttle across and boot the ball into touch. There was plenty of time. He was miles closer to the ball than Ieuan.

Unaccountably, and he cannot explain to this day what went through his mind, Rory refused to hurry, only sensing the danger when it was too late. Ieuan hacked the ball forward and dived on it over the line to score the try which proved decisive. Rory Underwood, the man who had saved England's bacon dozens of times in the past, had had one of his Hamlet moments.

Back in the changing room Rory was in tears, convinced that he had cost England the match, and it took Geoff Cooke to put it all into context. 'Hang on,' he told Rory. 'You have scored more tries for England than anyone else. Does that mean you won all those games?' That brought Rory round.

For England's most-capped international of all time, with an amazing eighty-five caps, Rory was a very strange guy. He used to room with Jerry Guscott. Jerry thought that arrangement was magic because Rory would always be up first thing in the morning making the tea or coffee. He even did Jerry's laundry for him for all I know. Jerry never had to do anything. Rory never turned up drunk, not difficult for a teetotal player who used to drink Coke by the gallon, never played loud music, never messed up the room.

I've known him for a long time now, yet have never known him. Within that quiet personality there are several clashing strands. There is no doubt that he was an incredible try-scorer, as good as anyone on the world stage, and over a thirteen-year career that is as fine a sporting epitaph as anyone is likely to get. He did care very much about playing for England and winning and he did care very much about scoring tries. He used to tell me his first thirty caps brought him two tries. It was something ridiculous like that, a complete waste of a special talent. Even towards the end we didn't give him as many opportunities as we should have done.

But for all his caps he could be incredibly naive and he always seemed reluctant to accept the responsibility within the squad which his experience warranted. He should have contributed much more than he did. I tried to involve him, so did Jack Rowell when he succeeded Geoff Cooke, but it wasn't Rory's style and it was a crying shame. He compensated by the diligent way he looked after the new boys. In any sport experienced players pass on tips to the younger men. It might be little things, the pattern of the wind in a particular stadium, which venues are especially noisy, the depth of the in-goal areas, how to cope with certain opposition players. Rory was quite happy to paint the pictures on a one-to-one basis but it was never completely natural with him. He regarded himself as the senior player, which he was, and that attitude tended to grate. He would try to do his bits and pieces, but always in a stilted way. I would have loved to have seen him let his hair down occasionally.

For all his experience he was very much a confidence player and it was important for me to stoke that confidence. I was not always successful and it was incredibly frustrating when he slipped into one of his lackadaisical moods and lost concentration. You had to appeal to his confident side, that was the way to get the best out of him. Not, 'Christ, Rors, you'd better play well today, or you're going to get dropped.' He just didn't respond to that at all.

Getting Rory back on track wasn't the only problem after the Cardiff débâcle. I had to tell Rob Andrew he had been dropped for Stuart Barnes. I had learned the lesson about not fighting selection battles on behalf of friends after my experience with Simon Halliday and I wasn't going to let my regard for Rob affect my behaviour. Dealing with disappointed players was far and away the worst aspect of captaincy. Geoff Cooke used to speak to them first and then I used to dig them out and sit down with them. As captain and in on selection it was my responsibility to be honest with them and explain the reasons why they were left out. It was very hard, especially when the individual up for the chop was a mate. At the end of the day, when difficult decisions had to be made and explained to people I liked, I always told myself that it was important for England to be successful even if the casualties were friends of mine.

Rob, as I knew he would, took it on the chin. He refused to accept responsibility for the defeat by Wales but there were no histrionics. He wanted to know if there were any aspects of his game which were deficient, so that he could remedy the weaknesses and come back a stronger, more complete player. But the issue was bigger than that. Selection for the Calcutta Cup was another episode in one of the great debates of English rugby: who was the better outside-half, him or Stuart Barnes, Bath's mercurial genius who now works as a rugby analyst/ commentator for Sky Television? The debate was as much about the style of the team as the strengths and weaknesses of the two individuals. In the end the argument was caricatured into Barnes, the flair man who would galvanise an under-performing back line, versus Andrew, the ultimate safety-first player who could coax performances from an ageing pack of forwards.

I did not get on that well with Stuart. I found him cocky and opinionated, unable to appreciate life outside Bath. There was no doubt that Bath were the most successful club in English competitions and had been so for a while, but there is another dimension to international rugby and I wasn't sure he appreciated that. However, I was determined not to let my personal feelings adversely affect our relationship on the pitch. It would have been ridiculous to jeopardise the team's chances because we didn't see eye to eye. Anxious to be fair, I deliberately went out of my way to clear the air with Stuart before that Calcutta Cup match at Twickenham.

Stuart had a stormer against Scotland. It was his first Five Nations match at Twickenham, nine years after his debut against Australia, and he played as if he had never been away. His personal high point was in manufacturing a try for Rory Underwood. Reaching for a high pass from Dewi Morris, Stuart stepped inside Ian Smith, Scotland's flanker, before accelerating over the halfway line. A precision pass allowed Jerry Guscott to cruise past the cover without breaking stride. Jerry found Rory, who scored to exorcise the Cardiff demons. As an example of what Stuart was capable of, it was sensational and England went on to win 26–12 in some style. But two weeks later, against Ireland, Stuart was desperate in a 17–3 defeat. It was a poor team display generally, but Stuart persisted in running the ball from suicidal positions when the forwards urgently needed a platform to settle in and work over the Irish pack.

That was the last game of the Five Nations Championship. Both outside-halves went to New Zealand with the 1993 British Lions and at the start of the next championship Rob was preferred to Stuart, as he had been throughout the Lions tour. Ireland beat England again in the second match of the 1994 championship and Stuart thought he would get back into the side. When Rob retained the shirt, Stuart went ballistic. Reckoning perhaps that his international career was over, he launched into a tirade of abuse.

'I can't believe you've picked Rob,' he began. 'I'm better than him at bloody everything.'

I pointed out that I didn't think that was entirely true, that he was a more accomplished broken field runner but that Rob was in a different class when it came to passing and kicking. I should have known better than to waste my breath.

'Don't bullshit me,' Stuart said. 'I'm better at everything, and you are just gutless,' and stormed off. That was the reason Stuart never fitted into the England set-up. He was a maverick, unable to work with players around him if he did not agree with the overall strategy. There was no doubt that he was an extremely gifted rugby player but his temperament meant that he could be a liability as well as a match-winner. Today he would have been an ideal choice at outside-half because England have achieved a certain stability in terms of their results and can afford to take risks. But in that difficult period when England were laying the foundations he was out of sync. He would probably say he was ahead of his time. Maybe he was, but the history books do not record what might have been. Rob went on to amass seventy-six caps, Stuart had to make do with ten.

The defeat by Ireland was the final straw. A championship which had promised much delivered nothing. The England team of which I had been so proud was on the point of disintegrating. The focus which had characterised the preparations over the

preceding five seasons had weakened. Several of the experienced guys were taking international rugby for granted. On the
Thursday before the game in Dublin a few of the forwards
slipped off for a couple of pints of Guinness to relax the nerves.
It was something they had done ever since I had known them
but this time they were unable to play their way out of trouble.
I, too, was jaded. I was offering nothing new in my team talks.
It was difficult when the same old faces had heard it all before,
but that was no excuse. The season finished with me losing the
ball in contact against Ireland. It was an appropriate image. I
was losing my grip on the team and the captaincy. And all this
before the biggest announcement in the rugby calendar.

— 15 —

A LUCKLESS LION

T HE Lions were looming again. Every four years Lions selection dominates the debate in rugby clubs and newspapers throughout Britain and Ireland. It starts before the Five Nations Championship and continues throughout that tournament right up until the tour party is announced. For many players playing in a Lions Test is the greatest honour the game has to offer. I did not see it that way. For me, the ultimate achievement was to represent my country but I was still keen to go. A shin injury had kept me at home when the Lions went to Australia in 1989 and I wanted to complete my rugby education. I was interested, too, in getting to know players from other countries. The dinners during the Five Nations are a chance to socialise but emotions are too high, the elation of victory or the depression of defeat too recent, for real understanding. That only comes through sharing experiences under a collective banner on a seven-week tour. I was one of three candidates tossed up by the media to lead the Lions. Scotland's Gavin Hastings and Ieuan Evans from Wales were the other contenders. Speculation about who would do the best job had continued for weeks in the newspapers.

England had experienced their worst season before that Lions tour, losing to Wales and Ireland in the Five Nations. You had to go back to 1988 to find a year in which England had dipped out twice and that run of results, plus the imminent retirements of those I had grown up with, badly affected me. I could not seem to get it out of my mind that I would be in an England team the following season which did not contain Peter Winterbottom, Mike Teague and Wade Dooley, all of whom had declared their intention to retire from international rugby. It even crossed my mind to give up the game and do something else and these feelings came to a head after the match with Ireland at Lansdowne Road where we were stuffed.

Geoff Cooke and I were together after the match. 'This Lions captaincy, you don't want it, do you?' Cookie said. He was going to manage the tour with Ian McGeechan as coach and he knew that I was tired. Geoff was not offering me the job but I wanted to be straight with him, to tell him how I really felt about the whole business, so he would be in a position to inform the tour selectors.

'Geoff, I'm absolutely knackered. I couldn't do the job if I tried but I would love to be considered as a player.'

Geoff asked who I would make captain if I had a vote and I said Peter Winterbottom. He had played on a Lions tour in New Zealand, enjoyed a fantastic reputation in that part of the world, and was hugely respected on the European circuit. It shows how much influence I had with Geoff that the eventual choice was Gavin Hastings. In my mind the fact that he pipped me for the job was never an issue because I had ruled myself out of the race. I'm not sure how Gavin felt about it, but I did see in his autobiography a picture of the two of us over a caption which read: 'Who got the Lions captaincy?'

I think Gavin did a reasonable job but for me he is not the same kind of guy as Ieuan Evans. Ieuan and I share the same sense of humour which is based on sarcasm. Gavin was not like that. He's pretty straight up and down. To be fair to him, being captain of the Lions is a hell of a job and there were loads of chores which required his attention and which meant we did not see a lot of him. He was either in meetings or he wasn't around. But when we did meet up on the tour it was not a fun-filled experience. He did come through in the main area, though. He did play very well.

Gavin likes to wear his nationalism on his sleeve. He is a fiercely loyal proud Scot, so much so that there is a bit of an edge in his devotion to his country. The England/Scotland encounters of the eighties and early nineties took over from the England/Wales matches of the seventies as examples of the dangers of being too partisan. Gavin was a part of that. After the 1990 match when Scotland beat England he was all for dressing up in kilts and claymores and going out on the town. In 1991 at the World Cup final, Gavin was instrumental in persuading the Scotland side to wear Australian clobber and support Australia. I could never forgive him for that. Scotland are not my favourite team in the world but if it ever comes to a northern hemisphere/southern hemisphere clash in a major competition and Scotland are involved I will be rooting for them. I thought Gavin was a bit mad at times with his Scottishness. I was very proud of playing for England but I didn't feel the need to ram it down everyone else's throat.

My own form on that tour was disastrous. Before we left I had just got engaged to Julia Smith and that weighed heavily on my mind. We had met years ago at a supper party, introduced by Nikki Turner, a girlfriend of mine who was also a friend of Julia's. Julia and I continued to see a lot of each other on a casual basis and gradually the relationship developed. We were poles apart but that was part of the attraction. She inhabited the glitzy world of PR and showbiz and had worked with or for some of the biggest names in the pop world. Her clients included Right Said Fred, INXS and Bill Wyman's Sticky Fingers restaurant. She had also been linked in the gossip columns with Mick Jagger, Eric Clapton and Bob Geldof and had lived with Jeff Beck for six years. Before I left for New Zealand with the Lions, Julia persuaded me to announce our engagement to the press. Victoria Jackson and I had split up in December, Julia and I had been spotted together and identified as a couple by the tabloids, and Julia wanted to bring everything out into the open. She was getting hassled by journalists ringing her three or four times each day asking for information on her love life. Against my better judgement I agreed to the photo opportunity and we were 'launched' as a couple. I had misgivings about the way we handled that at the time. It was a dramatic departure for me because I had normally refused to discuss my private life with the media, but Julia was in PR and she seemed to know what she was doing.

The misgivings grew on the Lions tour, even though Julia, who had been working in Australia, flew to Christchurch for a visit. I suppose I was suffering the doubts which everyone has when they are getting married for the first time. Is it the right decision? Is she the right girl? And, to be honest, it affected my game. In fact the whole business threw rugby into some sort of relief. Previously everything I had done, every decision I had made, was influenced to a greater or lesser extent by rugby. Now rugby, including a Lions tour, seemed less significant. I lost focus and my performances nose-dived.

I was one of four centres picked for that Lions trip. Scott Gibbs, Scott Hastings, Jerry Guscott and I would be fighting for the Test spots. Ordinarily I would have loved the challenge of competing against and seeing off two rivals. Proving yourself at the highest level is the attraction of top-level sport for me. Jerry's form was such that he was a dead cert for one of the centre berths. Scott Hastings was always reliable, efficient, defensively sound but lacked flair, so it looked as if my biggest concern would be Scott Gibbs, the Welsh centre. But I couldn't get into it. On the flight out I was more interested in the fact that Scott Gibbs, who had always impressed me as a centre, seemed to be a voracious reader, dipping in and out of a haversack to produce various notebooks and diaries which he devoured weaning his little round glasses. I was also tired and concerned about next season when England would be in a rebuilding phase. My depression became so bad that, ten days into the trip, I went up to Geoff Cooke and asked him if anyone had ever voluntarily left a Lions tour.

New Zealand is not the ideal place to visit when you're a high-profile rugby player on an important tour and palpably out of sorts. Virtually every New Zealander is passionate and knowledgeable about the sport. Hundreds turn out to watch the most mundane training sessions in the wind and rain, sessions which would only attract a few dozen fans in balmy conditions back home. My card was marked early on in the tour when I went into a shop to buy a tube of toothpaste.

'You're Will Carling, aren't you?' said the seventy-year-old lady behind the counter. I nodded. 'Well, I think your loosies are OK but you're a little slow in the front five . . .' and she went on to give a detailed analysis of the Lions' strengths and weaknesses coupled with potted biographies of several of her favourite players. What stunned me was that she was spot on with her assessments.

Wherever we went, we were besieged by rugby-mad New Zealanders who all appeared to share the same turn of phrase. Mike Teague and I were in a bar when we were asked whether we liked the beer we were drinking. 'Aw mate, what do you think of Steinlager? It's not a lot, but we like it.' Later, someone stopped us to point out his car. 'Aw mate, what do you think of it? It's not a lot, but I like it.' The constant interest and attention shown to touring teams in a country like New Zealand can be stimulating as well as oppressive. I found it oppressive, which was indicative of my frame of mind.

Scott Gibbs and I were paired together against North Harbour in the second game of the tour. It was an undistinguished beginning to my Lions career. The match was more noteworthy for the fight which disfigured the second half than the scintillating form of W.D.C. Carling and that was the beginning of the slippery slope. I picked up injuries in games against the New Zealand Maoris and Otago and made the team for the First Test only because there were no alternatives. Scott Hastings had returned home after fracturing his cheek bone and Scott Gibbs could not be considered because of ankle ligament damage. Grant Fox kicked a penalty for the All Blacks two minutes from the end to shade the contest 20–18 and that was my one and only Test appearance for the Lions.

The moment Scott Gibbs recovered from injury he was rushed back into the side and he and Jerry were selected together to play Auckland the Saturday before the Second Test in Wellington. That was the first time I had ever been left out of a team on form in my life and it hurt like hell. It was a situation I had witnessed many times before but had never been on the receiving end. The players gathered in the team room to wait for the team to be announced. When I realised I was not part of their plans my stomach dropped. It was a horrible empty experience. You feel exposed, as if everyone is staring at you, when the reality is that the players are just concentrating on their own reactions.

No one had prepared me for the disappointment. I did not expect preferential or special treatment but with England we always tried to break bad news to individuals before it became public. As I left the room Ian McGeechan came up to me and said, 'Listen, Will, you have not been dropped. For me you are still the man.' Geech probably meant well but I wish he hadn't tried to camouflage the truth. I knew I had been dropped and I would have preferred the facts to be delivered that way rather than be led up the garden path with a convenient explanation. The significance of the omission was that I never played for the Saturday side again.

Some good did come out of it though because it forced me to take stock. It made me sit down and work out whether I still wanted to be part of rugby. I realised I hadn't really enjoyed the last eighteen months, primarily because of the way I had been playing. I had stagnated to the extent where, as a centre, I had limited myself to taking the ball up the middle of the pitch to provide a target. And there was another reason for my lassitude. Maybe I had kidded myself that the burden of leadership and the hundred and one considerations which a national captain must deal with were responsible for my mediocre performances.

Peter Winterbottom left me in no doubt what he thought. He hadn't spoken to me much since our arrival in New Zealand but he, Mike Teague and I found ourselves in a bar the evening after I had been dropped for the Auckland match. I was looking for a few friendly shoulders to cry on but Wints was still withdrawn and uncommunicative.

'What have I done, Wints?' I whined. 'I don't need this now. I've just been dropped, my Test spot has gone and you've hardly said a word over the last hour and a half. How about a bit of support?'

'You've played like shit,' Wints said. 'That's what you've done. I told all my mates in New Zealand that you were a great player. I told them not to believe all the stuff they'd heard and read about you, that they should judge you on this tour, and you've played like a pillock. You've let me down and you're letting yourself down.'

It wasn't what I wanted to hear but he was absolutely right. I decided that if I could not force myself back into contention for the Test team I would go down fighting. I was determined to blast through the last two matches left for the dirt-trackers just to prove to myself that I was still a centre who was capable of operating at the highest level. I bumped into Geech on the morning of my last game and he asked me whether I was up for the match later that afternoon. 'I'm going to go out and play,' I said. The statement was as much for myself as it was for Geech but it had the desired effect. I rediscovered my lust for the game and convinced myself and a few others that I still had a future.

Later I was told that a lot of the England boys on the tour were interested in how I reacted to the disappointments. Some were secretly thinking that I was going to sulk. Winters made the most heart-warming comment when he said, 'Mate, you've earned more respect in the last few weeks than in two seasons as England captain. Players have seen you in a different environment, one in which you were struggling, and they have appreciated the way you have tried to work through the difficulties.' He was speaking to me again.

I may have been exonerated in that last game against Waikato but the defeat proved that some of the Scottish forwards were simply not up to it. And worse, they appeared not to care about playing for the team. I was captain that game and the 38–10 reversal has entered the record books as the worst-ever loss suffered by a Lions team. It is not a record of which I'm proud and out of frustration more than anything else I led the side on a tour of the local bars to see if a surfeit of alcohol would improve the picture.

Around 2 a.m. Mike Teague, Andy Reed and I were having a pee round the back of a bar when we were joined by a rotund, small, elderly supporter dressed in a blue V-necked sweater and tie who was accompanying the tour with one of the supporters parties.

'Evening, Will. Evening, Mike,' said the fan.

We exchanged greetings.

'Excuse me,' he said, turning to the 6ft 6ins Andy Reed. 'You're Andy Reed, aren't you?'

Andy nodded.

'Well, I don't think you gave it your all today.'

'I'm not taking that crap from you,' Reed said. 'Shut your mouth or I'll shut it for you.'

Mike Teague jabbed me in the ribs. 'My money's on the old bloke,' he said. Mike was a great comfort in New Zealand. I had admired his rugby ability for a long while, but it was his human qualities which sustained me in my darker moments. He kept me sane with his sense of humour. Nothing was too much trouble for him. I had experienced more than my share of fair-weather friends up to that point in my life and it was a privilege to get to know a man who was steadfast whatever was happening.

The Lions had given me a kick up the backside. Being left out of the side was a shock as well as a setback but it did provide the springboard at the bottom of the slump. Geech probably did me a few favours in that regard. For a long while I resented him, though I never quibbled with the thinking behind the decision. The blow was doubly painful because I respected him as a coach. Getting dumped was bad enough, but getting dumped by one of the shrewder rugby men around was doubly painful.

Although the 1993 Lions tour wasn't a great success for me personally it did give me a chance to get to know players from other countries. That is the special significance of the British Lions. In the preceding Five Nations Championship you do your level best to beat the living daylights out of opponents only to find months later that the very same opponent is now your best ally. In New Zealand I became friendly with a few Welsh players. I had always felt ambivalent about some of the Welsh players and public. The reasons were simple. England had not had a particularly good record against Wales, especially at Cardiff, and Englishmen and Englishness did not go down well in the Principality. So it was with some trepidation that I linked up with Ieuan Evans, Tony Clement, Robert Jones and Richard Webster. I needn't have worried. The moments with those guys were among the happiest I experienced in rugby.

Ieuan in particular was outstanding on that tour. We used to call him Randy because he invariably wore his atrocious old cowboy boots wherever he went. He also had comfortably the worst taste in clothes of anyone I have ever met and for the most part looked like an out-of-date cowboy. I had a bit of a dust-up with Ieuan on the pitch in 1993 which had coloured my perceptions of him but that tour enabled me to discover what a fantastic bloke he is. I was also able to make sense of my unease with Wales. We always used to have tea and stickies after training and chew the fat. One afternoon the conversation turned to nationalism and Robert Jones explained that the Welsh hated me.

'But I meet Welsh folk, Robert, and they invariably say how different I am from what they expected,' I replied, eager to set the record straight.

'That may be true, Will, but the moment you walk away they will say how much they hate you.' It was said in fun but there was a serious side to the jest. 'The trouble is,' said Robert, 'you've captained an England side that has beaten Wales so there is no way you are going to be flavour of the month. You are built up to be this arrogant, aloof English git because then the defeat is easier to stomach. If you were portrayed as a decent, caring, sensitive human being that would make it worse, wouldn't it?'

It was slightly cockeyed logic but what Robert was saying made sense. When you are involved in sport at national level you become a representative of a set of values and those values are attributed to you randomly. I was a symbol of all the injustices England ever perpetrated on Wales and there was nothing much I could do about it.

Richard Webster was less cerebral than Robert Jones. Webbie called me Billy Arse. The England lads had christened me Bum Chin for ages because of the dimple in the middle of my chin but Webbie wanted to go one step further. The man was incorrigible, a law unto himself. We were rooming together before one match and Webbie had decided to make a big night of it afterwards. 'Will, we're going to get into real trouble tonight. Real trouble,' he said. The words sent a shiver down my spine because trouble with Webbie was just that. I managed to avoid him after the game and went out with some of the lads, but when I came back, instead of returning to sleep in our room, I set off for the physio's room. The thought of a drunk and demented Webster returning in the early hours of the morning was too much to bear. It took me over an hour to barricade myself in the physio's room. I piled steel trunks and chairs against the door and made use of the equipment left lying around in case he tried to kick the door down and find me. The plan worked. I slept through until nine the next morning and returned to my usual room to be greeted with a sight which was a complete vindication of my actions. A nuclear holocaust would have done less damage and there was Webbie flat out in the middle of the mess.

'You bastard, Billy Arse,' was all he said.

16

BEATING THE BEST

THE trickle had become a torrent. The Lions tour had proved the expected watershed, signalling the end of the international careers of Wade Dooley and Peter Winterbottom. Mike Teague, Jonathan Webb and Jeff Probyn were also at the end of that particular road and would never represent their country again. I will always be biased about the team I first played in. They were the players who brought England out of the wilderness, who gave English rugby the self-respect it had lacked for so long. I have never come close to experiencing the affection and the trust those players had in each other in any other rugby environment.

It wasn't the same for me after the England side which I had grown up with began to break up. Martin Bayfield, Ben Clarke, Tim Rodber emerged but they never had that aura which Wade Dooley and Mike Teague had. In my mind they could never match up to my heroes whom they were replacing. It wasn't their fault. They were fine players – probably better – but, as far as I was concerned, they had not come through the lean years.

Yet I knew the old-timers had to go. Their reluctance to experiment with new ideas and ways of playing, which first surfaced in 1992, had proved costly in 1993 when Ireland exposed those shortcomings. There was no doubt that they were stuck in a time warp, used to the old ways where forward power meant dominance at the line-out and scrummage and anything else was a bonus. Those were the conditions under which they had played most of their rugby and it was impossible to get them to think about approaching matches in any other way, let alone putting the new ideas into practice.

The law changes which were introduced throughout the early nineties made their old skills redundant. Lifting in the line-out, the use it or lose it rule, changes at the scrum meant that it was impossible to control the ball for long periods. A wider range of skills and a different attitude was required. The game speeded up and it called for a new breed of forward, players who were as happy running with the ball as they were winning it. It was too much for Jeff Probyn and Wade Dooley. Retraining a ten-year-old dog would have been easier than convincing Wade and Jeff to move with the times.

One player was able to bridge that gap. Martin Johnson combined the vigour and athleticism of the new generation with the niggardly don't-mess-with-me attitude of the old. He was first called into the England team at very short notice in 1993 against France when Wade Dooley was injured and he fitted like a glove. Martin hardly said a word as he was rushed through the calls and line-out signals which were in use for that game. He just sat there silently with that hooded, furrowed brow of his, a malevolent, brooding presence. I did not know him well and found his silence disquieting. It didn't seem the silence of a player too overawed to open his mouth but I needed to be sure, so I checked with Dean Richards, Martin's Leicester team-mate. 'Does he speak, Deano?' Dean assured me that he did and that all was well. And to prove that this was the true Martin Johnson, that it wasn't just a reaction to being drafted in to win his first cap, it happened again on the Lions tour later that year when he again replaced Wade Dooley who had returned home for a family bereavement.

Martin rolled up, slotted straight into the Test team with only one national cap to his name and piled into the All Blacks. The impact he made was remarkable. Everyone sat up and took notice, simply because of the way he played his rugby. There was a general acknowledgement within the Lions squad that he was very good, capable of playing and dominating at any level, and that aura has surrounded him ever since.

Nevertheless, it was a tremendous punt from Fran Cotton and Ian McGeechan, the Lions' manager and coach, to ask Martin to front the 1997 British Lions tour to South Africa. Martin had never captained his country and had only recently taken over from Dean Richards at Leicester. A Lions tour was ideal for Johnners. He might not have made a good international captain because he wasn't too interested in all the aspects of the role but for a short, draining, one-off trip there was no one better. His approach was spot on. He wasn't bothered about getting involved in selection or working with the media. He just wanted to play, to lead the team out and get stuck in. His body language, his entire being, told the squad that that was what he expected from them all. On a Lions tour that approach works because there is no time to build real relationships. You need a figure to set an example at training and on the pitch and Martin was that symbol. He expected players to understand and emulate his standards and by and large they did.

I admire him immensely for that. Martin could not give a damn about the politics of the sport. Some may find that insular or unimaginative and in a way it is but his take-it-or-leave-it approach was highly effective. These are my standards, he said. These are my morals, the code I live to, and I'm not going to taint them for anybody or anything.

I approached the start of the 1993/94 season like a new kid at the start of a new term in a new school: excited and apprehensive. It was time to rebuild, to introduce new players and a new style of rugby, and New Zealand were first up to test how we were doing. Throughout my England career the All Blacks have always been the team to beat. Whenever they play they bring with them an implacable intensity and fury. South Africa might argue the toss but New Zealand have dominated the game for the best part of a century. Their whole approach is geared to producing the best national team and they lead the world in planning, coaching, everything. In Britain old players graduate into coaching roles under the assumption that those who've done can teach. In New Zealand much more is demanded in terms of theoretical and practical knowledge. Their systems are far more rigorous and they turn out competent, highly prepared sides as a result.

They also have a dedication to their sport and winning which is unmatched anywhere else in the world, except perhaps in South Africa. They will do anything they can to win and in the highly competitive world of international rugby anything means just that. On that 1993 tour there was an edge to the All Blacks which was unacceptable. When the South West played New Zealand in Redruth, Phil de Glanville's face was sliced open by a New Zealand stud, nearly blinding him, as the All Black forwards ran back to a defensive ruck.

Much less dramatically, I also experienced a touch of All Black skulduggery when they went searching for my eyes in a maul in the London match. The practice, though not widespread, is not uncommon and anyone who has played rugby at any level has experienced something like it. If you are trying to get the ball from a player who has wrapped both hands round it, the best thing to do is to claw at his face in the hope that he will let go of the ball to protect his eyesight. One of the photographers took a picture of my face as I left the pitch and the nailmarks round both eyes are obvious. To my mind those tactics are unacceptable. Rugby is dangerous enough at the best of times without stooping to those depths.

But that should not detract too much from the reputation of the All Blacks. All teams have their crazy men and New Zealand are no exception. Their better players content themselves with playing within the legal limits of the game, relying on legitimate intimidation to influence the mental battles. Zinzan Brooke, New Zealand's talented No. 8 now playing with Harlequins in London, was a player who enjoyed a verbal skirmish. He was always having a go. When I lost possession in that London game, Zinzan was there rabbiting away. 'Getting a bit old for this, Will? Keep spilling the ball do we? Not good, Will. Not good at all.'

All of which spiced the preparations for the international. The All Blacks had brought off a 51–15 victory against Scotland and we were turning out a kindergarten to face them. Kyran Bracken, Victor Ubogu, Phil de Glanville, Ben Clarke, Jon Callard, Tim Rodber and Martin Johnson were all either new or inexperienced at international level, or were returning to the side after a spell in the wilderness. But for once we won the propaganda battle. Geoff Cooke talked up the All Blacks and talked down our chances against them. He emphasised the fact that England were wet behind the ears and told the journalists that damage limitation was the order of the day. It worked beautifully. The media gave us no chance and we prepared with expectation at rock bottom.

I was winning the on-pitch battle, too. After a massive argument I had persuaded Dick Best to tone down the training routine. Dick wanted an eye-ball out approach, arguing that the only way to beat the All Blacks was to match them physically, to hit harder and more frequently than they did, to knock them out of their stride. He wanted training to mirror the intensity of the game itself. I agreed with his analysis but thought it was important for players who hardly knew each other to get the communication right before the game. I reckoned that the quality of opposition, the occasion and the atmosphere would be sufficient stimuli and, if the basics broke down, no amount of courage would dig us out of a hole. Instead of belting the living daylights out of each other, we walked through situations on the training pitch until we were word-perfect or as near as damn it.

It was good enough. Four penalties by Jon Callard, plus a dropped goal from Rob Andrew, against three penalties from Jeff Wilson, saw us home 15–9 and there was an added bonus. The triumph gave me the complete set of victories over the major rugby-playing nations. I had now played and beaten all the top teams in the world.

The atmosphere that November day was incredible. Twickenham has always been my favourite ground in the world to play at and the crowd did us proud. Supportive on most occasions, they are at their best when the challenge is greatest and they ripped into the All Blacks with nearly as much feeling as we did. This was a knowledgeable crowd, too. Not the day-tripping, corporate hospitality, uncommitted mob which gatecrashes big sporting occasions these days. The spectators knew that we were up against it and appreciated the effort which the side was making.

Victor Ubogu survived some sledging from All Black captain Sean Fitzpatrick, Kyran Bracken survived a gratuitously late stamp on his ankle from flanker Jamie Joseph but, more important than all of that, we survived as a team. Players grew up that afternoon. Tim Rodber came of age, Bracken kicked off his career with elan, Ben Clarke was a revelation, Martin Johnson confirmed that his debut performance against France and his form on the Lions tour were no flukes, and I was convinced that new England had a future. Brian Moore and Dean Richards were still around to offer a jolt of realism where necessary, Rob Andrew and Rory Underwood were still going strong, but my infatuation with the old days had gone. If this was typical of the fun to come, I was going to like it very much indeed.

The day ended with the normal post-match function, this time at London's Guildhall, and a howler from me. As usual I was on the top table, along with Sean Fitzpatrick. Sean was there with his wife and the Presidents of both the Rugby Football Union and the New Zealand Rugby Union were present, together with the New Zealand High Commissioner and various other guests. There was also a rather large lady on the far side of the circular table whom I did not recognise. She looked a bit out of place and as the evening wore on I became increasingly intrigued as to her identity. She appeared to be on her own and unconnected with anyone round the table.

Eventually I turned to Fitzpatrick for help. 'Fitzy, who is that woman over there?'

'Which one, Will?'

'That really fat one over there.'

'Oh her,' said Fitzy. 'That's my mother.'

What a disaster. Fitzy wasn't amused and when I looked to his wife for a hint of a smile and some moral support she looked away. In the end I could not think of anything to say to retrieve the situation, so I muttered some excuse about having to go to the loo and never returned to the table. If our win had not provided New Zealand with a reason to pay us back next time we met, my comments definitely had. Cape Town, 18 June 1995 at a World Cup semi-final would be the next venue and date where the two nations would clash.

The Five Nations Championship which followed the All Blacks was an anticlimax. France and Wales were seen off and we struggled to a one-point victory over Scotland, a match which reduced Gavin Hastings to tears after Jon Callard had snatched victory with the last kick. Gavin was not consoled by the television replays which showed that the referee had confused the blue cuff of Rob Andrew's shirt sleeve with the blue of Scotland's jersey and mistakenly awarded England a penalty when Rob handled the ball in a ruck. Those last three minutes at Murrayfield were heart-stoppingly tense. Gregor Townsend had knocked over an audacious drop goal to give Scotland the advantage going into injury time. Drop goals do not offer the chance to regroup. With penalties, or conversions following tries, there is always a couple of minutes to regain composure as the kicker prepares himself but with drop goals it is simply a case of going back to the halfway line for a restart. Even so, I managed to shout to Rob Andrew, 'Basics. Put the pressure back on them and see how they cope.'

Jon Callard was as white as a sheet when the referee blew for the penalty. He had already been successful with four penalties but he knew, as did everybody in the stadium, that his game would be judged by this kick.

'Jon, it's easy. You're kicking brilliantly,' I hissed, already composing the excuses for the post-match press conference. I needn't have been so pessimistic. As soon as he hit it, I knew it was over. Scotland had lost again.

The relief lasted a couple of weeks. That was the period between the Scotland victory and losing by a point to Ireland. The Ireland reversal was the first Five Nations Twickenham defeat in the six years I had been in charge. But if that was a shock to my system it was nothing to the blow when Geoff Cooke announced that he was stepping down as coach at the end of the championship. The man who had plucked me from obscurity and thrust me into one of the biggest sporting jobs in the land was on his bike.

As usual Geoff had kept his own counsel. He had not talked it through with me and the first I heard about it was at the end of a routine meeting in Geoff's hotel room leading up to the France match. Dick Best, John Elliott, a national selector, and I were confirming arrangements for the Paris trip when Geoff informed us that he had something to say. 'I've decided that's it,' he said. 'I'm going after the Wales game. I wanted to tell you first because it will be public in a few days.' It was as brief and matter of fact as that. There was no preamble, no explanation, just a short verbal statement and then silence.

I'm not sure the three of us quite believed what we were hearing. Geoff's news was so unexpected that we did not know how to respond. I asked him if there was anything I could do or say which would make him reconsider but I knew it was a futile question. Once Geoff had made up his mind that was usually it.

To this day I am not sure why he quit. I know that he did not enjoy his spell as manager of the 1993 Lions. Ian McGeechan ran the playing side on that trip virtually single-handed and Geoff's role was reduced to giving out ties and making pretty speeches. He had always enjoyed his time on the practice grounds, working in a tracksuit. But with England he was his own man, able to have as much of an input as he required. I just think he had had enough. Rugby was still amateur in 1994, there was no remuneration for managing the England rugby team thirty hours a week, and Geoff was finding it increasingly tough to devote sufficient time to his family and his job. There wasn't much else on offer within rugby for him. He had taken England, a side with no direction and organisation in 1989, to just below the top berth in world rugby in six years. Maybe he was happy with that epitaph, maybe he wanted to improve his golf handicap. All I knew was that I would miss his guidance, company and friendship.

We had never allowed ourselves to get close emotionally. Whatever people believed, Geoff and I were intensely aware that ours had to be a professional relationship. But despite that, not surprisingly, I was and still am fiercely loyal to him. I always had huge respect for him as a man and as a coach, and I would like to think, by the end, I had managed to earn a little respect from him, too.

Now, though, I would have to start all over again with a new boss.

— 17 —
MAN OF MYSTERY

THE phone stayed silent. Geoff Cooke had resigned in March, the Rugby Football Union had appointed Jack Rowell as his successor and England were touring South Africa in May. And still the phone did not ring.

I was in limbo. I did not know much about Jack; enough to recognise his achievement over seventeen years with Bath where he turned them into the best side in England, enough to applaud his successful business career with food company Dalgety where he had risen to become chief executive of Golden Wonder crisps, but nothing about the man himself. I knew that Jack had carte-blanche to choose a new captain and a new squad to take to South Africa. There wasn't much I could do about that. But I needed to know whether I featured in his plans because time was short and South Africa, with the World Cup taking place in that country the following year, was an important tour.

The vibes emanating from Bath were not good. Alex Hambly, with whom I had stayed in touch since our times at Sedbergh and Durham together, was working in Bristol and was in regular contact with the Bath players. Alex had heard that the word was that Jack was after Stuart Barnes to captain the side. There were even one or two rumours to the effect that Stuart was so confident that he had got the job that he had been out celebrating. It made sense. The pair had been close at Bath and Jack respected Stuart's rugby intelligence and his playing talents. It wasn't too fantastic a scenario.

With the phone still silent I made some calls of my own. I had contacted Simon Halliday and Jonathan Webb, both of whom had played under Jack at Bath, to pick their brains. Their feedback was more positive. Both pointed out that he did not select his mates, that he loved winning above all else, and would go for the man whom he thought would deliver that for him. They reckoned I was in with a chance. Three weeks after his appointment Jack called to ask if I would remain as captain. The delay had been one of his celebrated mind games. It was as if he were working out whether I would plead for the job, to see if I would crack. It was typical Jack.

I'll never understand him. We were together as captain and coach/manager for the best part of two seasons but we never had any kind of a relationship. Nothing was ever discussed formally in terms of roles or responsibilities. We just got on with it but the man used to drive me mad. He is a complex character, very bright, a massive fan of rugby but chaotic, too. He was so changeable that you rarely knew where you were with him from one day to the next. He could be vulnerable and amusing, insensitive and a bully, all in the space of a few hours. In his own way he cared about the people he was working with but he did not know how to show it. I found that quite sad. Less forgivable were some of the things he did with England which I thought were appalling. But I don't dislike the man. Far from it. I just find him very difficult to fathom, as did most of the England players, even the Bath men, come to that.

I once asked Sue, Jack's wife, why he bothered to accept the England job. It was early on in Jack's reign. His successes with Bath were well documented, as were his various business direc-torships, and I couldn't work out why he had stuck himself on the line again as England manager when the post was bound to bring with it all kinds of flak.

'Because he wants to be a star,' Sue said. I must have looked incredulous for a startled moment but Sue was adamant. 'You be careful.'

She would probably have made the remark to Jack's face but I thought it was an amazing thing to say. Jack revelled in the attention, the fuss, the column-inches. We all do, otherwise we would not put ourselves in the spotlight, but with Jack it was more than a consequence of a high-profile position. It was the reason for getting involved in the first place.

He also loved setting himself against the world. Jack liked nothing better than a fight, stirring things up to provoke a reaction and then standing back watching how people coped with the waves. In that regard he could not stand sycophants. The way to gain Jack's respect was to challenge him, to disagree and fight your cause, which was fine with some players but detrimental to others who needed reassurance and support.

The South African experience was a difficult one for all concerned. Jack and I were wary of each other, the squad was relatively inexperienced and the Springboks were a vastly different prospect from the outfit we had beaten at Twickenham nineteen months previously. That team was lumpy, one-paced and clearly unused to the demands of modern rugby after their isolation. A year and a half later they were sleek, fit and inventive. To make matters worse, the itinerary was close to suicidal with matches against the top provincial sides as well as national selections. The Super 10, a competition between representative teams from New Zealand, South Africa and Australia, had improved standards in southern hemisphere rugby yet again and it was no surprise that we headed into a match against Transvaal, a week before the First Test, having lost three games.

The Transvaal game proved critical. We went down 24–21 at Ellis Park in Johannesburg in a match we should have won. I had a perfectly good try disallowed but that was not the significant moment; nor, for that matter, was the incident when Martin Johnson was forced out of the tour through concussion after being hit by a Transvaal player. They were spurs to our renaissance, but the big motivating factor was provided by François

Pienaar, Transvaal's captain, who later went on to lead the Springboks to World Cup glory in 1995.

Pienaar came into our dressing room three minutes after the final whistle and said, 'Thanks for the game, we think you're a good side,' and left. It was a perfectly reasonable comment to make in the circumstances, one that most captains traditionally offer, but unaccountably it just got under my skin. 'Thanks for the game, we think you're a good side' – it was just so condescendingly dismissive. Clearly Pienaar and Co. thought that we were anything but a good side, otherwise why bother to mention it at all. You do not go to players or teams you genuinely respect and congratulate them for being competitive. During that week the remark kept swimming around in my head and I used it to gee up the team.

It worked because we stuffed them in that First Test with twenty minutes of some of the best rugby England has ever played. And to make a great day extra special we were introduced to President Mandela before the kick-off. Meeting Nelson Mandela remains one of my most cherished memories. Most dignitaries move quickly down the line with a routine comment for every fourth person. It is obviously not the time for protracted conversation but they appear to work to a formula. Not Mandela. He moved along the team and spoke to each player as he shook their hand. That was rare enough, but he also listened to what they said in return. The dignity and grace of the man were remarkable.

Tim Rodber played out of his socks that day and Rob Andrew made an idiot of the many critics who had rubbished him in articles published on the morning of the match. Rob collected 27 points in the 32–15 victory. And guess what? François took a real pasting in the first ruck as the forwards trampled all over him. That was England all over. If we got in the right frame of mind, we could beat anyone but we had to be underdogs, or have suffered some real or imagined slight to spark.

That's the essential difference between England and the

southern hemisphere countries. New Zealand, South Africa, and to a lesser extent Australia, will win the big matches three or four times on the trot. They have proved that by winning the three World Cups which have taken place. England produce world-class performances occasionally but are unable to sustain them. A week after that First Test victory against the Springboks we were hammered. Not much had changed apart from the fact that we weren't underdogs any longer.

Jack and I were still circling each other warily but I was beginning to understand him better and I was impressed with the way he stood up to the South African authorities when Tim Rodber was sent off against Eastern Province days before the Second Test. The match was a disgrace. Eastern Province were coached by Alex Wylie, a grizzled ex-All Black forward who was obviously still living in the dark ages, and it was clear that they were intent on softening England up before the final vital Test. Jon Callard needed twenty-six stitches after being stamped on the face and there were several running battles amongst the forwards which continued throughout the match, exacerbated by weak and ineffective refereeing. Tim was sent off when he retaliated after yet another fight during which he was punched repeatedly.

His dismissal was a blow. He had been the outstanding forward in the First Test and not to have him play in the Second would have been a huge setback. There was also the issue of natural justice. England and Tim had been grievously provoked by Eastern Province, Jon Callard had been scarred for life, yet the debate centred on whether Tim would pick up a ban which would rule him out of the last game of the tour. It did not seem fair or right. Jack obviously thought so, too. ITV had filmed the match for transmission back in England and Jack took the tape of the game into the disciplinary hearing and catalogued the incidents of South African violence. He demanded that no further penalty, other than the disgrace of then becoming only the second player to be dismissed in an English shirt, should befall Tim. Faced by a belligerent Jack and some incriminating evidence, the three-man tribunal, which included Jack, decided that the sending-off was sufficient punishment.

Jack's loyal and courageous stand in defending Tim was underlined by the response of some of the RFU committee who were accompanying the tour. In the hotel bar after the match, Dudley Wood, soon to retire as RFU Secretary, was bitterly critical of the panel's decision. Dudley thought Tim deserved a ban and said so, spouting the usual old nonsense of England needing to be seen to be beyond reproach, a stance which took no account of the exceptional circumstances surrounding the incident. It was his usual head-in-the-clouds response. All Dudley was concerned about was the reputation of the Union. It seemed as though he could not care less about a potential injustice to a player his Union represented and the fact that England had a chance of making history by becoming the first side to win a series in South Africa by two Tests to nil.

I was not surprised at the attitude of the committee and their inability to get near the wavelength of the players. At the start of the season I had been taken to lunch at the East India Club by Ian Beer, the new President. Ian had not been entirely helpful in England's cause. As headmaster of Harrow he had refused Roger Uttley time off to coach England in the autumn, insisting he put school duties ahead of any commitment to his country. Roger had to leave the team hotel and return to Harrow the day I led England for the first time against Australia. The newspaper pictures of him following the game via a radio clamped to his head as he watched his Harrow side play Wellington did not present English rugby in the best possible light.

Ian's main concern at the lunch was mind-boggling. At the head of his list was the content of my speeches at the post-match dinners.

'They have to improve, Will,' he said. I almost fell off my chair.

'They're not exactly top of my agenda, Ian. I'm more interested in what happens before and during the games, in how we can work together to improve England's performance.'

'Well, they should be important to you. The people at those

dinners are the guests of the Rugby Football Union. They come to hear the thoughts of the England captain.'

That lunch was the beginning of another disastrous relationship with an RFU big-wig which was not improved when we met up again after the South African tour. As we rambled round that country it became fairly obvious that professionalism was rife in the top strata of the game. After matches, during the formal parts of the proceedings when all our RFU committee men were present, the South African administrators actually thanked the sponsors for paying their players. It was as clear and unambiguous a statement of the way rugby was going as anyone was likely to get.

Afterwards Beer agreed to do an interview in *Rugby World*, Britain's biggest-selling rugby magazine. He repeated his and his committee's view that if South Africa wanted to take the low road to professionalism, the RFU would continue on the high road with amateurism. Pompous piffle most of it, but in the article he said, 'The likes of Will Carling, Rob Andrews and Brian Moore come to me and ask for things which the RFU, who believe in sticking to the regulations, cannot allow. They argue it's allowed elsewhere and I tell them that the other rugby nations are cheating. They then say we've got to cheat as well.' That really annoyed me. I never advocated dishonesty of any kind. The whole point of my argument about money was that it should all be out in the open, that the world of shamateurism was tacky and unsavoury. The last thing I wanted was to cheat, to continue the under-the-table deals.

So I collared him next time England met up, which was after the match with Romania in November. 'Ian,' I began, 'I'd like to have a word with you about something.' Jerry Guscott, who had just returned to the squad after a lengthy absence following a groin injury, was sitting next to me. 'I resent you implying that I told you to cheat. You should look at the *Rugby World* interview because it is in there in black and white, in quotes. I think that's out of order and it would be nice if you would apologise. I never told you to cheat.'

'Now listen here boy,' he started back. Just like a headmaster.

Jerry spluttered, 'Oh no,' but it was too late. I grabbed Beer and said, 'Don't you dare call me boy,' before letting off more steam. Luckily Colin Herridge intervened and pulled me off, otherwise I don't know what would have happened. Administrators like Beer had no idea of the issues which concerned the modern player. They remain glued to the era in which they played themselves.

Beer represented his country in 1955, so he should have known better than to thrust himself on the squad just when they needed the time and space to prepare without interruption. But he would make a point of accompanying the players onto the pitch when they first arrived at Twickenham. That time is precious, part of an established routine. You get off the coach about an hour and a half before kick-off, dump your kit in the changing-room, grab a programme, then wander onto the pitch to sniff the wind and test out the surface. Beer used to join us in this ritual and would try to talk to the players, when the last thing on their mind was a chat with someone they didn't know too well. At that stage you are beginning to focus in on the task ahead, closing off all extraneous interruptions, and that included talkative administrators.

Once Beer was unable to make it because the Queen was opening the new East Stand. He was responsible for welcoming her to Twickenham and looking after her. All fair enough, but the way he apologised to the players for not being there with them was hilarious. He sent me a letter explaining his temporary absence. 'Tragically, I can't walk the pitch with the players,' he wrote. 'Do apologise and say that I'll be with them in spirit. Today I'm up to my eyes in Royalty.'

I read the letter out to the team at the Petersham Hotel. An outbreak of manic laughter followed 'I'm up to my eyes in Royalty.' What planet are these guys on?

I couldn't be bothered playing politics with them. I took the view that I was the captain of the team and that was going to take all my energies. The committee were the committee and never the twain should meet. I admit that my approach was confrontational but I hated their empire-building and their little games. Making it on to the committee offered them a bit of power, a chance to invite their friends to the internationals. It seemed to me that was what turned them on, not whether English rugby was successful, or whether the England team were doing well. That may be unfair to some of those I worked with who did, and still do, a great job, but sadly it is certainly true of a very influential few.

The finest player I have ever encountered – Peter Winterbottom in action for England against Ireland in 1982.

Paul Ackford is tackled by Paul Burnell as our Grand Slam aspirations go up in smoke against Scotland in 1990.

'I hope they know what they're doing because I haven't a clue.' The England front row of (left to right) Probyn, Moore and Leonard.

Geoff Cooke – the man who gave a shy, twenty-two year old the chance to fulfil a dream.

A rare picture of a forward helping a back. Peter Winterbottom's excuse is that the game hasn't started yet.

'Excuse me guys, but can I get to the dressing-room?' Excited scenes followed our 21–19 win against France to clinch the 1991 Grand Slam.

The safe hands of the great Serge Blanco in his last match for France. We should have given him a more fitting send-off.

The champagne flows as we celebrate England's first Grand Slam for eleven years.

So the man can run as well as jump. Wade Dooley on the rampage.

Mike Teague and Mickey Skinner bust a gut against Australia in the 1991 World Cup final.

Michael Lynagh, the world record points scorer, was massively influential for Australia for over a decade.

Buenos Aires, July 1990 – Richard Hill in action against Argentinian side Banco Nacion. Not the happiest of games, or tours, for me.

Text book stuff – Dewi Morris fires out a perfect pass.

A rare moment of triumph against a southern hemisphere team after an inexperienced England side had beaten the All Blacks at Twickenham in 1993.

Sean Fitzpatrick, New Zealand's outstanding captain; indomitable, knowledgeable, intense. His mum's nice too.

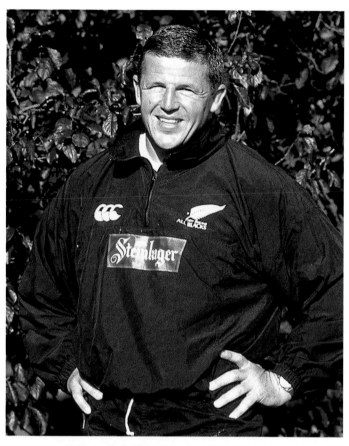

A typically belligerent Brian Moore.

'Anyone seen my ball?' The exploding golf ball always got a laugh as we relaxed during tours.

Gavin Hastings, an inspirational captain of both Scotland and the Lions.

(Left to right) Ieuan Evans, Gavin Hastings and myself were the media's three favourites for the captaincy of the 1993 British Lions. Little did they know I didn't fancy the job.

A hug is in order for Jon Callard who has just pinched the 1994 game against Scotland 15–14 with the last kick of the match.

Who suggested we had no chance against the Boks? South Africa 15, England 32 , 4 June 1994, Loftus Versfeld. Enough said.

David Campese talked a big game, but he played an even better one.

The one that nearly got away – I manage to hang on to Philippe Sella as England run out 31–10 winners against France in 1995.

The unacceptable face of rugby. Phil de Glanville gets in the way of an All Black boot on New Zealand's 1993 tour.

A concerned bench – Dean Richards, Graham Rowntree and I check the progress of the final pool match against Western Samoa in the 1995 World Cup.

Receiving the World Cup cap from RWC chairman, Sir Ewart Bell – must remember to look at the administrator, not the camera.

A reconciliation of sorts – Dennis Easby, Jack Rowell and myself at a press conference following my reinstatement as captain.

Australian scrum-half George Gregan is outnumbered as we attack en masse.

Drop dead gorgeous – Rob Andrew slots the kick that sends Australia crashing out of the 1995 World Cup.

Jonah Lomu *en route* to legendary status as he brushes aside Mike Catt in the 1995 World Cup semi-final in Cape Town.

So deceptive, so brilliant – Jerry Guscott was always a threat.

At least we made one tackle – Jeff Wilson is battered as we are clobbered 45–29 by New Zealand, 18 June 1995.

Left to right) Les Cusworth, John Elliott and Jack Rowell wonder if things are going according to plan.

Meeting Nelson Mandela on England's 1994 tour of South Africa was a privilege. He had time and a word for everyone.

18

THE BEGINNING OF THE END

JULIA and I were married back in England on the Saturday after the Second Test against the Springboks. It was a big wedding. The reception was held at Castle Ashby in Northamptonshire and many of my England mates were there. So were friends I had met outside of rugby. *Hello!* magazine had been on the phone asking if they could take pictures. They were prepared to pay up to £40,000, but I wasn't interested. I did not want the occasion paraded across the shelves of newsagents up and down the country. We were pretty sure that the paparazzi would not get more than the pictures we had agreed to because I had invited a few of my SAS friends and they had told me that uninvited guests would get short shrift.

I had approached the wedding the same way as I had other targets in my life. I was ready for marriage, was fond of Julia, enjoyed her company, found her physically attractive, thought we would get on well together and that was good enough for me. Later, when the story of my friendship with the Princess of Wales began to unfurl, the psychologists employed by the tabloid newspapers would work themselves into a frenzy, making much of the fact that I seemed always to be attracted to blonde, bubbly, vivacious women. If that is true I can think of a few hundred thousand men who are similarly drawn.

I did not take a particularly romantic or mature approach to marriage with Julia but that's the way I was then. For some reason I compartmentalised different aspects of my life – rugby, business, friendships, romance – and dealt with each almost exclusively of the others. It seemed the sensible thing to do. In a hectic schedule it was the only way I knew how to satisfy the various demands.

Julia and I had moved into a flat in Battersea before the wedding but we were not seeing much of each other. She was busy pursuing a television career which was becoming increasingly successful and I was heavily involved with England and Insights. We rarely sat down long enough to talk properly and, if we had, maybe we would not have gone through with the wedding. All I knew in the two to three days leading up to the ceremony, and as I walked up the aisle, was that I might be making a terrible mistake. The lavish scale of the occasion wasn't me. I did not want all the fuss. But I rationalised my apprehension in time-honoured fashion. Stage fright, I thought. Everybody has doubts on the eve of a major commitment. Everything would be all right and in any case Julia's father had committed a great deal of money to the venture. I had to go through with it. It was only later, after we had separated, and I had talked to my father and Andrew Harle, my best man, that I realised that they, too, had had serious misgivings. Still, as we headed off to Zimbabwe for a safari honeymoon I wasn't overly concerned. We were young, healthy, with the world at our feet. I was more worried about my relationship with Jack Rowell and the fortunes of the England team.

It was time once again to get our act into gear for the World Cup. Since its introduction in 1987, that competition had dominated the thoughts of everyone involved in international rugby. Careers, campaigns, lifestyles are all organised according to when and where the next World Cup takes place. I had been dreaming of South Africa ever since we lost to Australia in the final four years before. Team targets and my own development as a player were the two factors which kept me interested. I didn't give a toss about personal benchmarks. After the South African tour, England played Romania at Twickenham, a match in which I won my fiftieth cap, but it wasn't particularly momentous or significant. I cannot remember the game where I passed Nick Farr-Jones to become the world's most experienced national captain. Those ephemeral milestones are not important, of interest only as questions in pub quizzes. I wanted a more permanent memorial and a Grand Slam followed by a World Cup success under the new management of Jack Rowell would do very nicely thank you.

With that target in mind I said something at the start of the 1995 Five Nations Championship I had never previously articulated to the squad. It was a declaration of intent. I told them that I wanted a Grand Slam out of this season, that we were good enough and that last year we had let ourselves down by the way we capitulated against Ireland at Twickenham. It was a measure of the progress England had made. No one dared utter those emotive words 'Grand Slam' in 1991 after the defeat by Scotland in 1990. In 1992 the achievement crept up on us almost before we knew it, yet here I was deliberately setting out mine and the team's stall before a championship. Geoff Cooke would never have believed it.

Maybe I felt I needed to re-establish my authority, to make myself accountable to the team. I was no longer involved in selection, frozen out by Jack who never explained the reasons for the change in policy. I had helped choose the tour party to South Africa when Jack took over from Geoff, but thereafter Jack would ask my opinion of various players but refused to include me in the formal process. In a strange way it was a relief. That initial selection meeting had gone round in endless circles for the best part of three hours, seemingly without any decisions having been made, so not to be part of that would not be the end of the world. And I would finally rid myself of those desperate situations when I had to tell a mate he was out of the side.

I was also anxious to develop my own game. Rugby had

become more fluid through a series of law changes and it
was incumbent on players in all positions to get stuck into all
aspects of life on the pitch. The ball was in play more, opportunities beckoned. The new style suited me. I had always been
happy to take the ball up the middle and into the opposition
forwards. That was a strong part of my game already but now
I would get a chance to show the more creative side of my rugby
character.

Jack had brought in Les Cusworth to help develop the backs.
Life was turning full circle, repeating itself again. Les had played
outside-half for England against France when I made my debut
in the centre and we had both kept our places in the side for
the following game against Wales. It was weird dealing with
Les as a coach when only seven seasons previously I had known
him as a team-mate. I remembered looking across at Les, who
was as white as the proverbial sheet, as we sat in the changing-
room in Paris, thinking, 'Blimey, if he is petrified at what is
about to happen, what hope have I got?' My confidence was
not especially boosted when it came to the game. Les had five
attempts at dropped goals which all missed, probably because
he was reluctant to shovel the ball on to me in case I made a
hash of things. Eventually I yelled, 'For God's sake, give me
the ball and I'll have a go.' A hugely cocky comment from
a twenty-two-year-old playing his first game and not exactly
designed to build bridges with a veteran outside-half.

The Carling/Cusworth relationship was not improved by
defeat in the Wales match, though this time it was brother
Marcus who was to blame. Les missed a couple of crucial tackles
in that game which caused Marcus, sitting in Twickenham's
West Stand, to bellow, 'Jesus, that guy is absolutely pathetic.' It
was only afterwards when Dad was talking to several particularly disappointed people behind and either side of the Carling
family that the penny dropped. Marcus had not been aware that
the players' wives and families were all bunched together in a
block and that the lady in front of him was Les's wife.

The mantle of coach did not change Les. I was after a strong, knowledgeable, almost bossy, individual to lay down the law, whereas he was a quiet, almost diffident man who wasn't at his best when dealing with bolshy, strong-minded individuals. A tremendous amount of piss-taking goes on on international training pitches which, unless nipped in the bud, can become counter-productive and Jeremy Guscott was particularly hard on Les. After Les had outlined a new move, or suggested a change in the angle or line of a run, Jerry, laying on the sarcasm with a trowel, would comment, 'Brilliant, Les. That was revolutionary five years ago. Got anything up to date for us?'

It wasn't meant disparagingly, and it certainly wasn't intended to undermine his role or reputation as coach, but Les found it difficult dealing with that attitude. He seemed unable to prevent the mucking around or relate to the experienced characters. It was as if he were intimidated by the fifty-cap brigade who were exactly the players who would have benefited from an injection of new ideas and practices. I sometimes had to build Les up before he could coach the backs.

Yet there were times when Les did bristle and, when he did, he produced cracking sessions. That was the odd thing about him. When provoked or angry he could be especially assertive but it would take a lot to rouse him. He was like that with Jack Rowell. Les held Jack in high regard, was in awe of his intelligence and the way he toyed with the players, according little or no respect to age or status. But he was not Jack's poodle. Late one night in the bar of the Burnham Beeches Hotel where England were staying, Les and Jack were involved in a conversation with a senior executive of the supermarket chain ASDA. Tim Rodber was also present. The chat centred around England's prospects in the forthcoming match and the man from ASDA asked Les's opinion.

'Don't ask him,' Jack said, provocative as ever. 'He's only an ex-teacher.' Les did not flinch.

'Say what you like, Jack. At least I've done it. At least I've played for my country. You can only dream about it.'

Jack was so taken aback, so stung by the remark, that he

sprang out of his chair and let fly at Les with an unrepeatable tirade of abuse.

If arguments and disagreements peppered the season off the pitch, at least there was some harmony on it. Slowly England were progressing towards the style of rugby necessary for success in the World Cup. Much was made in the press of the search for the new-look England, provoked in part by Jack himself, but the reality was different. There was never a conscious desire to play any particular style of rugby. It was simply a case of making best use of the available resources.

During the first two Grand Slams England had probably the best set-piece pack in the world. Their replacements offered different attributes. It would have been madness to ask Ben Clarke, Victor Ubogu and Tim Rodber to play static, tightly controlled rugby. But to say that the change was born out of some messianic conviction to be the disciples of running rugby is ludicrous. Brian Moore, Dean Richards, Rob Andrew and Jason Leonard were still around and they were not about to sign up to the pretty-pretty stuff to appease the critics.

Ireland and France were our best performances that season. The first forty minutes into the teeth of a howling gale in Dublin were well nigh faultless, a fusion of pace and power with the forwards in irresistible form. The contest against France added another dimension. This time the backs did their stuff. Up 13–3 at the interval, two tries by Tony Underwood late in the game was more than enough for a convincing 31–10 victory. The try count was important. For years we had relied on battering the French half to death in order to subdue them but now it appeared as if we could match them in other areas. If only we could slip into, and sustain, that approach more often.

The Grand Slam was clinched against Scotland who also had that prize in their sights. But if the press were revisiting Murrayfield '90, we weren't. Half that side had disappeared, this match was at Twickenham, and we had moved on. Winning wasn't exactly a habit but we were getting there. Still, the echoes of Murrayfield '90 did the ticket touts no harm. A pair of the best seats in the stadium were reputedly on offer at £5,000. Grandmothers were being sold all over London and Edinburgh.

The match itself failed to live up to its billing. Seven Rob Andrew penalties plus a dropped goal added up to a 24–12 success. It was my third Grand Slam of the nineties, as sweet and as satisfying as the other two, and a tremendous fillip to our World Cup campaign. That was the good bit. Less promising was a row I had with Jack in Cardiff *en route* to that Grand Slam.

England had asked Austin Swain, a sports psychologist, to assist in the preparations. Austin was well liked by the squad and he did make a difference, especially to players coming into the side or those who were struggling with certain aspects of their play. Austin enabled players to see their problems from a different angle and he improved individual confidence considerably. I don't know whether or not Jack thought Austin's work was valuable but he blanked Austin in a way I found reprehensible. Austin had put in a lot of work before the Wales match and he wanted to attend the dinner afterwards because it would be a good opportunity to see his charges when they were completely relaxed. The other, equally legitimate, reason was that he simply wanted a good night out, to experience the social side of international rugby. But Jack turned him down, said there was no way he could come to the dinner, which meant that Austin would have been packing his bags to go home after the game as we were getting ready to party.

I first got to hear about it at 1 a.m. the following morning and I was furious. I found Jack, who was in his hotel room with Les Cusworth, and loaded both barrels.

'I think you were out of order, Jack. You should have treated Austin with a great deal more respect. He's a great guy and a valued member of the squad. You should not have mucked him about like that.' Jack was incensed.

'Don't you dare talk to me like that. I'm not Geoff Cooke. You can't twist me round your little finger.'

That did it. Maybe it was a combination of a tense match and a few drinks but I had had enough. People always thought that I could do no wrong in Geoff's eyes, that I was his little protégé, which was absolutely inaccurate. Geoff and I had plenty of disagreements and he was, after all, one of the selectors who refused to pick me for the Test side on the 1993 Lions tour to New Zealand. There was no truth that I had it all my own way with him, and Jack contributing to the myth finished me off.

'You've no idea of my relationship with Geoff,' I fumed and squared up to hit him. I would have done so as well which, given our respective sizes, me at 5ft 10ins, Jack at 6ft 6ins, may not have been too bright. But Jack, seeing that I appeared to be on the verge of belting him, backed off and offered me a drink instead.

That was par for the course for Jack, an episode where he had alienated a valued member of the England entourage in Austin Swain, provoked a confrontation with me, and then eased off. It may have been stimulating for him but I found the incident terribly depressing, and a blazing example of how not to conduct business in international sport. Twelve months into a partnership with Jack, I wasn't sure if I was going to be able to make the partnership work.

— 19 —
ME AND MY BIG MOUTH

I T wasn't clever and it wasn't accurate. There were fifty-six old farts on the committee of the Rugby Football Union, not fifty-seven. The comment was made off-air and used in a Channel 4 documentary about the state of rugby and the direction it should take. The programme was recorded before the Calcutta Cup match with Scotland in March 1995 as part of the *Fair Game* series commissioned by Yorkshire Television. I thought I was sharing a private conversation with Greg Dyke, the interviewer, but it was included in the final cut and caused a massive fuss. I suppose it was the day Dudley Wood nearly got his own back because he was the inspiration for the comment.

I was annoyed that the remark was broadcast because I never intended it for public consumption. I had finished my interview with Greg and the production people had turned the camera off. We had both unpinned our microphones and laid them on the table. I had no idea that the mikes were still live, still recording. Dyke asked me a general question about the merits of running sport through committees. 'If the game is run properly, as a professional game, you do not need fifty-seven old farts running rugby,' was my response. As far as I was concerned that was not on tape. I wouldn't have said it on tape and I left relieved that I had not slipped up and said anything controversial. Little did I know that my remarks were going to be used over the final credits as the programme ended.

On the Thursday before the programme was due to go out on the Friday, Hilary, my secretary, phoned saying that the *Sun* newspaper was intrigued as to why I had labelled the committee fifty-seven old farts. They had got wind of a press release due to be issued by Channel 4 to promote the programme. I didn't know what the hell she was talking about. On the Friday that it was broadcast I was playing golf with Gary Lineker and Jon Holmes. We were constantly interrupted by phone calls from journalists and news organisations who had received the publicity hype and wanted a reaction. To be honest we all thought it was a bit of a joke and that the furore would die down but it didn't. Finally Jon's phone rang again as we were having a cup of coffee on the ninth. It was the RFU Secretary, Tony Hallett, who had succeeded Dudley Wood, this time. 'Things are getting a bit out of hand here. You'd better come back.'

Gary and I looked at each other and Gary said, 'Will, not even your lot are stupid enough to react to a thing like that, even if you did say it.' He couldn't have been more wrong.

We finished the round and Jon suggested I spoke to Colin Herridge on the way home. Colin was a close friend, was on the committee himself as Surrey's representative, and had a good nose for trouble. 'You'd better ring Jack and the President and apologise,' Colin said. 'Everyone is hopping mad.'

How right he was. Senior figures within the Rugby Football Union had convened at the East India Club to decide how to respond. Dennis Easby, the President, was in the chair and he had vice-president Bill Bishop, assistant honorary treasurer John Motum and former president Ian Beer alongside him. Dudley Wood was present as an observer and the late treasurer Peter Bromage and vice-president John Richardson offered comments over the telephone. I felt that I couldn't have had a worse bunch of men to try my case. I had had run-ins with Wood and Beer and the others were not known as Carling supporters. Clemency seemed out of the question.

I rang Jack Rowell, hoping he was going to support me. 'You've been a prat,' he said. A normal reaction from Jack. There I was seeking help and he was having another pop at me. I knew I had been stupid. I didn't need to be told that but I could have done with some advice, a way out of the hole I had dug myself. It was quite obvious from our conversation that Jack was intending to sit firmly on the fence. He wasn't going to move one way or the other until he could tell which way the wind was blowing.

That Friday I rang Dennis Easby, the President, to apologise but I was unable to speak to him personally because he was in a meeting. Instead, I sent him a fax explaining the context of the remarks, telling them they weren't intended for broadcasting. In return I was told to ring him the following morning which was a Saturday, and the day of the Pilkington Cup final between Bath and Wasps. Julia and I then went out for dinner with Hugh Laurie and his wife Jo, convinced that the affair would blow over. Hugh even made a joke about it. Raising his glass, he said, 'I would like to toast the ex-England captain.'

Bright and early on Saturday morning I called Dennis Easby. I was halfway through the phone call, full of humble pie, when Easby interrupted me. 'That's very kind of you but it's unnecessary now. I'm sorry to tell you, you've been relieved of the England captaincy. You'll still be able to go to South Africa as a player, but not as captain. Thanks for all you've done.'

I don't think I took it all in straightaway. 'Right,' I said, and put the phone down. My initial reaction was to think, 'Shit, that's that. It's all over.' But then I saw the silver lining. I could still go as a player and maybe it would do me good after seven years in the job to concentrate on my game and enjoy the experience as part of the team rather than the side's front man. I called Hugh. 'You bastard, you were right. I'm now the ex-England captain.' There wasn't much he could say.

The RFU made it official at 11.30 on the morning of the

Pilkington Cup final in a terse press release. 'It has been decided with regret that Will Carling's captaincy of the team will be terminated forthwith and an announcement concerning his replacement will be made shortly. In the light of the views Will Carling has expressed regarding administrators, it is considered inappropriate for him to continue to represent, as the England captain, the Rugby Football Union, England and indeed British sport.'

The timing of the RFU's statement was symptomatic of their cack-handedness. Pilkington must have been furious. For years they have pumped money into the game as major sponsors and on their biggest day, English rugby's final end of season flourish, the RFU had hijacked the agenda. They could have made the announcement on Sunday or, better still, on the Monday and allowed Pilkington their day in the sun but they chose not to.

All hell broke loose when the press release confirming that I had been sacked was issued. The phone lines and faxes at Twickenham went berserk. I was told that the majority of the comments were critical of the RFU's decision. Then the press descended on the house (a taste of things to come when my marriage encountered difficulties), asking for comment and reaction. I told them the truth, that I had apologised, that I was very sorry, that the comment was never meant to be on the record, but that the matter was now out of my hands. There was nothing more I could do.

I remember lying on the carpet at home watching the final on TV. The crowd were chanting something but I couldn't make out what it was. I had the volume down and wasn't paying close attention but I heard later it was all supportive of me. Looking back, it was the crowd's reaction and the response of the Sunday papers the following day which may have per-suaded Easby and chums they had not quite captured the mood of the nation. And when the England players became involved it became clear that, far from being congratulated on upholding the power of the administrator over the player, the RFU were embroiled in a damage-limitation exercise.

Rob Andrew called me on the Sunday. He had been playing for Wasps in the final and he took the mick saying that I had ruined the game for everyone. But then the conversation turned to my sacking. 'Take it from me,' he said, 'no one is going to accept the captaincy.' Rob then went on record saying that he wasn't interested in the captaincy, even if it were offered to him. Dean Richards did the same and the RFU were left with the appalling prospect of taking a team to South Africa and a World Cup without a captain.

It was on Talk Radio that the prospect of peace was first mooted. Jon Holmes was driving his wife back from lunch with his daughter when he was contacted by host Gary Newbon, asking him to talk about the situation on his radio programme. Jon pulled over to the side of the road and spoke with Gary live on air for a couple of minutes. Then out of the blue Jon was asked to stay on the line because Dennis Easby had also agreed to take part in the discussion.

Dennis trotted out his line about how I had insulted the committee and it was only when Jon reminded Dennis that Dudley Wood had allegedly insulted athletes earlier in the year in a lunch-time speech to newspaper editors that Dennis appeared to alter his position. Dudley's defence at the time was that the speech had been off the record and should never have been reported, which was identical to the position I was taking. Gary Newbon suggested to Dennis that it would be a magnanimous gesture if he were to rethink his decision, following an apology from me, and in an amazing volte face Dennis agreed. The radio conversation was the olive branch the RFU had been waiting for. By this stage they were in a hell of a predicament. None of the players was going to accept the captaincy, there was a huge public outcry against their decision and there were even calls for mass resignations.

Jon called me in a right state. 'Look we can sort all this out,' he said. 'I've been talking to the President on the radio and you can apologise and we can rescue the situation.'

I was not convinced. 'Jon, what are you talking about? I've

said sorry once. It didn't work the first time, why should it work now?'

'I can get you back as England captain,' he insisted. 'You've got to ring the President between 4 p.m. and 5 p.m. and you've got to apologise and they'll have you back.'

The whole business was crazy. I had already apologised once but I had to do it again publicly for them to appear magnanimous and reconsider their original decision. I rang Dennis at home. 'Apparently I've got to ring you,' I said.

'Yes,' he answered. 'This is a hell of a mess. We feel if you publicly apologise, maybe we can sort something out. Can you come to Twickenham tomorrow?' The change in tone between our conversations on Saturday and Sunday afternoon was marked. Dennis was now much more conciliatory.

I travelled to Twickenham for a late afternoon meeting. Colin Herridge accompanied me and Dennis Easby and I went into the Secretary's office and sat down. 'What are we to do?' he said. 'Will you publicly apologise. If you do, I think we can have you back.'

'Of course I will.'

'What is it all about anyway, that remark of yours? What provoked it?'

So I explained about the tremendous resentment among the players, how it was all to do with Dudley Wood, how they were sick of the way he was trying to stop professionalism. 'He's blocking the whole thing. If the RFU continue to fight the players there will be resentment. There are many problems brewing and we don't feel we are getting a fair crack of the whip.'

This dispute ended there. I agreed to a statement in which I apologised to the whole committee and I was reinstated. We drove down to Marlow, where England were training, for the press conference. Before that began, I walked into a room for some peace and quiet and to compose myself before facing the media. Who should be in there but Jack Rowell. It was another bizarre twist to a weird episode.

'You could at least smile,' he said.

'Why's that, Jack?'

'Because you are bloody captain again.'

It was as though he hated the thought of me being captain once more. I told him I didn't want to appear pleased or smug because I thought the press conference would be difficult enough for Dennis without me grinning all over the place. Jack mumbled something and walked out. Well, I thought, he's pleased I'm back.

People have said the whole experience must have been very flattering but I don't think it was about me as an individual or about me as a captain. The players didn't suddenly get together and claim that I was a great guy. They weren't prepared to be dictated to by the RFU two weeks before setting off for the most important tournament rugby has to offer. As far as the public reaction went, that was a pretty apposite comment on the egos of a few old men. How anyone could be so upset, react so strongly, at being called old farts is beyond me.

I felt sorry for Dennis Easby. He copped the flak but he was the one person who acted honourably throughout. When it became apparent that the East India Club cabal had misjudged and mishandled the matter many of them dived for cover. Dennis did not. He never distanced himself from the decision and he had the grace and guts to admit that a mistake had been made. The abuse he received that weekend in the newspapers, through letters to the RFU and his home address, and via his telephone, was cruel and vicious. That was an unpleasant consequence and one I would never have wished on any administrator.

Dennis and I patched up our differences soon afterwards. He came out to the World Cup and was treated like any other member of the official RFU party accompanying the England team. Better than most. Dennis was very much part of the team celebrations which took place in a Cape Town restaurant following our quarter-final win over Australia.

I think the players handled what became known as the old farts affair remarkably well. They didn't confront the RFU, they released a statement saying we hope you can reconsider your position. It was lucky Brian Moore was away for the weekend because he would have stirred things up good and proper. Rob Andrew and Dean Richards were the key men. They kept in constant contact with Jon and played hard ball with the RFU, yet at the same time gave them a way out which allowed them to retain some dignity.

Certain people in the press thought it was a plan by Jon Holmes to boost my profile but that's a stupid theory. Since when do all the newspapers do what Jon tells them? Or all the players for that matter? And how can you orchestrate all that public reaction? The press might have said good job Carling's gone and the players might still be cheering, but it didn't happen like that and I was very grateful.

— 20 —
LOMU LOOMS LARGE

THE 1995 World Cup was when it was all supposed to come together. I was very confident going into that competition. I didn't think we were out-and-out favourites but with a following wind and a large slice of luck there was a chance we could go all the way. The tea-leaves were propitious. England had notched up another Grand Slam in the Five Nations and performances in the preceding two years against South Africa in 1994 and New Zealand in 1993 had shown that when it came to one-off occasions we could beat the top sides. We would still lose three or four games out of five against those nations but World Cups are one-off competitions. Three big matches in the final stages and the deed is done.

There was another reason why I was upbeat. The shadow of Jonah Lomu had still to fall across world rugby. Before South Africa '95 Jonah was just a freak of nature who was making a name for himself on the Sevens circuit. After South Africa '95 he was the most famous rugby player on the planet.

I was happy in South Africa. I knew it was going to be my last shot at the big time. There was no way I would last until 1999 and that knowledge was curiously uplifting. So were the arrangements for the first three matches. We were based in Durban, staying in a hotel just metres away from the Indian

Ocean. The weather was kind, training conditions first-class and the stadiums outstanding. Take the politics out of South African rugby and it is the finest country in the world to tour. And in 1995 the authorities had massaged apartheid out of rugby politics. The World Cup was portrayed as the event which would unite a country still trying to live down the horrors of the past.

For a few short weeks it did. Inside a national sporting team is not the best place to make a judgement on the health of a nation. You never know what will happen to the kids introduced to rugby in the shanty towns when the PR circus and the cameras move on, whether donations and interest will dry up, but I was impressed by the buzz of the place. It was impossible to manufacture or fake the enthusiasm shown by all sections of the community as South Africa edged towards the final. And that searing image when Nelson Mandela, wearing François Pienaar's No. 6 jersey, handed over the Webb Ellis Trophy to Pienaar will go down as one of the great moments of the twentieth century.

All that was a mile away as we plodded through our pool games. The first-round matches were always going to be difficult. General standards had risen in the four years between the World Cups. In 1991 we had waltzed past Italy but in 1995, although the result was never really in doubt, the task was much harder. Close victories by 24–18 against Argentina and 27–20 against Italy had the critics carping, but I wasn't particularly concerned. In World Cups you have to peak at the right moment; there has to be steady improvement. Sides who blast out of the blocks in the opening rounds rarely last the distance and a 44–22 win against Western Samoa in the last pool match was proof that we were moving in the right direction. We were not flat out but we did not want to be and that, in part, accounted for our diffidence on the pitch.

There was also a strong feeling within the squad that these were not the make or break games. We were aware that the fast direct style we were seeking was not in place and that we weren't putting sides away in the manner in which we hoped, but time was on our side. We all knew that the first big test would be against Australia or South Africa in the quarter-final. That was a dead cert ever since the Rugby World Cup committee published their seedings and groups two years before the tournament kicked off. And when South Africa cruised past Australia in the opening game of the tournament we knew that Australia would be the first major hurdle. That was the moment for pieces to fall into place.

Yet as we prepared for that match the alarm bells were tinkling softly in the back of my mind. England were still relying on the old soldiers to lead them forward. Rob Andrew, Brian Moore and Dean Richards were the movers and shakers at a time when other players should have been giving a lead. Martin Johnson was becoming more influential in terms of strategy but England was still a side defined by its past. The environment was not right for players like Mike Catt to come through and assume responsibility. I am to blame for that because my inclination was to listen and trust those who had battled by my side since the late eighties rather than lean towards the new generation. Jack Rowell, too, did not help. His coaching style was very much off the cuff. He was reluctant to issue directions to players. But when he did, I felt that those directions were invariably confusing and limiting to the players concerned.

In 1995 Mike Catt was developing as England's full-back. Mike is an instinctive and gifted runner, and full-back was the ideal position to make best use of his qualities. Jack would acknowledge Mike's qualities and tell him how important they were to the team's attacking potential, yet in the same breath he would instruct Mike that on no account must he get caught with the ball in his own half behind the forwards. For a player like Mike who thrives on confidence the orders were confusing and contradictory.

Jack still appeared very nervous and insecure when it came to the big matches and his anxieties about himself communicated themselves to the squad. Before the World Cup quarter-final against Australia he was so uptight at the final meeting that he could not read from the piece of paper in his hand because it was shaking so much. Some of the players at the back of the room actually started laughing. The more nervous he became the more he relied on an established routine. He would make the same points over and over and over again in the team sessions. The flip chart would be summoned and Jack would scribble key phrases – 'back three, front five, first phase'. They were valid points in themselves but they did not need to be rammed down our throats on a daily basis. The team used to get frustrated with him. It can be incredibly boring preparing for World Cups and internationals. Most of the hard training has been completed and there is little to do apart from resting and attending meetings. It is very easy to get lethargic and stale and the best antidote is to inject something new and different into the preparations. Jack never seemed to grasp that principle. It was very strange behaviour for a man who was such a hit in the business community.

The quarter-final against Australia will be remembered for Rob Andrew's drop goal which won the match but of much more significance was the spying mission which went on before-hand. Austin Swain, our sports psychologist, was in South Africa to assist with the mental preparation. Not content with contributing to the mind games which are part and parcel of international rugby, Austin took it upon himself to help out in a far more practical manner. Dressed as a backpacker, he sneaked in to watch Australia's last closed training session before the quarter-final.

His disguise was so effective that he befriended the grounds-man and ended up drinking some of Australia's isotonic drinks with him by the side of the training pitch, while noting down Australia's strike moves and defensive patterns. Australia blithely went through their pre-match repertoire blissfully unaware that every last detail was being recorded for the con-sumption of the England players later that evening. When Austin returned he showed us which way Australia preferred to attack from certain areas of the pitch and who were the key men in different moves. In practical terms it probably made little difference to how the game was played, because matches rarely reflect training programmes, but as a psychological boost Austin's information was invaluable. We went to bed that night secure in the knowledge that we were unlikely to receive any major surprises the following afternoon.

Austin also helped out in more orthodox ways. After giving us the low-down on Australia he asked each of the twenty-one players in the match squad to write why he thought that a particular member, Jason Leonard say, was a great player and why he was happy Jason was in the side. Austin collected up the pieces of paper and posted them under the doors of the relevant players' rooms. Reading the comments before turning out the light to sleep was massively uplifting. It may sound corny, and some of the comments might have been less than completely honest, but as a world tournament enters its final knock-out stages, when matches turn on the smallest details, it was reassuring to read the scraps of paper. They created a sense of well-being, as did the probability that all round the hotel team-mates were doing and feeling the same thing. Australia were the common enemy and we were bound together by the thoughts on the scraps of paper. Three years of planning and dreaming were about to be tested.

The drop goal which won it was nothing to do with me. With only seconds left and the score tied at 22–22 apiece we were awarded a penalty just short of the halfway line. Rob Andrew shouted that he thought he could smack one over but I thought it was too far out. Instead I told Mike Catt to kick to touch to set up an attacking line-out. Then Dean Richards piped up. As we were running towards the line-out, Deano scuttled past and said, 'We'll drive it from here.' That wasn't much of a surprise. Deano had been saying, 'Will, we'll drive it from here,' ever since the Dead Sea was sick. It was his catch phrase. But Rob liked the idea. 'Drive the line-out and I'll go for the drop,' he ordered. That is how most significant decisions take place on a rugby pitch. They are never totally pre-planned. The state of the game, the form of the players, their mental state, field position and luck are all considerations. Everyone likes to think that the drop goal was played for step by step, but it wasn't. We might just as easily have asked for quick ball off the line-out and tried a miss-move to expose Australia on the flank. The fact was that Dean's initial call, the one he always made, suited Rob and that was the option he went for.

The rest, as they say, is history. The ball sailed through the posts and we had avoided the early flight home. Relief is the emotion which dominates such moments for me. Elation and satisfaction all come later. To go home at the quarter-final stage would have been a disaster. As Dean, Rob and I relaxed in the whirlpool bath in the Cape Town changing rooms, England's World Cup hopes were very much alive.

A night of celebration followed but not before one of Australia's greatest players received a dose of his own medicine. The RFU had flown out the girls for a relaxing weekend round the quarter-final stage and they also contributed to Australia's woe. Through some administrative cock-up their coach pulled up outside the Australians' hotel. Before they discovered their mistake and drove away, David Campese, thinking it was Australia's official transport, hopped on board and was subjected to a barrage of abuse from the girls. It was a good couple of minutes before Campo realised he was on the wrong bus and it was kind of fitting that the scourge of English rugby, who had dished far more than his fair share of dirt over the years, was told exactly how and where to get off by a group of players' wives. Campo would not have liked that one bit.

The rest of the players and I trooped down to Cape Town's waterfront area, a warren of bars, nightclubs and restaurants. The Barmy Army, that bunch of Anglophile nomadic sports fans, had beaten us to it and the sight of the 6ft 10ins England lock Martin Bayfield towering over the masses to conduct the singing sessions will stay with me for a long while. But after a time the crush became too oppressive and I slipped off for a beer with Peter Winterbottom. That was the point where the celebrations ended and the anxieties surrounding a New Zealand semi-final hove into view.

Winters had watched the quarter-final and was concerned about the form of Brian Moore. 'He's past his best,' he said. 'You shouldn't pick him against the Blacks.' The significance of what Winters was saying seeped through my alcoholic haze. Brian was the most competitive player I had ever known. If Winters thought he was losing it, and he was right, then against New Zealand we would be in trouble. Brian was invariably at his best against the best and we needed him on top form.

The news leaking out of the New Zealand camp was worrying. The talk was of revenge following our victory at Twickenham two years previously. Losses are usually remembered long after the greatest of victories fade away and this All Black side was no different. On top of which their form in the pool games had been nothing short of awesome. Ireland and Wales were beaten 43–19 and 34–9 respectively, while Japan were hammered 145–17. A comfortable 48–30 over Scotland was equally ominous. New Zealand were three games down the road to a Grand Slam without breaking sweat. If my theory about teams needing to peak towards the end of a tournament was right then we were in for a tough time. The reputation of Jonah Lomu, too, was growing game by game.

I first sensed the mood wasn't right on the bus going to the match. The self-belief wasn't there. On the surface everything appeared OK. The bus was quiet, but not unduly so, and the team seemed to be concentrating on the task ahead. But I could not shake loose the impression that New Zealand were a team too far, that the emotion and effort involved in beating Australia had taken too much out of the side. It was as if that result, feted back home, had justified our World Cup.

The three days we spent in Sun City, one of South Africa's top holiday resorts, after the quarter-final might have been a mistake. No one went on the lash, or behaved irresponsibly, but the concentration had been fractured. I had campaigned for that break, believing that you can get too intense, too withdrawn at times, but mixing with a load of tourists may not have been a good idea. The sense of foreboding continued into the changing room. Nothing was palpably amiss but it didn't feel right. I am powerless at this stage. Players are too far gone to be preached to. If the self-belief is not there, no amount of haranguing from me will get it back. This is the time when a captain trusts in the routine of past victories, hoping that whatever it takes to win games will explode onto the pitch. I have never been able to define that ingredient. Sometimes it's there, at other times it isn't. Noisy dressing rooms do not signify victories, neither do quiet ones. There are no barometers. The only moments of importance are the first five minutes of action and they were to be the worst I have ever experienced in an England shirt.

In 1991 England were beaten 40–15 by Australia in Sydney but that wasn't a World Cup semi-final. This was, and it was a disaster. Even the kick-off went wrong. New Zealand kicked left to Lomu and the ball dropped in the space between Tony Underwood and myself. Neither of us called. I left it to Tony as he was the player coming on to the ball but in the confusion Tony dropped it. And that was the nearest we got to the ball in that opening spell.

After fifteen minutes we were history. The Blacks had scored four tries. They tore us to pieces. We were in shock. I could see it on the faces of the players. After the second score I gathered the team round and told them not to panic, that we had to get hold of possession and retain it, establish our own rhythm and pace. But after the fourth try I was unable to convince myself that we were still in with a chance. I only wanted us to play with pride. New Zealand's pace and power was phenomenal. We did not so much as sniff the ball. It was quite incredible watching Lomu run over people. We'd seen the videos before the match, thought yes, he's a big strong boy, but felt we could deal with him.

The reality was something else. I had never played against Jonah in the flesh and very early on I saw him coming down the middle channel. The angle of his run made him my man and I lined him up as I had done a million times in the past. But he blew me aside. I did not get near him. It wasn't just his strength and his speed which made him such a formidable athlete. His balance was also special. Jonah could step off either foot and all he needed was to check a defender by the slightest amount and he was gone. Tony Underwood carried the can for Jonah's four tries that afternoon but Superman on a steam-roller would have come off second best.

New Zealand were touched with genius that day and, if we'd stuck three men on Jonah, they'd have gone through somewhere else. At least in the second half we came back at them but that was the best side I have ever played against. They were untouchable. It was like fifteen-year-olds against a men's side. Embarrassing. They were as quick with their thinking as they were over the ground. One of their tries came from a simple No. 8 pick-up from the blind side of the scrum on the halfway line. That is just not meant to happen at international level. Everything was performed with clinical precision. I could see them thinking where are England weak or slow? There, there. Try!

Should we have factored Jonah into our game plan, devised a strategy to neuter his effectiveness? I don't think so. We would merely have opened the gate for another All Black to write his name in lights. An early encounter with Frank Bunce, my opposite number, convinced me of that. During the first half, I made a break down the right-hand side of the field and put Tony Underwood away only for Tony to be caught by Jonah Lomu. A few seconds after I had shipped the ball on to Tony I was flattened from behind, pole-axed right in the kidneys.

I didn't have to look. I knew immediately who it was. I also knew that I had to get up because the player concerned would have been standing over me seeing if I could hack it. As I rose groggily to my feet I saw Bunce smiling and then watched as Jonah threw Tony one-handed into touch. Bunce knew he had hit me late, but it was a mental thing. Are you going to get up

177

or are you going to stay hurt was the question he was asking. All of New Zealand were asking that question. The entire team.

Which was why we had to treat Jonah the same as the other Blacks. We refused to double team him, or tinker with selection to pitch a more physically powerful player than Tony against him. If we had done that, we would have denied our own capabilities. Most international teams, and England are no exception, are more concerned with what they can offer rather than stopping the opposition. Sure, you respect your opponents, acknowledge their strengths and skills, but no more than that.

We believed that New Zealand were vulnerable, that the physical presence of our forwards, Tim Rodber, Martin Johnson, Jason Leonard, Martin Bayfield and Dean Richards, would be enough to rein in the Blacks. We also thought Andrew Mehrtens and Walter Little in their midfield area were vulnerable. Those assessments turned out to be way off beam but to prepare for an international on the basis of what New Zealand would do to us would be tantamount to handing over the game before it had started. Elevating Jonah above his team-mates would also have shattered the already fragile confidence of Tony Underwood before Jonah got round to doing it himself. Both Tony and Mike Catt took a long while to recover from that game. I didn't enjoy the experience much either.

But there was still one humiliation to go. As New Zealand travelled to Johannesburg to prepare for their titanic clash with South Africa, we travelled to Pretoria for a more muted game. Whoever invented the play-off game to decide third and fourth places needs to be shot. No one enjoys the experience. After the disappointment of losing the semi-final it is virtually impossible to anticipate the encounter with anything other than profound gloom. Even the carrot at the end is meaningless. The winner gains automatic entry to the next tournament, missing out on the qualifying rounds, but as World Cups are four years apart it means that the majority of the side is endeavouring to ease the passage of players who will come after them. Not exactly the most motivational of circumstances.

Nevertheless, the final game against France was still a Test match and a chance to tighten morale and confidence after the New Zealand débâcle. It was important that we took something positive back from South Africa with which to start the new season. It was a match to blood new players, for individuals to show they had character and that England was important to them. Jack didn't see it quite in that vein. He acknowledged the significance of the match but he refused to experiment. He wanted the tried and trusted men on board.

It didn't work. Some of the players couldn't get up after the New Zealand match and we lost to France for the first time in eight games. Three or four people had shocking matches, Victor Ubogu especially. Victor was a complicated character. His privileged background and many distractions, including a financial interest in Shoeless Joe's, a fashionable London wine bar, occasionally dulled his appetite for rugby. When roused, he was sensational but, I thought, he also had a tendency towards laziness, content to coast the next few matches if he had played conspicuously well in one game. France was Victor at his worst. I lost it completely for the second time in my career. To go down against a better team was liveable with. Against New Zealand we had fought back to score four tries and retain some dignity but against France there was nothing. No passion, no pride. Nothing. Victor copped the tidal wave of my frustration at the half-time interval.

'Look mate, do you want to play? You're doing absolutely nothing for this team. If you're not up for it, say so, and you can go off injured.' I really tore into him. The rest of the front row were getting hammered in the scrum but Victor was particularly poor. In my view he should never have played for England again.

And what did Jack do? He picked Victor for the very next international against South Africa five months later. I thought, that was a terrible decision. It sent out all the wrong signals. The squad knew of his poor performance against France and here he was back in contention again. Perhaps it is not quite fair to single him out, but when you're aspiring to becoming one of the best sides in the world, you need the best around. I was absolutely livid.

Brian Moore was another player who did not have one of his better games in the play-off against France. He was enduring a turbulent episode in his personal life and it became obvious that these problems were getting to him. Peter Winterbottom's observations had proved prophetic. Brian was simply unable to tap into the fury which made him such a great player. The desire had deserted him and that communicated itself to the rest of the forwards. I've never seen England get hammered up front as we did against France. The backs didn't perform either. We just weren't hungry.

Afterwards I sat in the changing room totally demoralised. I had thought we were competitive but we weren't. The planning had been poor and we had failed to learn from our mistakes in the early matches. We should have looked at the faults arising from the Australia match rather than using the victory as a validation of our tactics and methods. There were also too many egos and vested interests in and out of the squad. World Cup '95 had not gone according to plan.

— 21 —

A VERY FAMOUS FRIEND

O NE year into our marriage and Julia and I were experi-encing problems. The relationship wasn't working. It is easy to be wise after the event but I should have taken time out to think it all through before I made that commitment. After we were married I had this terrible feeling that I was trapped in something that I didn't want to be in. Julia began to devote more and more time to her media career which was taking off. I was still heavily involved in all my activities and, even though we were man and wife, nothing fundamental had changed. There was no real partnership, no sharing. We tried to talk but that was our main weakness. We didn't know how. I certainly did not know how to communicate within a relationship, how to resolve problems when they were wrapped in so much emo-tional baggage. Eventually we both agreed that it wasn't work-ing and decided to split up.

All this happened before the news of my friendship with Diana broke. I had known Diana for two years before Julia and I separated and, despite what people have said and written, she was not the reason for the break-up of my marriage. Julia and I had concluded that our marriage was not working, and had agreed to go our separate ways three weeks before the story first appeared. As I have recounted, I met Diana first in 1993 in

Wales in front of 56,000 people at Cardiff Arms Park, and later that year at a charity function for Help the Aged and then at a Buckingham Palace reception. On none of those occasions did our conversation get past the 'Hello, nice to meet you' stage. We became friendly when I joined the Harbour Club, a fashionable gym in west London. Diana was already a member there and occasionally our training sessions coincided. She used to work out really hard, especially on the weights, and that was the subject of our first real conversation. I was fascinated by her routine. I've always been a bit of an anorak in that regard, eager to pick up new ideas from other sports and disciplines.

Diana had her personal trainer with her offering advice and I was monitoring what she did. I told her that she did more weights than any other woman I knew and her fitness consultant, obviously taking this as some sort of endorsement of her training methods, said, 'She looks good on it, doesn't she?'

'Not really,' I replied and moved away. It was a light-hearted remark but true nevertheless. I thought she was putting too much emphasis on her weight-training and she did not need to.

The comment did not faze Diana in the least. 'You cheeky bastard,' was her immediate response. Maybe that was why we got on with each other. She could not stand pomposity and liked to be treated, when appropriate, informally.

The Harbour Club was a haven for her, a place she could relax away from the spotlight without having to worry about her appearance, or what she said and did. The vast majority of the members respected that and let her get on with what she had to do, but there were a few idiots who tried to impress her. One middle-aged man in particular timed his training schedule to coincide with hers and he would regularly sidle up to Diana and boom, 'Morning,' in as deep a voice as possible. She could not stand him and I often used to hear this bloke telling his friends how he was with Diana the other day and she said this and told him that. It was a complete fabrication and a small example of what she had to put up with.

I got to know Diana better when, during another routine training session, she asked if I fancied a coffee. That was the start of our friendship. I found her immensely attractive and I was flattered that she occasionally sought me out for a coffee. It was fascinating to chat to her because of where she had been and whom she had met. She had a unique perspective on the world scene, having entertained all its leading public figures at one time or another. Our conversation was gossipy. She said she found President Bill Clinton impressive in private but she considered Hillary, his wife, to be over-ambitious. It was fun just to sit back and hear her talk about these people because she was good at fleshing them out as human beings, enlarging their public personas.

She was also a great listener. Somehow, and everyone who has ever met her has remarked on this, she had this quality of making you feel as if the views you were expressing were interesting. Once or twice a week we would sit and have a coffee after training in the very public Harbour Club restaurant/coffee lounge. I also went round to Kensington Palace for lunch – once with Ieuan Evans because she wanted to meet him – but there too we were surrounded by other people – butlers, cooks, policemen. Believe me, the palace is pretty crowded.

Those were special occasions, though. Diana was incredibly relaxed and would fool around with her children, William and Harry. She was particularly interested to hear some rugby stories, to find out what really happened in games, who the jokers were. It was overwhelmingly normal, very much a jeans and tee-shirt affair – no different from a Sunday lunch at home with family and friends – and at times it was difficult to believe that one day William would be the king of England.

When I met William he was fourteen going on twenty. Harry was just mad, a real laugh. There's a lot of Diana in both of them. They share her mannerisms and her sense of humour. Both had a dignity about them without being in any way starchy but William was really impressive. At Diana's request I arranged for them all to come to Twickenham to train with the England side. It was a major coup because, with the help of Colin

Herridge, we brought the whole thing off without the committee finding out. Diana and the boys came into the England dressing rooms after training and chatted to many of the side. She joked that she had always wanted to see the inside of the men's changing rooms and the day went off really well. It was exactly what they had wanted, a normal day out without any fuss or protocol, but within hours Colin was besieged by irate committee members who wanted to know why they hadn't been informed of the visit so that they could have attended.

We did discuss my marriage to Julia. One day, out of the blue, she said, 'Listen, I don't want to pry, and you can tell me to mind my own business if you wish, but you're not happy, are you?' It was the overwhelmingly natural way which she had with people which made it so easy to talk to her. 'No, I'm not,' I said.

'I thought so, I have a bit of experience in that area.' Her remark broke the ice. That was her gift. Inoffensively, humorously, she had shown her concern and indicated that she probably could relate to what I was going through because of her own situation. She and I talked through the issues and she gave me moral support just when I needed it most. At the time I was in self-flagellation mode, blaming myself for our problems, but Diana put it in perspective. She said it was only a relationship involving two people that had gone wrong. There were no children, no one else involved on either side, and while that was very sad it was not the end of the world. She pointed out that no one enters into a relationship with the intention of it failing. Simple stuff, but I found those comments curiously reassuring. Looking back at those meetings now, her advice appears pretty low-key and logical but at the time I felt isolated and it was just such a relief to be able to talk to someone.

Diana was such a good listener and there is no doubt that she helped me over a difficult part of my life. I will be forever grateful to her for that kindness because she did become a good friend and I will always regret that the media's discovery of our meetings ended that friendship. Once the publicity blew up there was no way that we could remain buddies. It was just too good a story. The captain of England and the Princess of Wales was what mattered to the press, not the feelings of the people trapped inside those titles.

The story broke in the *News of the World* on 6 August 1995 and it was my former PA Hilary Ryan who leaked it to the press. Hilary had worked for Insights for over a year but had left the company because I considered her disruptive and confrontational. She spilled the beans either for money or revenge, but her scam backfired. She gave her real name to the press and this was used in the article, so she has since found it almost impossible to get another job.

The night before the story was published in the *News of the World* there were five or six journalists outside our house posting a first edition of the paper through the letter box and asking for comment. The story was splashed across the front and two inside pages, with tales of clandestine meetings, private rendezvous and pet names. The avalanche of media attention far exceeded that provoked by the old farts affair. The story dominated the Sunday newspapers, even the broadsheets were excited, and led most of the TV and radio news bulletins.

That Sunday Julia decided we would retaliate. So we collaborated with the *Mail on Sunday* the following week which was the only time I've said anything about the situation publicly before now. 'My main feelings are about what it has done to the people around me,' I wrote, 'the people I really care about and love, Julia, what it has done to her. That is unforgivable. It was a perfectly harmless friendship. But, as a high-profile person, I should have thought about it differently. It was flattering that the Princess was interested in me. That is probably where I made my mistake.'

The inference was unfortunate. I did care about Julia and nobody in their right mind would visit all that speculation and innuendo on to their worst enemy, let alone a person they had shared their life with, but insinuating that Diana had somehow forced us apart was wrong and I did not consider her friendship a mistake. I regret making that statement because it was less than honest. I allowed those comments into the public domain via the paper in the hope that it would allow Julia and me to end our relationship with dignity but I was naive to believe I could manipulate the media in that way.

Julia's contacts and PR skills stood her in good stead during those dark days. On one occasion she returned from a conversation with a knot of journalists outside the house and said, 'That's it. I've told them you won't visit that woman again.'

'Julia, she's a friend. Why have you told them that?'

'You won't be able to see her now.'

In the end Julia was right. It became more and more difficult for Diana and me to meet. For a while we talked regularly on the phone but that did not last for long and we drifted apart. Not only had I lost a marriage, I had also lost a good friend.

It is difficult not to feel bitter over what happened. Certainly there were several developments which were difficult to explain away. How, for instance, did a copy of our private phone bill end up on the editor of the *Sun* newspaper's desk? It became a game as to who was going to outwit whom. My overriding feeling is one of sadness and regret that a situation developed where two people I cared about were hurt and in which everyone, bar half of Fleet Street, lost out.

Some papers don't give a damn about the facts. Some are not interested in a balanced tale. If they get both sides of the argument that is a bonus but their main concern is to keep the story going and if certain people are talking to them they run with that and to hell with objectivity. Because I didn't say anything publicly, apart from that single regrettable instance, my side was never put forward. That may have been a mistake. I still think the media is almost impossible to influence but not to try to do so gives you absolutely no chance of a fair hearing. At times I felt a horrible game of tennis was going on around me with me as the ball. I never knew from which direction the next development or attack was coming. The papers had all the aces because they were being nourished on a daily basis.

I made mistakes. Delivering two of my rugby shirts to William and Harry at Kensington Palace before they returned to school was stupid. But I had made a promise and was damned if I was going to let the media dictate what I should and should not do. My marriage had gone bust, it was no longer possible to stay in touch with Diana, so the least I could do was to fulfil an obligation. Asking a friend to do it or using a courier service seemed almost tacky and I decided to play the delivery man myself. It wasn't as if I was seeking a clandestine meeting. Diana was engaged elsewhere on official duties and after a cup of coffee and a thirty-minute chat with Paul Burrell, her butler, I left. But that was enough for another mountain of newsprint to come tumbling off the presses.

And when I failed to feed the beast they manufactured the copy themselves. At least one alleged meeting was a complete fit-up. There was a celebrated newspaper photograph of me peering round a door looking furtive while, in an adjacent picture, Diana was seen scurrying to her car from the same building. The story which accompanied the photographs was that we were still seeing each other, despite both pledging that we were no longer in touch. The offices in question were those of Bimal and were used by Alan Watson, my physiotherapist. Alan also works with Damon Hill and Daley Thompson and I had recommended him to Diana in one of our conversations at the Harbour Club because she was unhappy with certain aspects of her fitness. Diana had booked an appointment with Alan which coincided with one of my routine training days at Bimal's gym and the paparazzi who were her constant companions nearly dropped their long lenses when I turned up at Bimal an hour or so after Diana had entered the building. We met briefly as she came down the stairs from his consulting rooms for a two-minute conversation after which she left via the front door and was snapped by the photographers.

Shortly afterwards a bloke in a tee-shirt rushed into the offices and collared me. 'Listen mate,' he said. 'There are a bunch of journalists outside. You'd better watch yourself.' And with that he grabbed my arm and ushered me towards the door indicating that I should take a look. I fell for it hook, line and sinker. He held on to make sure it was only my head that was poking out the door frame and the picture was in the bag – Carling and Diana together again, guilty by association. Within seconds the bloke in the tee-shirt had darted across the road into the back of a van which the paparazzi were using as their base and roared off with his scoop.

One day I went out for lunch with Colin Herridge at the Compleat Angler, a hotel in Marlow which was occasionally used by the England squad when they trained at Bisham Abbey. Later that afternoon Jon Holmes rang to enquire if the food was good. He had been called by a *Sun* journalist who presumably had been tipped off, either by another guest or one of the staff who had recognised me or seen the name on my credit card. It was just another example of how any attempt to live a normal life in the midst of such a media storm is impossible. I was shocked by the whole experience. I'm a fairly private person and I could not comprehend that this was going on. It got to the stage where I closed down emotionally and retreated inside myself. I did not know who to trust, who was on my side, who would be swapping tales with Julia or the press.

The only solution was to move out of the house we shared together, which I did. Julia and I had agreed a while ago that a trial separation could provide us both with thinking time and space, and I moved into a flat in Covent Garden to clear my head. Everything about the move was top secret. Colin Herridge organised the flat with underground parking. I did not want any journalist seeing the number plate on my car and putting two and two together. Both the flat and the phone were in Colin's name and only he, Jon Holmes and Andrew Harle knew my phone number. I stayed in that flat for nine months and never once opened the blinds. Journalists used to follow me from England training sessions or from a Harlequins club match but I invariably lost them round the back streets. It was the nearest I ever came to experiencing life in the SAS! I adopted anti-surveillance techniques, never taking a taxi to my address but asking to be dropped off half a mile away so I could check for pursuers. I became paranoid. Every time I walked out of the flat and saw two people sitting in a car I would think they were journalists.

By a horrible coincidence the phone number to the flat was only one digit different from that of Stringfellows, the nightclub. So naturally there were plenty of occasions when the phone went because of a wrong number. I never answered the phone in my own voice in case it was a reporter on the other end. I'd put on my best Australian accent, declare that they had the wrong number, and then wonder whether it was a reporter who knew it was me and was using the Stringfellows misdialling as an excuse to see whether it was me.

If anything positive came out of that period, it was the knowledge that I had real friends. Colin Herridge was fantastic. Before he arranged the Covent Garden apartment, he and his wife Sandy took me into their home in Esher. Colin was up to his neck with his business interests and associated RFU matters, yet he dropped everything to help out. Even when the press found out where I was and started pestering his family and friends, his attitude did not change. His phone never stopped ringing for two or three days, and there were people camped permanently outside his house, but he remained his usual calm smiling self. Without support like that I probably wouldn't have pulled through. Colin was the one person I could rely on. He'd been around a bit, seen a lot, and in that sense was better placed than my parents to help out.

Julia had never taken to my mum and dad and I had allowed her opinions to influence me. I had always been reasonably independent but throughout some of 1994 and most of 1995 I cut myself off from them. I didn't want to know what my parents thought. They had been married and nothing had gone dramatically wrong in their relationship. So how could they understand my position? They wouldn't know what to say or do. I closed down completely and refused to tell them anything. It was a mistake and an episode of my life which I deeply regret.

I know that Julia has blamed Diana for the collapse of our marriage but I don't share that view. That assessment of our difficulties seems to me to be too glib, too much a convenient excuse. A relationship fails when two people cannot get their act together – and in that respect it was as much my fault as hers – or if one of the parties becomes involved with a third party. That certainly was not true in my case and I don't think there was anyone else in Julia's life at the time. For Julia to see Diana as the cause of our problems was to misread the situation. Julia and I were not meant to happen. Simple as that.

I do resent the manner in which my life was influenced by some sections of the press. Their interest effectively killed off my friendship with Diana. She had lived under this intense scrutiny ever since she became engaged to the Prince of Wales and was more matter of fact about the attention. She did not like it but knew that there was precious little she could do to control it. There is something terribly debilitating about having your lives dissected and gossiped over in public. Eventually both of us realised that it wasn't worth the hassle. How can you sustain a friendship when every phone call is noted down, every visit monitored? It became impossible and we drifted apart. Diana was also entering a very traumatic phase of her life. She was negotiating her own divorce and had enough to keep her occupied.

I just hope she found some happiness towards the end of her life because she struck me as an incredibly lonely person. She was able to alleviate emotional and physical suffering in so many people, yet retained a curious air of sadness herself. I don't think she ever quite came to terms with her existence. There was a sense of isolation about her, a sense that she was trapped by her situation. She was able to live with it for the most part, but it still rankled. Everyone had a view on Diana, everyone would judge her, without having the slightest idea of what her role or her life was like, or how she fitted into the complex private/public relationships within the royal family. She found people's willingness to comment and to moralise difficult to comprehend.

There was another side to her as well. She was very demanding on the people who worked for her and she was well aware that she could be very awkward and difficult. Her brother Earl Spencer hit the right note in his funeral address. Her appeal was magnified because she was frail and vulnerable and made mistakes. She wasn't perfect and that made it easy for everyone to relate to her but I did get the sense that underneath it all she was very lonely. I always felt that after the public appearances had finished, after the flurry of her daily activities was over, she would return to her private apartments in Kensington Palace to sit in front of the television with her TV dinner. There seemed to be no stability to her life, no inner peace. A week before she died in the Paris car crash the papers were having a go at her because of her relationship with Dodi Fayed. Some of the comment was pretty harsh. Yet a week after her death she was almost beatified by those same journalists and commentators.

Her death was shocking. I had been out on the beer with Harlequins the night before and was staggering around, heavily hung over, getting some golf gear together for a charity day, when the news came through. It did not sink in at first and the numbness remained over the next few days. Initially I was shattered because it was a reminder of mortality. The royals were not meant to die. They were cosseted and protected by teams whose job it was to make sure no harm befell them and here was the most famous woman in the world who had been killed in a car accident.

I only experienced a small part of what she endured daily when our paths crossed. I remember sitting sometimes in the Covent Garden flat and reading what allegedly I was up to. It was completely unconnected with the truth. I'd think who is this guy they are writing about? It's not me. The tabloids used to get so-called psychologists to write profiles of me. This is who Will Carling is, this is what he is suffering, that sort of thing. I tried to dismiss it out of hand but that is difficult to do when people who have never met me write authoritative analyses of my character. In the end it gets you down because it is so personal and because there is so much of it. Sometimes you begin to wonder whether there could be any truth in what these people are writing.

I had to put up with that for a relatively short period of time, she had it for much of her adult life and when that occurs you tend to lose touch with your sense of reality. You become disorientated, your perspective goes. That was the Diana I met. On the surface she was fantastic fun – warm, loving, caring, indiscreet, great company. But, sadly, apart from her boys and her devotion to them, I think she was a very lonely person.

22

MONEY, MONEY, MONEY

Rumours had been flying round South Africa about a possible rugby circus during the World Cup. The detail was
unclear but it involved the top level of the game signing en bloc
to play professional rugby for serious money. Ross Turnbull
was the man doing the talking and it was believed that he was
the front man for the Australian TV mogul Kerry Packer.

I had heard nothing officially while in South Africa. I was more
interested in the deal announced by Australia, South Africa and
New Zealand on the eve of the World Cup final. Those three countries had sold sponsorship and broadcast rights for international
and provincial tournaments to Rupert Murdoch media outlets.
They would play each other twice a year home and away at Test
level in a Tri-Nations competition which was viewed as the
southern hemisphere equivalent of the Five Nations. One tier
lower, in 1996 provinces from the three countries would compete
in a tournament which became known as the Super 12. The sums
involved were staggering. South Africa, New Zealand and Australia would share US$550 million over a ten-year period. And
rugby union was still supposedly an amateur game.

I had been fighting that particular battle since 1991. Together
with Brian Moore and Rob Andrew I had campaigned for the
England squad to be allowed to make money from their status

as England players. We knew it was going on in other parts of the world and we weren't relying on hearsay evidence. Chris Butcher and Peter Winterbottom, team-mates at Harlequins, confirmed the stories of cash changing hands in dressing rooms or at after-match functions when they returned from various trips to South Africa.

Although the money was important, there was a point of principle at stake. We were angry that we were denied the opportunities which were available to players from the southern hemisphere nations. If the sport had been strictly amateur across the board no one would have kicked up any fuss, least of all me. But it wasn't and the inequality stank. The New Zealand and South African Rugby Unions allowed their players to be paid for adverts or promotions in which they endorsed products or goods in their national strip. They also condoned trust funds where money could be stored and distributed at the end of a career. The Rugby Football Union opposed both.

The regulations regarding remuneration were laid down by the International Rugby Board, the sport's governing body. The rules were incredibly complex but basically they allowed players to earn cash, provided they did not receive money for physically playing the game and provided the money-making schemes were not directly rugby-related. I could appear in an advert recommending a certain drink dressed in a suit but I couldn't do so wearing rugby kit. I could not be paid for speaking at a rugby club dinner but a speech to businessmen, or indeed at a football or tennis club, was perfectly legitimate. The whole business was a complete nonsense and the IRB, perhaps aware of the iniquities, gave individual unions discretion to police the activities of the players. The RFU observed the letter of the regulations down to the smallest detail.

That was the context in which Brian, Rob and I negotiated with the RFU. We'd have fared better if we had struck out on our own, set up the deals, and then challenged the RFU to do something about it. They have always had the whip hand simply because of the veiled threat, unveiled in some cases, which was their bottom line. They had the power to get rid of me or any member of the team. That ultimately scuppered our more militant plans.

It is enormously difficult to make a stand over a point of principle when you know there is a very real chance that the stand will kill off your England career. Other teams round the world have taken on their unions. The All Blacks once refused to leave their dressing room to play a Test against France unless the French authorities improved the standard of their hotels and travel arrangements. We never possessed the organisation or the bottle to issue ultimatums. Who knows what might have happened if we had? The public condemnation which surrounded the old farts affair showed that we did not lack support. If only we had realised that earlier and had the courage of our convictions. But we played by the rules. Brian, Rob and I entered into an interminable series of meetings with Dudley Wood and Bob Rogers, the RFU committee man responsible for enforcing amateur regulations, where we were alternately either stonewalled or fobbed off. Every time we came up with a new idea or scheme we would be told it was not permissible under the guidelines.

Eventually we were allowed to work with a sports marketing company called Parallel Media Group who agreed to represent the England squad during the 1991 World Cup. A poster campaign followed which raised the profile of the squad and made household names of Rory Underwood, Dean Richards, Rob Andrew, Brian Moore and Jerry Guscott, but as for the financial rewards, forget it. A figure in excess of £2 million was the target at the start, based on selling eight sponsorship packages at £300,000, but those figures were never attained. They were grossly over-estimated and the start-up and running costs grossly under-estimated. At the end of the 1992 season the England players received £5,000 per man, £1,000 of which was the reward for playing in and reaching the World Cup final.

For the next few years the money issue festered. We were still bombarded by glaring examples of overseas players blatantly abusing the regulations with the connivance of their governing body. In 1993 I went with Harlequins to play in a televised competition in South Africa. Each time a try was scored the giant screen flashed up how much it was worth. The going rate for that tournament was 500 Rand a try. Just my luck that Quins did not score any.

But it is the four-year global circus which invariably focuses attention on any unrest within the game. World Cups are a hotbed of gossip and intrigue, simply because all the top players and administrators are in the same place at the same time and it is easy to arrange meetings. Ross Turnbull was making the most of this opportunity as he floated his rugby-circus ideas to the South African and New Zealand squads. I met him back in London. The meeting took place in his massively lavish suite at the Ritz and Andrew Harriman, a mate from Quins, Brian Moore, Rob Andrew and Jon Holmes also attended. Turnbull talked a good game. A former Australian prop, he knew that he would have to convince us of the integrity of his proposal rugby-wise before revealing numbers. And he did just that.

His plan was to create a number of franchises, super clubs if you like, all over Europe. Players would be allocated to each club to even out resources. Every effort would be made to keep players in their own geographical areas but if a French club needed a centre and an English club had one spare, then that individual would be relocated to France. There were a number of small glitches but basically the playing structure was sound. A credible competition could be created involving the world's top players with the ultimate aim of finding the top franchise by a league and knock-out system. The extravagance and daring of his scheme was breathtaking. Rugby would be destabilised overnight with the old governing bodies stripped of their most precious asset, the players. National squads would desert *en masse*, leaving the unions to fill stadiums with teams of second-division players. The image was certainly seductive and made more so for me when Turnbull said I would be paid a million pounds over two years if I came on board and persuaded the rest of the England squad also to jump ship.

The prospect of emasculating the RFU was tempting but I rejected the offer. Turnbull had put the cart before the horse. He needed the players' signatures on letters of agreement secreted away in bank vaults round the world before he could approach his backers. It was the wrong way round and, although many of the game's superstars, including the majority of the England squad, signed on the dotted line, I refused to do so. I wasn't going to be used as a bargaining device in some global mega-deal. If the rugby circus was a goer, and I thought much of it was, then Turnbull should have been able to raise the finance before approaching the players.

The truth of the matter was that Turnbull had no sponsors or television companies in place for the northern hemisphere part of his circus. Those major players were more likely to side with the administrators with whom they had done business for years. The Five Nations TV contract was coming up for grabs and anyone seen negotiating with Turnbull was bound to be black-listed by the RFU, and that fact was a considerable disincentive to anyone seduced by Turnbull's blandishments. He was much more advanced down south where he was known and his con-tacts were good but in Europe he was regarded very warily.

There was another aspect to the deal, too, which I didn't like. Kerry Packer, Turnbull's backer, and Rupert Murdoch were locked in a massive fight over who controlled the sport of rugby league in Australia. I thought this plan might be part of that larger enterprise. I wasn't convinced that Turnbull or Packer would give a toss about the future of a few dozen rugby players on the other side of the world who would eventually be isolated and cast out.

Turnbull's brazen scheme forced the rugby-union authorities to act in a way which the strident calls of their players over the previous decade had failed to do. Scared stupid by how close Turnbull had come to running world rugby, the International Rugby Board met in Paris over a weekend in August 1995 to consider the whole business of professionalism. Their decision to allow the game to go open, to enable players to be paid for playing rugby union, was a huge shock. Most commentators, myself included, expected another fudge. Instead, the IRB, confronted with the reality of what was happening in the southern hemisphere, opened the floodgates. The hypocrisy of their devotion to amateurism was exposed when delegates from the major rugby-playing nations were asked, hand on heart, to declare whether or not the existing regulations were being observed and enforced. The negative replies as the question was answered round the table gave them no alternative. Rugby was now a sport running around in the same marketplace as football, tennis, golf and athletics. But if that was the good news, there followed a prolonged period of chaos and mismanagement which is still with us today.

The decision to go open took the Rugby Football Union by surprise. They had instructed John Jeavons-Fellows and Peter Brook, England's IRB representatives, to vote for the continuation of rugby as an amateur sport, based on their confident prediction and hope that rugby would remain relatively unchanged. When the professional bomb dropped, the fall-out was massive. The RFU were completely unprepared for the shift to an open sport and hastily introduced a moratorium to buy thinking time. International players were allowed to receive money during the first year but club men would continue as they always had done.

I thought the moratorium was a good idea. It would allow the authorities to set up a framework in which the game could flourish but I should have known better. The RFU established a series of commissions which, in the hope of satisfying everybody, appeased nobody. Their deliberations amounted to a succession of compromises. I was part of the consultation process and with Jon Holmes met with Tony Hallett, the RFU Secretary. Our advice was simple. The players were the key. The RFU had to move quickly to contract the top eighty professionals and then they could dictate terms to the clubs and establish the primacy of international rugby. Jon pointed out that rugby was unlike football in that only at international level was it attractive to sponsors and television companies and therefore commercially sustainable. As the body responsible for controlling the international element, the RFU would be well placed to reap rich rewards from professional rugby, if only they could deliver the players.

What happened? The RFU allowed the contracts of the England squad to lapse at the end of the first year, whereupon a few shrewd businessmen, headed by Newcastle's Sir John Hall, swooped. Over the next few months Sir John and fellow entrepreneurs Nigel Wray of Saracens, Chris Wright of Wasps and, later, Tom Walkinshaw of Gloucester and Ashley Levett of Richmond signed up the players, and the RFU have been fighting a rearguard action ever since. Despite the recent Mayfair agreement between the union and the clubs which sought to rationalise the structure and agree power-sharing within English rugby, it is still the clubs who hold the whip hand. The 1998 summer tour when England were thrashed by Australia, New Zealand and South Africa is just one consequence of the dispute which has bedevilled the game over the last three years. The players have had to serve two masters and in doing so have served neither properly.

The great irony for me in this whole sordid business was that for once I was on the side of the authorities. I have never hidden my desire to place England above club rugby and I did not think professional rugby was sufficiently sexy to attract enough money to keep twenty-four English clubs afloat. I could see a future in a professional tier of the top European clubs but anything beyond that I considered unsustainable. I was all for the RFU controlling the players. That was the only way we could evolve a culture and a structure to challenge the southern hemisphere. So when representatives of the clubs came calling to solicit my support, I gave them short shrift.

My desire to remain on the outside was more than a matter of conscience. I had been fighting these battles for so long that, quite frankly, I had had enough. I was also in the fortunate position of having an income outside rugby through Insights, so I was lucky enough to be able to take a view without worrying about mortgage repayments and the financial considerations which invade everyone's lives. And there was a third consideration. I did not like the way in which the clubs were using the players as pawns.

Donald Kerr, chairman of English Rugby Partnership, the body representing England's top clubs, used to invite the players to secret meetings, ask for their help and support, and then usher them out of the back door forbidding them to discuss the issues. I declined to attend. Sure, there were concerns over confidentiality, but to prevent the players talking to the media and other informed observers was to treat them like dumb school kids. What many of the players failed to understand throughout this great debate was that they had the power. Whoever controlled the players, dictated the terms, and the players should have been far more vocal and responsible in contributing to the debate. Instead, they were abused by the clubs, who used to threaten to exclude them from England squads, include them and exclude them again. In the end the players, the clubs and the RFU all lost the support of the rugby public and that was unforgivable.

Throughout this period rugby needed men of stature and statesmanship. Instead the sport was saddled with Donald Kerr and Cliff Brittle as the chief protagonists. As national captain, I came into contact with both men. Kerr, who championed the cause of the clubs, was a Harlequin. I've yet to understand how he came to assume such a central role in the fight. It was as if he had drifted into rugby in the hope that it would tie up a few loose ends in his life. From what I could see he had little background in the sport and no feel for it. That came through in the tone of his disputes with Brittle. Kerr was in my view far too aggressive and it was only when he was removed from the clubs' negotiating team that progress was made.

Brittle was not much better. In his RFU role he had fought a number of battles with senior RFU figures to establish himself as Chairman of the RFU management board. His authority came from a series of special general meetings when he appealed to the member clubs and counties to endorse his policies and confirm his authority to run English rugby on behalf of the RFU. The fact that he was overwhelmingly successful in getting the support of the junior clubs was proof of his considerable powers of persuasion but it was also a reflection of the contempt in which the RFU was held by those it was supposed to represent. Brittle was openly critical of the RFU, the organisation he was meant to lead, and that endeared him to the masses.

I first met Brittle in the team bus after the England/France match in Paris in 1996. He had just come to power and Jack Rowell obviously considered it a prudent political move on his part to let Brittle forge a relationship with the national squad. But Jack's timing was lousy. The hours immediately after an international are not the best time to make political small talk, especially after a narrow defeat. And, in any case, the team bus should have been sacrosanct, a no-go area for administrators and hangers-on alike. As I got off the coach to go into the dinner, Jack introduced Cliff to me. We shook hands, looked each other in the eye, and I said, 'Hi.' That was it.

Shortly afterwards, as we were preparing for the Wales match, Cliff asked to meet the squad on a more formal basis. We assembled in the River Room at the Petersham Hotel and listened to Cliff as he gave a ten-minute resumé of his playing career. If he was after the credibility factor he did not get it. Then, towards the end, he said to the squad, 'I met your captain recently. Will, I know what you think of me, but when you looked into my eyes in Paris I hope you saw into my soul so that you know I am for the game. We must meet. If you want a low-profile lunch somewhere, that's fine. You should know that I, too, am a member of a gym.' The last remark said it all. Here was the RFU Chairman trying to curry favour with the England squad by a cheap crack at my expense, and I can honestly say it did not go down well with the players. 'I want to be your friend,' Cliff concluded. Some friend. We never saw him again.

I didn't shed many tears when Brittle's bubble finally burst and he lost the chairmanship to Brian Baister when Baister was voted in as the new Chairman at the RFU's 1998 annual general meeting. I hope Baister is more successful in the role, but he would be the first to acknowledge that there is still much work to be done. Professional rugby union could have been, should have been, an opportunity to start afresh, to put the game on a sound philosophical and financial footing to enable it to develop and prosper. Instead, we have a situation where both the clubs and the RFU are on the verge of bankruptcy and the game as a product is becoming devalued. The owner/investors have much to answer for. I am constantly amazed that successful businessmen have this fascination for chucking money at club rugby when there is little hope of a return on their investment. Either they are the greatest philanthropists in the history of sport, or they have taken the view that, as football is virtually a closed shop, it is a lot easier to get a toe-hold in rugby.

Sir John Hall and Nigel Wray paid well over the odds to get François Pienaar, Rob Andrew, Michael Lynagh and Va'aiga Tuigamala to join their clubs. And while there is no doubt that the policy has brought results on the playing field with Newcastle and Saracens dominating the 1997/98 Premiership, the inflated salaries have proved too much for Bristol and Moseley who, in trying to keep up, are facing financial ruin. A Joe Average England international can expect to earn £150,000–£175,000 if he has a good year for club and country, while the superstars are in the £200,000 plus bracket. The game cannot even begin to sustain that level of remuneration, given the income coming through the turnstiles.

There have been benefits. There is no doubt that the players are fitter and more technically accomplished. The standard of play in the Premiership has risen steadily since the introduction of professional rugby, and is rising still. I am also a fan of the bright and breezy marketing schemes in operation to put more bums on seats. Rock music, motorised buggies which bring on kicking tees, fireworks, improved fast-food outlets and crèches are all part and parcel of sport as entertainment. The old-timers may not like it but if clubs fail to attract more women and youngsters to their games, then rugby is dead in the water.

It will not be easy. The figures for those tuning in to watch club rugby on Sky Television are dire. That may be as much a comment on the British public's attitude to satellite television as it is on the attractiveness of the product but, whatever the reason, the trend is not promising. The RFU, in their rush to conclude a deal with Sky Television and forsake terrestrial coverage, made a grave mistake. It is easy to sit on the sidelines and criticise. I take no comfort from that. But when you have seen the RFU from close-up, been a party to the discussions and deliberations for the best part of a decade, you learn not to be too surprised at the chaos which has ensued. The single most woeful example of mismanagement was to allow the contracts of the England squad to expire in the first season after the Paris declaration, and part of the fault must lie with Don Rutherford, the RFU's director of rugby. He should have recognised that out-of-contract players would be swallowed whole by the clubs.

Rutherford is a low-key figure who has lurked in the background, powerful and apparently unaccountable, for nearly thirty years. Coaches and captains, presidents and managers have come and gone in English rugby but Rutherford has remained throughout as a paid professional. His job was to provide technical and administrative support for the national side as well as overseeing the way rugby was coached and organised, but I found him obstructive and unhelpful. It was the little things initially. Early on in the captaincy I wanted to take the team out for a meal, to get them away from the hotel so that we could all relax together. Don refused to sanction the money. Later, when I got to know him better, I believed that he tended to take the credit for ideas that worked but distanced himself from those that didn't. After the 1995 World Cup one of the players got hold of a report Don presented to the RFU committee which was fiercely critical of Jack Rowell, me, the team, everyone and everything. Some of his observations were valid but he refused to accept responsibility for any short-comings himself. The following season I banned him from team meetings. What was the point in involving someone when you knew he wasn't supportive? The decision was childish on my part but I knew I was on the way out and it was the only way I could express my disapproval. Here was a man who could have offered English rugby so much yet seemed more interested in safeguarding his job.

He's still there now. Rutherford must have been aware of the campaign to oust Jack Rowell, during which Jack's job was publicly offered to some of the world's leading coaches, only for them to turn it down. That was significant in itself. If Rutherford had done his job properly there would have been a queue of talented, qualified English coaches desperate to work with England. Instead Rutherford travelled the globe trying to inter-est foreigners to come to England. Clive Woodward, the man who followed Jack as England coach, was third or fourth choice. I have no problems with Clive but the circumstances in which he was appointed were embarrassing and a blazing example of how Rutherford has failed English rugby. Heaven knows, Jack and I didn't exactly hit it off but he should never have been treated so abominably badly. At least he put his head on the block.

— 23 —
LETTING GO

ROB ANDREW and I were having a coffee in our Pretoria hotel before the play-off game against France during the World Cup and in walked Jack Rowell. He was brusque as usual.

'Are you going to captain the side next season?' he queried. The question was unexpected. I was used to Jack's ways by now but we were days away from a crucial game and next season was the last thing on my mind. 'Because I want you to,' Jack continued.

'I don't know Jack. I haven't really given it much thought and I'm not sure it's the right time to be thinking about it now.'

'Fair enough,' agreed Jack. 'Why don't we have lunch when we get back and the dust has settled?'

And so began the will he-won't he, is he-isn't he saga which dominated much of the build-up to the 1995/96 season. Rob was typically supportive when I asked his opinion. 'If you're up for it, if you really want to carry on and you feel fresh enough to do so then I think you should,' he said.

A couple of months later back in England, before the season had started in earnest, Jack and I met up at the East India Club over lunch to hammer out the captaincy issue. The East India Club is the London home of the Rugby Football Union. A lot of business takes place there in the dining rooms downstairs and the committee rooms on the first and second floors. It was the venue where the decision to sack me had been taken a few months earlier and the place where I had been upbraided by Ian Beer for my poor speech-making. It was a long lunch, the best part of two and a half hours, but Jack took no time in getting to the point. 'Well, what's it to be?'

I had made up my mind before the meeting. 'I would love to continue, Jack, but we need to sort a few things out,' I said. 'I think Austin Swain should be with the England squad full time. We need a new fitness consultant and we need to improve our preparation. We must create a better environment before internationals, pay greater attention to detail and be more positive.'

It was massively arrogant of me to make those demands on Jack but I had nothing to lose. This season would be my eighth in charge of England and I needed new stimulation as much as anyone. If Jack didn't agree to those terms I would happily stand down but I thought that there were areas which needed reforming if we were going to move on as a side. Some of the advice on offer during the World Cup in South Africa had been plain wrong. We had been told to take a combination of tablets each day to prevent dehydration and to combat the detrimental effect of altitude, yet everyone in the squad felt incredibly lethargic for the first two matches. It was only pure luck that a chance phone call back home to Alan Watson rectified the situation. The pills we were taking were an either/or combination and under no circumstances should they be taken together. I felt that cock-ups of that nature should never befall an international side preparing for a major tournament.

Jack seemed to agree. At the end of the lunch he said, 'Fine. I'll put my thoughts for the season in writing and send them to you within a week.'

I left the East India Club confident that I was still in charge and that the season would herald many improvements. It was a done deal as far as I was concerned. When Terry Cooper, the Press Association's rugby correspondent, made his annual start-of-season phone call to enquire if I was remaining as captain I told him yes, that it had not been officially confirmed, but that Jack had asked me to continue. Cooper put the story out over the wires and that was when the trouble started.

Jack was upbraided by several members of the RFU committee, plus Don Rutherford, for not clearing the decision through the normal channels. And instead of apologising, which would have tidied the matter up within seconds, he went on the offensive. He called me from his mobile phone. 'Will, you've placed me in a very embarrassing position with the captaincy. I can't remember asking you to carry on.'

I was flabbergasted. I could hear voices in the background and thought he was making the call for effect but he refused to elaborate. 'Whatever you remember, Jack,' I said, and put down the phone. It would have been pointless arguing and I wasn't going to beg for the captaincy on the phone.

I did not need this hassle. My private life was in turmoil at this stage. My marriage was disintegrating, there were all kinds of innuendoes and speculation flying about over whether I was having a relationship with the Princess of Wales and the last thing I wanted was a public debate over my captaincy credentials. But Jack did not see it like that. I don't really know why he reacted as he did because, weeks later, after his recommendation had gone through the various sub-committees, I was confirmed as captain for the 1995/96 season.

I should have walked away then. That would have been the act of a sensible man but I did not want to be forced out. I wanted to go under my own steam. The captaincy had played such an important part in my life, meant such a lot to me, that I was damned if anyone was going to wrest it from me without a fight. But deep down I knew that it was time to quit. The next World Cup was three years away, too far for me to remain competitive. The more I agonised over the decision, the more I knew it was the right time to go. I was taking short cuts, not spending as much time on the phone to players and friends whose opinions I respected. When I first started I used to learn a lot from Kevin Murphy, England's long-serving physio. He was closer to the players than anyone else, heard their problems as they lay on the treatment table. Murph had wonderfully sensitive antennae. He could tune into the mood of the squad, could gauge when the players needed a rest. His advice and experience have always been crucial to me but I couldn't be bothered to chat to him. I was running out of energy.

When I began to ask myself why I still wanted the job I was appalled at the answers I came up with. I wanted it because I had always had it, or so it seemed. I wanted it because I didn't want anyone else to have it, to forfeit something which had been mine for so long. Those realisations came as a shock. I was treating the captaincy as a plaything and that wasn't right.

The season had started with yet more evidence of the distance between England and the southern hemisphere sides. World champions South Africa came to Twickenham in November and won 24–14. The final margin of 10 points flattered us. We were outgunned in every department. The Springboks scored three tries and had one legitimate score disallowed, while we could only manage one through Phil de Glanville at the death. A 27–9 victory against Western Samoa failed to lift the spirits. They played the more inventive rugby, enchanting the crowd so much that they jeered at our feeble effort. Then came the big one in the Five Nations, a match against France and a chance to set the record straight following our disappointing effort in the play-off game. When that too went down the pan 15–12 it was obvious that we had to rethink our strategy.

We had been too tight going into matches and needed to lighten up. A few of the senior pros came up to me and proposed some extra-curricular activities to relieve the tedium before the contest with Wales. Jack did not want to know but we eventually prevailed and organised go-karting one afternoon to enable the squad to relax and have fun. Jack came along but did not participate, just sat rather forlornly and watched what was happening. I've no idea why he turned up, perhaps he felt he had to, but it was the only fun we had all year and we won the match.

Days later I read a big interview in one of the newspapers in which Jack identified the change to the build-up as one of the reasons why England had won and claimed credit for the new approach.

I had to balance this side of Jack's character with the many occasions when he had the full support of the squad. He was outstanding company. He made some great speeches as England manager, irreverent and witty, and he was the master of the one-liner put-down. A favourite target of his, which went down well with all the players, was the rugby press. Jack had no time for some of the rugby writers and was happy to ridicule them at press conferences. While it was great to listen to, I am sure that Jack's relationship with the press was one of the reasons why he was eventually frozen out of his job.

But it was his cavalier dealings with the players which tipped the scales against Jack for me. Matters came to a head before the Ireland match that season. We had assembled for a squad session at the Petersham Hotel late on the Saturday evening. It was the usual routine, one I'd enjoyed countless times in the past. The match was important but no more than usual and I was alarmed at Jack's state of mind. He seemed on edge.

I had been tipped off that Jack had been reported in the *Sunday Telegraph* criticising the team, and in particular laying into England's young half-back pairing, Matt Dawson and Paul Grayson, along with Ben Clarke, the No 8. Jack did not raise the subject so I decided to leave things well alone to see how the weekend panned out. On Sunday morning Jack was up early, scouring the hotel to find and get rid of all the copies of the *Sunday Telegraph* so none of the team would be aware of his comments. He'd missed my copy though. I had read the article and told Jack that I had. We met to talk it over on the balcony outside the River Room overlooking the Thames. Jack was seething. 'The article was disgraceful,' he said. 'You know what journalists are like. You can't trust them. They write lies, make up stuff which is not true.'

I knew differently. I had heard that there was a tape of the interview and I told him this. He changed tack immediately.

'Those comments were off the record. I never gave permission for them to be aired publicly,' he said.

But that explanation did not wash with me. Here we were, seven days away from an international, and the England manager was shafting his young half-backs in public.

The crazy thing about the episode was that he had made a similar mistake before, though in private on that occasion. Despite his reputation as an innovative and lateral thinker, Jack was extraordinarily conservative in selection and choice of tactics. Before England played Western Samoa earlier in the season Jack had taken Paul Grayson and Matt Dawson, both of whom were making their debuts, to one side. For the best part of an hour he told them not to run from their own half, not to do this and that. It was exactly what inexperienced players did not want to hear twenty-four hours before their first game and Paul and Matt's self-esteem took a hammering.

But a public condemnation was much, much worse. 'Have you apologised to Matt and Paul? Have you talked to Ben?' Jack shook his head. 'Don't you think you should?' And that is how we left it. Jack did try to repair the shattered confidence of the players but by then the damage had been done. It was an unnecessary distraction, an example of a problem we did not need. The fact that it followed so soon after another embarrassing incident confirmed my suspicions that Jack was on the verge of irrevocably losing the confidence and trust of the squad.

We were nowhere near our full potential going into the Scotland game and one of the reasons was that there were too many discordant voices in the back row. Talk about backs with handbags, these were forwards with egos. Tim Rodber, Lawrence Dallaglio and Ben Clarke all wanted to control events and the pack were confused and rudderless as a result. I suggested to Jack at selection that the way round this mess was to bring back Dean Richards who would give direction and leadership.

Jack was aghast. Picking Dean would be seen as a regressive

step, especially as Jack had gone public on the need for England to develop an expansive game if they were ever going to compete successfully against the southern hemisphere nations. Jack fought tooth and nail against returning to Dean but I was adamant. I knew I was going to retire at the end of the season and therefore had nothing to lose if I carried through with my challenge.

'You pick him or I'm off,' I said. He looked at me as if he couldn't quite hear what I was saying. 'I mean it, Jack. I'll resign, retire. We have to win this game. We have a pack with no leadership and you have to pick Dean.'

And he did. Dean had one of the great games of his career and England beat Scotland. That match probably saved Jack's job which would have been very much on the line if the Scots had triumphed. Did he mention it, did he say, 'Good decision, Will, thanks a lot'? Did he heck!

By now I had made up my mind to quit and that decision was confirmed when I met up with Jon Holmes in London's Groucho Club. 'You're thinking about standing down, aren't you?' Jon said. 'It's the right time. You've done it for long enough and there are people who are after you. Unless you really want to fight for it, really want to hang on, it makes sense to finish.'

I knew Jon was right yet I hated hearing him say it. What would life be like without the captaincy? I was voluntarily standing down. No one had ever done that before. In some ways it would have been simpler if I had been stripped of the honour but that wasn't how it was. Was I completely mad? The answers to those questions lay in the future. The business now was to set the wheels in motion. I called my best mate Andrew Harle and told him he'd better get down for the Ireland game because it would be my last as skipper. That conversation meant more to me than the one in which I told the powers-that-be that I was resigning. I went downstairs into the wine cellars of the Petersham Hotel on the Saturday night where Rutherford and Rowell were holding a planning meeting.

'I thought I'd better let you know. I'm stepping down as

captain. I'm announcing the decision in the *Mail on Sunday* tomorrow.'

There was complete silence as I walked away.

— 24 —

A LEADER OF MEN

A CONFESSION. In my eight years in charge, I never made much difference on the pitch as a captain, never turned disgraceful defeat into glorious victory, never inspired a revival with an incisive, witty half-time team talk. And this is not an outpouring of self-modesty. It's just that I don't believe in modern international rugby that a captain has that much influence. Rugby has always been infatuated with this notion of captain as superman, the intelligent leader able to stand back from the storm raging round about him, able to cast an analytical eye at the chaos and then tweak one or two areas which change the direction of the game. Usually this mythical man was also a father figure, a raconteur, a serial-womaniser and a bloke who would play a blinder on a gallon of ale and two hours' kip. Well, if this figure exists, I haven't met him.

My attitude to captaincy was, I hope, more realistic. I always believed that England possessed enough great players but those players never fulfilled their potential through lack of belief and poor organisation. They shied away from taking responsibility for their own sporting destinies. When history judges my role in English rugby, if it can ever be bothered, I'd like to think that I will be viewed as someone who started to turn English rugby round, that with Geoff Cooke I put some backbone into the national side and gave it direction. But as for me as this comic book, cavalier hero, forget it. Geoff Cooke and I read from the same script. We both believed in identifying what we considered to be the most talented group of players and sticking with them. Once they knew they weren't going to be booted into oblivion on the back of a poor performance their trust grew and they opened up more. That experience was crucial because from that point they were willing to pool ideas and share knowledge.

It is rare in international sessions for coaches to talk about the minutiae of performance. They can say that the tight-head prop is not leading the scrummage into the important hit when the packs collide, or that the backs' angles of run are not challenging defenders, but they are rarely able to suggest detailed technical remedies. That comes from the players themselves, players who are at the sharp end. Step down from the top end of the game for a couple of years and it might as well be twenty. That's how quickly knowledge becomes outdated. That's why I tried to use the know-how contained within the pool of players. For me, that was the only relevant information. I saw myself as a conduit. I would spend time with someone like Paul Rendall, also known as the Judge for his role in the players' courts which were held on tour, to find out how he saw things. Paul was a vastly experienced prop, a position with which I had no familiarity. That's another intriguing aspect to rugby captaincy. There are so many idiosyncratic, mystifying parts to the game that a captain is nominally responsible for areas of performance which are alien territory. I would never in a month of Sundays understand what it took to become a competent scrummager, so the next best thing was to pick the brains of those who did. 'You've been around a long time, Judge. What do we need to do to improve? How should we train? Where are our weaknesses up front? Tell me. I'll get it done.'

That was my approach to the job. I was for planning, preparation, empowering players, getting them to communicate. Anyone can lay down the law as captain and insist on a course of action, and there are times when that is appropriate, but very few captains listen. I spent a lot of time listening and when I had assimilated the various views, I tried to set standards. I painted a picture of us being the best in the world. We never got there but I truly believed we had the capability.

To me captaincy was never about half-time set-piece speeches. Why wait until half-time to make changes? By then you've wasted half a match. In an ideal world key players would be making adjustments throughout the game without reference to me. If hookers, locks, wingers or flankers cannot see that a strategy is not coming off and have to wait until half-time before attempting to rectify matters, the team is not functioning properly. Half-time was a chance to take stock, for everyone to chip in free from the frenzied action. It was questions, questions, questions. 'What's working? Has anyone seen anything? Where are their weaknesses, how are they organising their defence? Are they tiring up front? Do we need to tighten up for ten minutes to finish them off? How are we feeling?'

The issue then became honesty. Self-doubt does not feature highly in the make-up of international sportsmen. It can't. Start thinking you're crap and before too long you will be. But England never arrived at the stage where problem areas were acknowledged. The pack would never admit that they were not going to out-scrummage the opposition, the wingers would never own up to the fact that they were unlikely to roast their opponents on the outside. And without that ruthless self-assessment, the attempts at team analysis were futile. It was probably a hangover from the days when England players were burdened by insecurity but it stalled the side's development. In the end it became an in-joke. We used to watch the videos, see the pack get moved about by Argentina, and the forwards would say there were no problems. The excuses would come rolling in. The camera angle was making it appear worse than it actually was, the referee let the opposition get away with murder. Never a hands-up, yep, it's my fault response.

The England side today is far more confident and capable

than virtually all of its predecessors. They expect to win the Five Nations Championship and run the southern hemisphere nations close, if not beat them. It is not the arrogance of the fool. Their self-assurance is based on a few years of decent recent results, certainly in Europe. Three Grand Slams in the nineties have instilled conviction. Some say it is harder for a team to win when great things are expected but it is far harder to win when everything is new and there is nothing to fall back on. Early on my role was to build confidence, to try to get players believing in their and the team's ability. It wasn't easy, especially when I had to convince myself before I talked to the rest of the side.

I used to have this regular battle with myself on a Friday night. The opposition, whoever it was, would grow large in my mind and they would all appear enormously capable, impossible to beat. I would compare our team man-to-man in an attempt to find reassurance but it was always touch and go. The nearer I got to kick-off time the more confident I became but I was a bag of nerves about twenty-four hours before the start.

I shared this dilemma with Wade Dooley once. We were staying in Versailles, due to play France in the 1992 Five Nations Championship. Wade saw that I had something on my mind and drew me into a small lounge just off the main bar area in the hotel.

'What's the matter?' he asked. 'You look worried.'

'No, no, I'm fine,' I lied. Ridiculously, I thought that I couldn't tell Wade because as captain I was not allowed to have any doubts.

'Come on, Bumface. What's wrong?'

'I think we're going to lose tomorrow. They're so bloody good. I can't see us winning.' Wade looked at me as if I were mad. 'Don't be so stupid,' he said. 'We'll beat this lot, easy. We don't lose to frogs.' And with that, he swallowed his coffee, got off his bar stool and moved away with his John Wayne walk. It was classic Wade. 'We don't lose to frogs.' What was the point of me getting het up when that conviction, born from either confidence or ignorance, existed?

Not the most glamorous of farewells – limping down the Twickenham steps after my last match as captain of England, against Ireland, 16 March 1996.

Never one to make a fuss – the injured ankle gets the full treatment.

Rory Underwood, here rounding Simon Geoghegan, could always be relied on to deliver when it mattered.

'Do as I say not as I do!' Me in training mode.

We may have had our differences, but Roger Uttley's contribution to English rugby has been enormous.

Kicking for victory, 1996 – Paul Grayson smacks over one of his six penalties as Scotland were beaten 18– 9. The critics weren't happy with the style of the win.

The attitude of Harlequins' director of rugby, Andy Keast, made it impossible for me to continue club rugby.

Dick Best's tongue could be sharp, but his record as England coach was outstanding.

Trying to wrong-foot Leigh Davies when playing for Quins against Cardiff.

Whatever he did, wherever he was, Jeremy Guscott invariably exuded class.

Lawrence Dallaglio, who made such an impressive start against the southern hemisphere nations, makes a point.

Dean Richards beat Scotland on his own after Jack Rowell and I argued over his inclusion.

Geoff Cooke's organisational abilities, vision and clarity of communication turned England around in the late eighties and early nineties.

The man behind the revolution – Ross Turnbull's plans for a global rugby circus forced the administrators to agree to professionalism.

Don Rutherford, the RFU's director of rugby, about to make a point at a press conference.

Former RFU president Ian Beer and I didn't see eye to eye over the issue of amateurism.

RFU chairman Cliff Brittle was involved in a series of battles with the top clubs.

Dudley Wood was a staunch defender of amateurism which made our relationship decidedly awkward.

Jack Rowell could be difficult, but he was genuinely witty and always good company.

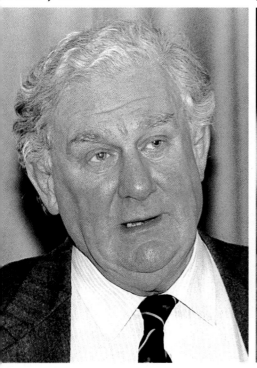

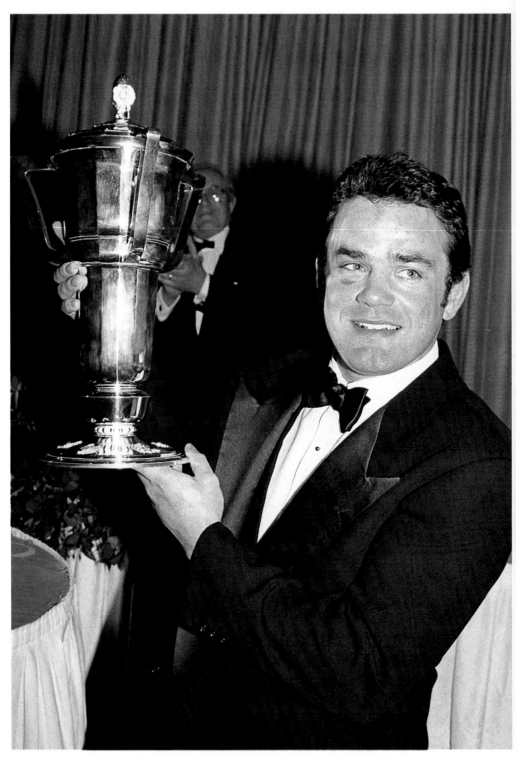

It was worth the effort – holding the Five Nations trophy after the 1996 campaign.

I changed my approach to motivation as I grew to know players better but in the first couple of years I relied on attention to detail. That and a common call to arms would be the theme of the Friday night team talk at the hotel. It was fairly predictable early on. 'They said we're no good, let's prove them wrong,' that kind of thing. Not particularly inspiring, just a variation of the us against them mentality which all sporting contests have. I would run through the strike moves and the various calls to ensure that all the parts of the team knew what was happening. That kind of information would just about go in on a Friday night but any later and the players' minds would be closed as they prepared in their own way. Detailed information was useless on the morning of the match.

The trick as kick-off approaches is to raise the emotional stakes, while still allowing the brain to function. I was never one for great rabble-rousing speeches. By the time the side reached the changing room ninety-nine per cent of the preparation was complete. You don't win games by screaming and shouting in the changing room. I've seen people kick shit out of kit bags and tackle bags five minutes before they went out to play an international, do absolutely nothing on the pitch, then come back and kick shit out of the same bags when they had lost. The more I played the less respect I had for players who made a lot of noise.

You need people to be focused, aware of their role within the team. A few reminders, a word here and there, is all that is necessary. Instead of banging the emotional drum, I asked the players to visualise the contribution they would make in the first five minutes, what they would get right and how that would impact on their opposite number. The important thing was to set the right tone.

As far as individual players went I would get to them before Saturday morning. I would try to make time for as many as possible during the build-up, sit next to them on the bus going to training, chat to them at dinner or over a coffee. Some didn't need any cajoling whatsoever. If I had told Peter Winterbottom that he was an exceptional player and that we needed him to go out and show John Jeffrey what he was capable of, he would have walked away in disgust. With Winters you just had to underline his role and he would do the job. There was no fuss or fanfare necessary.

Mick Skinner wanted both. He flourished when he was the centre of attention. I would tell the Munch that he was the best No. 6 in the world, that he was the best tackler in the universe and that the team were depending on him to make the big hits and provide a focal point for our forward effort. You had to pump Mick up, feed him lots of positive stuff before the game.

Brian Moore required something personal, a target to get his teeth into. You had to be careful with Brian. You had to imply that you thought his opposite number was a good player, a key member of their side. But it had to be reasonably subtle or Brian would see through the ploy. Even then it only occasionally worked against someone like Phil Kearns or Sean Fitzpatrick whom Brian saw as credible rivals. If he didn't rate his man the strategy would not work. But if you got it right, made it personal, Brian would play out of his socks.

I could also get to Brian by loading him with responsibility. He saw the forwards as his own domain, a team within a team. Making him pack leader gave him official as well as unofficial responsibility for their performance and it brought the best out of him. He took it upon himself to unearth and focus the forwards' aggression. Their problems became his problems and he was an accomplished motivator and analyst. Brian was also one of the few men to appreciate and understand what Jeff Probyn offered the side. And as I didn't have a clue why Jeff was so respected and how to get the best out of him I was quite happy to leave all that to Brian.

Brian remained pretty stable throughout his career but some of the long-term stayers needed a different approach from first cap to fiftieth. Early on Jason Leonard was the ultimate team man, fiercely proud of representing his country. There is an apocryphal tale about Jason. The story goes that he was so chuffed with his England shirt after winning his first cap that he sat in front of the washing machine the following day as the shirt was cleaned, refusing to move until the cycle was complete. I believe it. I tried to enthuse Jason by explaining his role in the team context. Once he knew that dominance in the scrum provided space out wide which made it easier for the backs to function, he would shove all day. He did not want praise or recognition, just the knowledge that he was contributing to the team. I'd come off the pitch and say, 'Mate, that second-half try, it came from the scrummage.' That was enough for Jason, that and thirty pints.

That approach worked for the first few years of Jason's career. But the older he got and the more caps he accumulated, the more he tended to play in a comfort zone. Towards the end I didn't get the best out of Jason. Maybe, because we had been through so much together and I like him so much, I didn't ride him as hard as I should. In my last couple of seasons I tried to needle him, to prick him out of his comfort zone, but I wasn't overly successful. Jason hasn't played to his potential of late because he has struggled with a neck injury. He is still hugely accomplished but a player as young as he is, with all his associated experience and knowledge and with a sensational physique, should be killing opposition front rows. Jason should have been one of the world's pre-eminent props but the fact that he was passed over on the 1997 Lions tour to South Africa is proof that he is not doing himself justice.

Dewi Morris was different again. Dewi suffered from tension before big matches. Nine times out of ten he was physically sick with nerves in the changing room. It was important to calm Dewi down, to impress upon him that, as a scrum-half, he was the eyes and ears of the team. His job was to look up and see, to assess options and make decisions. Two hours before kick-off it would have been insulting to tell him that, because he was an intelligent player and knew precisely what his duties entailed. But as kick-off beckoned that advice became more and more relevant as Dewi grew increasingly manic.

Sometimes the way into a player's mind was to connect with their value systems, tapping into their own opinion of themselves. Telling Tim Rodber that he wouldn't pass an army selection course if he didn't perform to certain standards was guaranteed to get him fired up. Agreeing with Victor Ubogu that he was capable of far more than any other prop on the planet, then asking him to prove it to people who weren't as well informed as I was used to get him going. In recent seasons I was happy to make use of the specialist consultants employed by England. When Tony Underwood had a crisis of confidence, Austin Swain put together a video tape of Tony scoring tries and overlaid it with a soundtrack of his favourite music. Tony used to watch this tape before matches to remind himself how well he could play and it demonstrably increased his self-esteem. And so it went on. Right through the team, right throughout the years.

It never stopped, even with the stalwarts who had played for England before I did. Rob Andrew was one of the great technicians and would endlessly work on all aspects of his game, but it was important to free him up, to rid his mind of the clutter and turn him from scientist to artist. He was never a naturally instinctive player but he was far more effective off the cuff than when he was the precision kid. He and Richard Hill were bad for each other. They would pore over game plans and charts before matches, blinding each other with detail. The challenge with that pair was to get them to loosen up, to react to what was happening on the day.

Jerry Guscott, on the other hand, just wanted to be left alone. Deep down he was quite insecure but it was pointless trying to do anything about it. Jerry played when he wanted and there was neither rhyme nor reason as to when that day would come around. I stayed clear of Jerry, smiled at him and left him to get on with it. He hated fuss, hated meetings, wasn't particularly interested in tactics. All he wanted was the ball and some space. In that sense he was a dream to captain.

But the man who impressed me more than any other over the last two seasons was Lawrence Dallaglio. There was something about Lawrence the minute he walked into the squad. He had steel, an arrogance about him right from day one. He didn't need to be mollycoddled. Quite the opposite, in fact. I had to persuade him not to get on the backs of the other squad members. If players weren't performing, Lawrence would tell them. Often he used to lift standards as a result, but occasionally he became too prescriptive and interfering, more interested in how those around him were performing than in his own game. But I admired what he stood for. He was confident, focused, a man with an easy natural authority. Clive Woodward was obviously of the same opinion because when he was appointed as the new England coach he chose Lawrence Dallaglio as captain in preference to Phil de Glanville. Lawrence's captaincy style reflects his maturity. He is very direct, up front. His preferred way of working is to say, 'This is the way it will be,' and expect players to follow him.

No doubt, as the side develops as a unit, Lawrence will soften and canvass opinion from those close to him, because he is a bright guy who listens. I found that, as players get experience, they have views and they have input and it is important to get them involved. I think Lawrence will do that. I think he learned a hell of a lot from his time at Wasps when he took over as captain after Dean Ryan and Rob Andrew were lured away to Newcastle. He had to learn incredibly quickly just to survive.

And he has made a creditable start in his national role. Beginning with four matches against the top southern hemisphere sides in the autumn of 1997 was just about the hardest baptism possible and, even though England did not win a match, Lawrence, as player and captain, came out of those game with enormous credit. Ground was lost in the disastrous tour to the southern hemisphere the following summer when England suffered record defeats but Lawrence wasn't tainted by that. His absence through injury means that he won't carry the mental scars from those hammerings. England have to come to terms with a considerable list of their inadequacies as they build for the 1999 World Cup in Wales but with Lawrence in charge there will be little room for false optimism, and none whatsoever for any complacency.

— 25 —

THE LAST TIME

I was determined to play it down for two reasons. I didn't want to lose it in my last game as England captain, for the bottom lip to wobble as the emotion swept over me. Heaven knows I didn't want that to happen. I didn't think it would. I've always been able to shut out the feelings. I did it in my first game in charge against Australia and I would do it again against Ireland, eight seasons and fifty-nine matches later. But I didn't know. This might be the occasion I crumpled and let go completely and that would be terrible. The other reason was more pragmatic. So what if it was my last game? This team would carry on, so would English rugby. What's the point of trying to halt the juggernaut, to celebrate the past when sport is concerned with what is happening now and in the future? I'd always said the team is more important than the individual. That was my mantra. If I were to go all soppy in my last game, all self-indulgent and congratulatory, how hypocritical would that make me? I resolved to do nothing, say nothing. It would be business as usual. We had an international to win.

On the Friday in the team hotel the whispering started. The team wanted me to run onto the pitch on my own, a courtesy I had extended to team-mates on their fiftieth caps. I didn't fancy it. 'Please, Deano,' I pleaded. 'Don't. That would really piss me off. I would hate it.' Dean Richards smiled.

I stuck to the same routine. Later that evening I went for my customary stroll up Richmond Hill with the Walkman and the tape which had been with me throughout. It was a compilation tape, an eclectic musical memory-jogger of some great rugby moments. I listened to the theme tune from the film *The Mission*, *The Planets* by Holst, 'Eye of the Tiger' by Survivor, but my favourite was 'Tragedy' by the Bee Gees. Sad really! That always took me back to the days at Terra Nova prep school and the first strong recollection of the rush which winning brings, of an Under Elevens Sevens competition against Barlborough Hall. We had won that day and as I went for a shower I could hear 'Tragedy' playing in the background. The feeling was as fresh now as it was then, exhilaration and satisfaction mixed together. Wonderful. If only tomorrow could be as good. But why wouldn't it be? I had been incredibly lucky. Tomorrow would bring more special memories. I was determined to enjoy it.

Back at the hotel the newspapers were unread. Another conscious decision. I had had enough press coverage to last a lifetime. There was nothing I could learn from the profile or career resumés which appeared that week. I had long since learned to be wary of the media. What could they tell me about myself which I didn't already know? It was pointless getting inflated by the positive comments and flattened by the knives in the back. I knew most of the journalists well, knew what they thought of me. I wasn't going to let them intrude on a private moment.

I kept talking to myself in the changing room. 'It's only another game. Concentrate. Do what you've done for the last seventy odd matches.' The last thing I wanted was to look around, to glamorise the event. I was still unsure if I could keep the emotions in check. There would be time to reflect afterwards.

Deano hadn't obeyed orders. I should have guessed. He always did things his way. The team stopped in the tunnel, leaving me to enter the arena on my own. Head down, I raised an arm in the air to acknowledge the reception. I was right. It was embarrassing. Desperately, desperately embarrassing. Then the rest of the guys ran out and three or four said, 'It's been a privilege,' as they raced past. That got to me. The band struck up and I couldn't sing, couldn't trust myself to use the anthem as the passionate key I had in the past. There was too much emotion swirling round my veins. Another verse and the walls would have crumbled.

Then disaster. Ten minutes before the end of the first half, I twisted my ankle. There wasn't a ball or a player within ten metres of me as I tripped and fell awkwardly. The pain was sharp. I knew the injury was serious. This wasn't how it was meant to end. We were losing for God's sake and I was getting carted off the pitch on a stretcher. Where was the fairy-tale ending? With me in the stands, England staged a revival to beat Ireland 21–15. It was an appropriate message. No one is indispensable. Life goes on. It's a team game. All clichés, but nonetheless true for all that. Now I was able to relax, to take stock, to drink in the occasion one last time. Dean let me hobble up to collect the Millennium Trophy and I was touched by the ovation. That was special. Standing at the bottom of the West Stand, waving to the crowd, made it real. Twickenham has always been a special place to me, has meant so much. I was grateful for the chance to say thank you. I had had my time and wouldn't have changed a minute of it.

The car park was full of friends. Mum, Dad, Andrew Harle, next to the Range Rover with the champagne. Deliberately low key. I had talked to Dad before the game. 'Enjoy it,' he had said. 'You've had a good run.'

Off to the Hilton Hotel and the final top-table, boring post-match dinner. People were very kind, back-slapping, wishing me well, a few thank yous. Some meant a lot others less so. I hadn't enjoyed this side of the captaincy role, bridging the team and the Union, and I wasn't about to start now. It hadn't been all bad. There were plenty of good guys but an official dinner was not the best place to review a career.

As quickly as politeness allowed, probably quicker, but who

cares, I left the Hilton and strolled the hundred yards or so to the pub round the back. Jerry Guscott had also made his excuses. As we opened the door, Jerry, rolling his eyes in mock astonishment, gasped, 'This pub is full of legends.' He was right. They were all there. The special people. Dean Richards, Mike Teague, Brian Moore, Wade Dooley, Peter Winterbottom, Dewi Morris, Rory Underwood, Jonathan Webb, Simon Halliday, Simon Hodgkinson, Paul Ackford, Colin Herridge, Paul Rendall, Rob Andrew. They had all turned up. I was touched.

Quickly, almost as a reflex action, I tried to downplay their attendance. They had only come because they had been to the game or were on rugby earners. Wade would have graced a couple of hospitality tents, Brian spoken at a lunch, Rob fulfilled his radio commitments. It wasn't me they had come to see. But I couldn't dampen the glow which their presence brought. I had not always seen eye to eye with some of these guys, yet we had battled together, lost our Grand Slam virginity together. To see them now taking the piss, cracking the same tired old jokes, falling back into the roles they used to adopt within the squad was magical. The exuberance of the rest of the evening closed the mental scrap book. It was just fun. There was not a drop of sentimentality left in my body. When the Rose and Crown kicked us out we headed for the Atlantic Bar and Grill, a Soho nightspot.

By now the more recent players had left the dinner and joined the party. Garath Archer, England's lock, had announced his engagement and he and his girlfriend were oscillating between the tender celebration of a blossoming romantic liaison and the boisterous, aggressive out-of-your-brain partying of an international victory. There was no dilemma for the old-stagers. They just partied. Dewi Morris and Rob Andrew staged a mock fight, well, it looked mock to us, slapping each other round the face, after Dewi had alleged that Rob had poured away his last drink into a plant pot instead of down his neck. My disagreement with Peter Winterbottom was more serious.

'All right. Let's go outside and sort it out,' I said drunkenly.

'Will, what *are* you talking about?'

'Outside. Now.'

Someone, somehow, lowered the temperature. The next day Winters called. 'Will. Last night. What did I do? Why the huff?' I didn't know. The alcohol had kicked in and half-drunk I had harked back to the 1993 Lions tour when Winters had not spoken to me for three weeks because I had let him down. Maybe there was still something around that memory for me. He was the one player, above all others, whom I most respected. Maybe I was just tired and emotional and didn't know what I was doing.

But there would be no more fights, arguments, prizes as captain. That part of my life was over. Next season I would survive, if selected, as any other player. Captain Carling had ceased to exist.

— 26 —
FREEDOM AT LAST

THE next eight months were decidedly odd. My last game as England captain was on 16 March, yet the new man was not announced until 5 November. For those eight months I was in limbo land, captain by default. I was still the media's fall guy whenever they wanted a comment on the latest shenanigans in the row between the clubs and the RFU. It was a strange period. The reality of life on the back benches had not yet sunk in. England had not played a game, so I had no experience of being part of a team instead of in charge of it. In any case, without the captain's badge to tip selection, there was a distinct probability that I might never represent my country again. Jack Rowell might decide to get out the new broom and sweep all the old debris away.

I was never consulted about the identity of my successor and it was a huge relief. I might have been tempted to flag up someone who wasn't up to the job. I wouldn't have done it consciously but there was something inside me which wanted my record as captain to stand untarnished. I wanted people to think, 'That new bloke's not as good as Carling.' But in the end it wasn't an issue. Nobody sought my opinion. According to media speculation, Jason Leonard and Lawrence Dallaglio were the two main candidates with Phil de Glanville as a decent outsider.

Jason was a hugely popular figure within the game and had proved his leadership credentials when he captained Harlequins. But there were difficulties with Jason. One of his more endearing qualities is his refusal to ignore some of rugby's more riotous traditions. And with media interest in national sporting figures increasing almost by the hour, there was more than a slight chance that Jason would find himself splashed across the tabloid front pages following an all-night drinking session with a few of his Barking chums. He might have taken some of the heat away from Paul Gascoigne or David Beckham but the RFU would have had their hands full keeping him in check.

Phil de Glanville was an altogether more sensible choice. Another player who had captained his club, Bath, Phil was a shrewd tactician who handled the media side well and cut a dash in public. Crucially, too, he had worked with Jack Rowell at Bath. But there was a massive millstone round Phil's shoulders. Most commentators thought he could not be guaranteed a place in the side, that he would struggle to keep either myself or Jerry Guscott on the bench. In my book that ruled Phil out. Putting personal considerations aside, the one thing I did know about captaincy was that a captain has to be beyond reproach on the field. He can be tactically inept, politically naive, monosyllabic to the media but he must have respect and be worth his place.

Phil could not deliver that and for that reason my preference was Lawrence Dallaglio, the Wasps flanker. Lawrence made a significant impact when he arrived in the team. He first came to notice when he toured South Africa with England in 1994, although he did not feature in either of the two Tests. Straightaway you could see he had the necessary qualities to do well on the international stage, but as usual with England the instinctive response was to nit-pick. He's too inexperienced, I was told, too young. Give him a few years and he might make something.

England have traditionally taken that view. As a nation we are reluctant to take risks, to chuck youngsters into the cauldron and see how they fare. I was still meeting significant resistance from those who thought Geoff Cooke had been mad to thrust the captaincy my way at twenty-two. Lawrence might have been inexperienced but isn't everybody until they are given the chance? Lawrence was left out of the 1995 World Cup squad which probably was a mistake because he was very impressive during the Five Nations Championship which followed seven months later. He is a hell of an athlete and he also has the natural arrogance which prompts him to strive for excellence. In his early career he filled all the positions in the back row. Very few players have the confidence and flexibility to do that.

At the start of the 1996/97 season Lawrence was in form, had enough experience of international rugby and should have got the job but I felt he dipped out because he was badly advised. He should have been told to keep his head down when Jack Rowell was musing over the next England captain. Instead, whenever you opened a newspaper or turned on a radio or television there was Lawrence pontificating on all the subjects under the sun. He probably only acceded to the requests out of politeness or a sense of duty, because that's the way he is, but it raised his profile too high. The last person Jack Rowell wanted as captain was another media monster. Lawrence was undoubtedly the best man for the job but he talked himself out of it. Jack was after someone more discreet, someone who would be more malleable, and that wasn't Lawrence.

When Jack plumped for Phil, I thought my international career was over. There seemed no way I would remain in the side. Jerry Guscott and Phil were the natural pairing. Both had bags of experience as a partnership at Bath, with Phil at inside and Jerry at outside centre. As a natural inside centre myself, I thought it would be crazy to pick me alongside Phil. We would not complement each other. But, as ever, Jack took great delight in doing the unexpected. He left Jerry on the bench for much of the season and played Phil and me. I was as embarrassed as hell that I was preferred over Jerry but I wasn't about to argue. It allowed me a season of international rugby without the burden of captaincy. Watching Phil de Glanville in his first few matches as captain was a bizarre experience for me. It felt great to be free, to be able to concentrate on myself and my own game, but part of me longed for that involvement.

People think that the new captain automatically turns to the old one for advice but that is not the case. Phil did ring me early on, though. Within two days of his appointment the press were hunting because some girl was trying to sell a story to the tabloids. Having journalists outside his house was obviously new to him and I talked him through that bit, but he never again asked me for any help. I found that strange. I would have sought advice in his position but that was my style. You can captain a club side for ten years but captaining your country is a completely different ball game. If the positions were reversed and I were Phil taking over a side which had been led by one individual for so long, I would have sat down and said, 'Hey mate, can you give me a rough guide as to what this is like, what that's like.' But he was his own man, he ran the show his way. Phil was far more assured than ever I was. He didn't worry about things which would have concerned me. He didn't worry what the guys thought. He just explained what he wanted, where he thought England were heading, and said that's the way it is. I thought, 'Christ, I admire your balls because I just couldn't have done that.' And the guys did it. It confirmed that I probably did worry too much about what people thought.

But no matter how well he led the side Phil could never escape the large shadow of Jerry on the bench. Jerry came on twice as a replacement during the 1997 Five Nations but he should have started every match. Phil's best rugby occurred in the season 1993/94. At that time he was worth his place in the England side. Jerry's long-term absence that season with a groin problem meant that Phil was never competing directly with his club colleague but his form was such that he could have made a convincing case for getting selected ahead of either Jerry or myself on merit. When the captaincy came up in 1996/97 Jerry was fit again and simply awesome. He should have been the first name on the team sheet.

I think Phil recognises that now, although it was very hard for him at the time. It was painfully obvious to people that Jerry should have been included and the players knew it, too. Players aren't stupid. They know better than anyone else who makes a difference on the pitch, who the really class boys are. In the mid-eighties there were countless occasions when inadequate players were drafted into the England side because selectors had no idea what it took to build an international team but Geoff Cooke had changed all that which made it all the more puzzling why Jack chose to make an issue out of Phil. It made it very hard for Phil to stand up in front of the squad to do his captain's bit. However, it never became a major factor. The guys were honest enough to ask themselves what they would have done if Jack had turned to them and offered them the greatest privilege in English rugby. They knew, like Phil, that they would have jumped at the chance. They knew that the problem wasn't of Phil's making, and this, coupled with the fact that Phil was such a great bloke and an effective captain, deflated the issue.

The debate over the captaincy and the exclusion of Jerry Guscott dragged on throughout the whole season until, finally, I got a chance to confront Jack Rowell about it. It was after the Welsh game, about 2 a.m., and we were both slightly the worse for wear. I was sitting in the hotel with Colin Herridge and Paul Grayson. Jack asked me a question, something about why did I want to retire, and I answered him. Then I said, 'OK Jack. My turn to ask you a question. Did you get the captain right?' An ambiguous answer came back, giving me the impression that he knew he hadn't.

Another senior rugby figure was also musing over the issue of captaincy that season. Fran Cotton was due to announce his initial Lions squad of sixty on the Monday following the England/Scotland international. Fran had been asked to manage the party and, quite rightly, was cock-a-hoop. He believed totally in the concept of the Lions, having toured himself in 1974 and 1977, and was clearly determined to do everything in his power to make the South African extravaganza a success. The first squad wouldn't be set in stone. There would be additions and subtractions as Fran and the selectors finalised or revised their thoughts over the coming weeks but it was nevertheless an important announcement in the rugby calendar. Except for me. The Lions were never in my plans for that summer for a whole host of reasons and I had made no secret of my intention to stay at home.

It was nothing personal, nothing to do with Fran. It's just that the Lions have never meant as much to me as representing my country. I can't get worked up about it in the way other players obviously do. That's not to knock the concept, or the history of British Lions rugby. I didn't fancy it and I was saying exactly that in my newspaper column on Sunday. But, as a courtesy call more than anything, I wanted to tell Fran personally before the paper was published the next morning.

Towards the end of the post-match dinner I trawled round the ballroom of the Hilton Hotel trying to find him. It was the old needle in the haystack job. As the formal part of the evening deteriorated, people slipped off into different corners to hatch various plots and conspiracies. Fran was nowhere to be seen but in my travels I did bump into Peter Rossborough who was England's representative on the Lions selection panel.

'Peter, I'm off out with the boys in a minute and I wanted to put Fran in the picture regarding my availability for the trip. I'm not going. I can't find the energy or the motivation for the tour and if I went I would be an embarrassment to you and myself. I've said as much in the paper tomorrow but I wanted to tell you personally.'

'I appreciate that, Will,' Peter said. 'Are you sure we can't persuade you to reconsider?'

'No. I'm too old.'

Conscience cleared, I was heading out of the Hilton when I bumped into Fran. 'Will, can we have a chat? I hear rumours you are not available for the Lions. I take it that's a PR stunt dreamed up by Jon Holmes for maximum exposure and publicity.'

'Not at all, Fran. It's nothing like that. I'm not available. I don't want to tour.'

Fran was incredulous. 'But this is the British Lions. It's the pinnacle of any rugby player's career.'

'I know, Fran. The Lions are great. But to go on such an intense tour I would have to be raring to go and I'm not. I'm being honest with you. I'm not belittling the tour or anyone who goes on it. I'm just saying I'm not up to it.'

But Fran wouldn't take no for an answer. He seemed to think my decision was part of a grand plan to raise my profile.

'You've got a problem, haven't you?' he said.

'What are you on about?'

'It's the captaincy, isn't it?' he continued. 'What about it?'

'Look, Fran. When you get to a certain age you become a bit cantankerous. I'm at that age. If I were to captain the Lions I would want a say in selection, tour itinerary, how the party was managed, the whole caboodle. You know that doesn't happen with the Lions. The captaincy isn't a factor. I've explained my reasons to you and I'll be doing the same in the paper tomorrow.'

I must have been talking double-Dutch. Either that or I had completely lost the power to communicate, because Fran said, 'OK, ignore the article. Give me a week. I'll go and talk to the other selectors about the captaincy.'

'Up to you, Fran, do whatever you want but it will not make any difference.'

We left it like that. I thought the matter was dead and buried but it was just the start. Over the course of the next week rumours flew back and forth that Fran had offered me the captaincy. It was typical of the way the media feed off a story. Gossip and tittle-tattle become validated by a response to the speculation. It's the easiest game to play in the world. Say, for instance, there is a rumour that Lawrence Dallaglio was considering a transfer of clubs, from Wasps to Bath. Journalists would ring up Lawrence who would deny it because it wasn't true and the next day the story would appear as: 'Dallaglio denies Bath move,' with the inference that the rumours must have been true in the first place for Dallaglio to deny them.

That was how it was with this story. The following weekend, again in the paper, I was asked by John Taylor, the *Mail on Sunday*'s rugby correspondent, whether my decision not to tour would have been different if I had been offered the captaincy. I said no, it wouldn't, and everybody made two and two make about six hundred and assumed I had been offered the job. This was relayed to Fran and he rocketed straight into orbit, accusing me of lying, misrepresenting a private conversation, of manipulating the media, anything he could think of really.

But Fran got his knickers in a twist. If I had invented the conversation why did he refer to it in his book published to celebrate the Lions Test series victory against the Springboks. 'I could have told him the truth,' Fran wrote, 'that not only would he not be going as captain, he wouldn't be going as a player either. I didn't want to do that and thought I would let him down lightly. That's why I told him there would be a selection meeting the following Sunday and that I would raise the captaincy with the other selectors. I said that after we had discussed it I would ring him to let him know if there was a chance we might consider him in that role.' That was how Fran explained our conversation at the Hilton in his book, *My Pride of Lions*. Why talk about the captaincy to someone who's not even going to make the tour party? Where's the logic in that?

I think Fran's version of the events was prompted by his infatuation with the Lions. He took it as a personal insult if any player would not leap through rings of fire for his beloved Lions team. He felt that I was deliberately belittling the tour. In fact, I was doing the opposite. I was saying that I didn't want to waste a place on the tour. I could have made myself available, played in the Wednesday side for two months, gone on the piss and picked up the fat cheque at the end, but I chose not to. That would have been the dishonest position to take, not turning them down from the outset.

Fran and I saw each other in Cardiff six weeks later after the Wales/England match. It was the first time we had met face to face since Scotland and it was clear that Fran was still seething. He later claimed in his book that I had been drinking and that I said I would have hit him if we had been in the same room when his comments, which appeared in several newspapers, were published. He must think I'm stupider than I look. Me, a 5ft 10ins and 14 stone centre, hit an ex-prop who's 6ft 4ins and approaching 20 stone. I'm not that dull, even if Fran's chin is a tempting target.

I was delighted that the Lions won and Fran should take some of the credit for that, but the greater share should go to Ian McGeechan, the coach. The feedback from the players whom I spoke to when they returned home was that it was Ian who made them tick. Fran never really involved himself with the rugby side because it was obvious he never had a clue what modern rugby is all about. Fran was excellent administratively but that was the extent of his involvement. He continually referred to his exploits in 1974 and 1977 with the Lions in New Zealand and South Africa. Those were special periods for him. But he couldn't come to terms with someone who might not view playing for his Lions as the greatest honour life could bestow on a rugby player.

— 27 —

ALI AND HENRY

L IFE in the fast lane was over. England's last Five Nations match of the season was also the final international of my career. I hadn't resolved to call it a day in Cardiff but it was appropriate to do so. I hadn't enjoyed the season as much as I had hoped I would. The row with Fran Cotton hadn't helped, nor had the uncertainty surrounding Phil de Glanville's stint as captain, but those weren't the only reasons. Squabbles and spats had dogged me for the last decade and I was accustomed to putting them on the back burner when necessary.

The truth was that I hadn't enjoyed the rugby. The games themselves were OK but I was bored with the extended preparations surrounding a match. In the old days England assembled on a Wednesday night and dispersed on the Sunday morning following the post-match dinner. That was fine. Long enough to hone the training and enjoy the players' company, short enough not to get enveloped by the tedium and get on each other's nerves. But since the game went professional England gathered and prepared for a week. The first three days were spent in a hotel in Marlow near the training facilities at Bisham Abbey before we were bussed up to Richmond to stay at the Petersham Hotel. A week of meetings was too long. As captain, the days would be filled with planning sessions, press conferences and a host of other time-consuming items. As a player it was a case of staving off the boredom.

I found myself watching day-time TV in my room after training. Initially it was fun to be selfish, to prepare as an individual with no concerns or thoughts about others. It was enjoyable, too, to spend more time with Jerry Guscott and Jason Leonard, to slip away for a beer without feeling guilty. The initial unease between Jerry and me had disappeared. We were in the same boat, two ordinary players fighting for a place in the team, and we enjoyed each other's company. But they were the only compensations. As the season developed I lost focus.

The personnel had changed, too. Colin Herridge was no longer part of the set-up, Don Rutherford was playing a bigger role and the players coming into the England side had little to offer apart from rugby. Some had gone from school to college to club without experiencing other employment. Rugby was their life and they lived it day and night. After training they would kill time with computer games. The characters did not seem to be around and the piss-taking between the players had disappeared. Guys playing for England would still die for their country but it was more of a business to them. We were talking mortgages. Little things like the use of substitution and the bigger match squads had fractured the sense of a team. Players hopped on and off the pitch with monotonous regularity. At times I had to check to see to whom I was passing the ball.

The more I thought about it the less I liked it. International rugby had changed and I wasn't changing with it. It wasn't necessarily better or worse, just different. The new guys were as excited and overawed as I had been when I first made the side. Jon Sleightholme, Alex King, Phil Greening, Andy Gomarsall and Tim Stimpson hadn't known the old days. All they knew was what they were experiencing and they were loving every minute of it. My decision to quit was confirmed when Jack Rowell picked Rob Andrew on the bench for the Wales match. We were two old farts in a young man's world. I was still friendly with Paul Grayson, Tim Rodber and Matt Dawson but I didn't feel strongly connected to the bulk of the squad.

I had also achieved the objective I had set myself for that season. In the past I had used the burden of captaincy to excuse patches of indifferent form. Now that I was no longer able to offer up that excuse I wanted to see if I could still hack international rugby as a player. The first match of the championship against Scotland proved that I could. It was one of those games where the ball runs for you. I scored near the end, made half a dozen breaks and acquitted myself well. I never came close to that sort of form during the rest of the championship but it didn't matter. I could leave on my terms.

I had something to move on to now and she was called Ali Cockayne, a qualified aerobics teacher and fitness consultant. In 1991 I got to know Gary Lineker. We first bumped into each other at an awards luncheon and six months later our paths crossed at a photo shoot. On the back of that we went for lunch and the friendship developed. Through Gary I met his wife Michelle and through Michelle I met her sister Ali. It was around the time that Gary and Michelle's son George was being treated for leukaemia so Ali's attention was naturally elsewhere, but we seemed to hit it off. She was incredibly easy-going and fun to be with. There was no edge to her, no side. Her behaviour was always natural whether she was in the middle of a Cartier polo function, having lunch with Hugh and Jo Laurie, or mucking about on the beach with a group of children. There was never any attempt to show off, to say the right things. I admired that about her. I also loved her stability, the fact that she was part of a big family with two brothers and two sisters, and had lived in Leicestershire for most of her life. Nothing seemed to get her down or rile her. All of which was in stark contrast to my upbringing which was topsy-turvy and nomadic.

We started going out together around September 1995. I had separated from Julia but the fuss surrounding my friendship with Diana was still simmering and Michelle was not impressed. Michelle is three years older than Ali and at that time very much the big sister. So much so that I used to call her mum. She was very protective towards Ali and didn't like the idea of her going out with a bloke whose relationships were habitually splashed over the front pages of the tabloid newspapers. I could see her point. In her eyes I was damaged goods.

And so began a period when I spent as much time getting on the right side of Michelle as I did wooing Ali. Michelle was distinctly frosty in the beginning. 'Don't go near him. He's trouble,' she told Ali. On our first proper date I picked Ali up at the end of the road rather than at the Linekers' house where she was staying. We had decided on that somewhat unromantic start to the evening partly to fool the photographers who were following me in order to get a picture of the new girl in my life but mainly so as not to alert Michelle. Yet it was Gary who cottoned on first. Thinking that Ali and I might be becoming an item, but not totally sure, he decided to bluff Ali. 'Listen Ali, Will's told me all about it and I'm really delighted. How long have the two of you been going out together?' Ali fell for it and spilled the beans. When Michelle found out she read the riot act once more and threatened to throw her out.

Gary can be a bit sneaky like that. Football's Mr Clean, television's Mr Nice Guy, stroker of furry animals, cuddler of children, is not as unblemished as he sometimes appears. Recently Gary and I have formed a golfing partnership which has defied challenges from all-comers. Two years ago that dominance came under the severest pressure. We were playing at Wisley against a pairing who were giving us a hard time. As we stood on the par five fifteenth tee we were one down and in danger of seeing our record disappear. I smashed my drive left over a small hillock, Gary pushed his towards the water bordering the fairway, while our opponents' balls both sailed serenely down the fairway to land in perfect position.

'Will,' Gary said. 'When you find your ball, tee it up, and belt it onto the green. No one's going to see you. If we lose this one it's curtains.'

I realised this was an example of Gary's special brand of humour, but decided to call his bluff and followed his advice to the letter, only to hack the ball twenty metres into the thick rough. Thankfully I did not have to live with the cheating scandal hanging over my head because Gary got home from the edge of the water with an eagle three, while our opponents made do with birdies. I'm still never absolutely sure if Gary is having a laugh, or is serious in what he is saying. Bear that in mind when you next see him presenting *Grandstand*'s Football Focus.

The first date which Ali and I ventured out on was a trip to the cinema to watch *Species*, a sci-fi film. A visit to Zianni's, an Italian restaurant just off the King's Road, followed. Those early outings were difficult because they were conducted in a cloud of secrecy. Even Ali's first experience of Five Nations rugby was surrounded by subterfuge. She flew to Paris in 1996 to watch England play France in the company of Amanda Herridge, Colin's daughter. The pair deliberately kept out of the way of the official RFU party and after the dinner I met up with Ali and spent the night in her hotel. I have never received a welcome like it when I returned to the team hotel at 9.30 a.m. the following morning for breakfast still wearing my dinner jacket. The lads thought I had been out on the town all night and hadn't yet gone to bed. It was a Carling they hadn't encountered often before and I did not bother to set the record straight.

Ali moved into the Covent Garden flat I had rented after Julia and I separated and it was that period which made me think that I really could maintain a worthwhile relationsihp. I was a complete mess, battered emotionally and almost paranoid about media intrusion to the extent where I refused to open the blinds for the nine months I was there. There was all the time in the world to talk and we discussed everything. Nothing was sacrosanct. Ali saw all my fears and insecurities and took them in her stride.

It was around this time that our relationship became public knowledge. Shortly after we had returned from the France match, I was approached by a journalist from the *Sun* newspaper as I came out of a Covent Garden restaurant. 'Congratulations,' he said. 'I understand you're seeing Gary's sister-in-law.'

'I've no idea what you're talking about,' I replied, but it was no use. The next day Ali and I were on the front page of the newspaper. The *Sun* tried to contact some of her old boyfriends to see if there was any dirt flying about but they found none and after a day or so we were old news.

Our son Henry arrived, kicking and screaming, into this world on 5 October 1997. It was yet another event with which Ali seemed to cope with supreme equanimity. During her pregnancy I often used to catch her stroking her tummy with a faraway dreamy look playing across her face. I used to joke that I would have to give her a cushion as a baby-substitute to ward off any withdrawal symptoms after the birth, but the reality was better than the anticipation. She bonded with Henry within seconds and I am convinced her instinctive natural way with him is the reason he is so content most of the time. For me, Henry's arrival was altogether more traumatic. I was still playing for Harlequins and walking round the house at 3 a.m. trying to quieten an occasionally fractious baby was not an experience I was used to. It made me realise how ludicrously pampered and privileged my life had been up to this point.

— 28 —

THE PRICE OF FAME

N OTORIETY crept up on me. When I was appointed England
captain in 1988 the impact on the world was so huge that
only seven or eight journalists turned up to report the event.
And these were the dyed-in-the-wool rugby correspondents.
No one else was interested. There were no feature writers, no
journalists from general sports magazines, no news men. Now,
when rugby has a big announcement to make, a new England
coach or captain, a development in the battle between the clubs
and the RFU, the press conference is attended by sixty to seventy. The contrast between then and now is massive.

The change is due to the growth of the sport generally but it
is also an indication of how the media and the public at large
has become infatuated with its sporting figures. Men such as
Alan Shearer, Paul Gascoigne and Michael Atherton only have
to sneeze too often in public before some sparky editor will
order an article about the importance of alternative medicine in
the lives of top athletes. International sportsmen are now regular
guests on the talk-show circuit. I went on ITV's *This Morning*
programme during the 1991 World Cup where I was given an
embarrassing grilling on my love life and I had to sit through
an appearance on *Wogan* in the company of Ian McGeechan and
John Jeffrey the Monday after England lost that famous match

in 1990 against Scotland. Neither were particularly pleasant experiences but they were part of the package which went with the job.

Other appearances have been less testing. I've raced, and beaten, a turbo-charged Lotus Esprit over twenty-five metres in Battersea Park to help raise £10,000 for the Royal Marsden Cancer Appeal and I was a guest on Sue Lawley's *Desert Island Discs*. My choice of music – including the theme from *The Mission*, Eric Clapton's 'Layla', the Police's 'Every Little Thing She Does is Magic' and Louis Armstrong's 'What a Wonderful World' – was not especially revealing, nor was my preferred book, Tolkien's *The Hobbit*, or my luxury, a flotation tank. But I make no excuses for that.

Some of the spin-offs from rugby have been faintly embarrassing. In 1992 I was awarded an OBE on the back of England's 1991 Grand Slam and our appearance in the World Cup final of that year. Jeff Probyn was particularly incensed that I was singled out, stating that he thought Geoff Cooke was a more worthy recipient. Jeff was probably right. It is invidious to single out one player, especially as rugby is so self-evidently a team sport. But what should I have done? Said thanks, but no thanks and refused the honour? I accepted it on behalf of the side. The letters might sit next to my name but that is the way the system rewards teams who have performed creditably. They give the gong to the captain.

The ceremony itself was curiously matter-of-fact. I arrived at Buckingham Palace with my parents as guests. The OBEs were asked to wait in one room, the MBEs in another. A Palace official places a hook in your jacket to receive the medal and I waited in line with people from many other walks of life until one by one we were called forward. Then it was a quick left turn, a bow to the Queen, she placed the medal on the hook, I backed away and returned to the room where the hook was removed and I was handed the medal. The Queen asked, 'Did you enjoy the World Cup?' I said, 'Yes,' and the entire ceremony took about ninety seconds. The medal is now in the attic of my parents' house with a trunk-load of other rugby memorabilia.

Back in 1988 the England rugby captain used to change so frequently that a new one was never worth talking about. In fact the England captain himself was not a figure of any consequence. I suppose I changed all that. Because I was in the job for so long and because I outlasted several other prominent figures, including other famous players and RFU presidents, I became synonymous with my sport, defined and restricted by rugby. Initially I was very much a curiosity for those trying to get a handle on me. Because I played rugby people tried to slot me into a category. It was a bit like the attitude some Americans have to their sporting figures: virtuosos in their particular disciplines but unsuited for any contribution outside of that environment. I was portrayed as the pretty boy England captain, a piece of meat, thick as a brick and about as interesting. And in 1988 those assessments weren't too wide of the mark.

But the longer I hung around, the more people's perceptions changed. It was largely a cultural shift. Gradually people accepted that some sportsmen had other things to offer. Various athletes went into the media or diversified into business and flourished. I, too, benefited. After three years in the job people I met started to treat me differently. There was a general acceptance that some of the principles which lay behind a successful team had relevance in business and other disciplines.

In recent years I have used that interest to develop relationships personally and, through Insights my company, with some of Britain's top businessmen. It became possible to write to the chief executive of British Airways and get him to come to lunch. I'm sure that one of the reasons he came was out of curiosity to see the man behind the public persona, but I would also like to think that the experiences I had had in management and leadership were similar to his. Jon Holmes and I developed this idea to the extent we held irregular dining clubs. Gary Lineker would turn up and Jon and I would invite Sir Colin Marshall or Richard Branson along for lunch. It was all terribly informal. There was never any hard sell but it was immensely useful and a great privilege to talk to these guys and to get an inkling of how they operated. Much of what I learned was filtered back into the England rugby team.

Most of the chairmen and chief executives of the big companies have no lives of their own. Their diaries are booked up to three months ahead to the extent that each lunch and dinner will be taken care of. They are also driven. You do not get to be chief executive of a multi-national company by accident and there is something about them that makes them want to be different, to stand out in a crowd. They are not interested in the humdrum, the ordinary, but that is not the same as saying they rarely let their hair down. All those I met had a tremendous capacity for enjoyment. They like nothing better than going to internationals, getting excited about the occasion and the match and talking about it afterwards. That is the all-embracing quality which sport has. It can offer something to everyone. It took a while for me to understand this, because my instinctive reaction to meeting public figures is to hold them in artificially high esteem, but that is precisely the wrong way to get to know them.

If there is a characteristic which sets them apart it is the way they deal with people. There is a respect there, an understanding, a desire to soak up someone else's point of view. Lord MacLaurin, English cricket's supremo, and Sir Colin Chandler, the top man at Vickers, are prime examples. They are obviously powerful people, have fought many a battle in their ascent to the top, but there is a stillness about them which is captivating. It is easy to see why they are so successful in their own particular fields. They are direct, purposeful, organised, assured and very straight. Natural leaders. If the shit hits the fan I immediately know who I want around to handle the problems and the Sir Colin Chandlers of this world would be high up on that list.

Through rugby I also got to know celebrities from the world of television and entertainment and now, I suppose, I have a number of so-called famous friends. Hugh Laurie and I attended the opening game of the 1998 soccer World Cup and later I was lucky enough to meet Sean Connery. I see John Cleese and Rory Bremner occasionally, too.

After the Scotland/England match in 1996 Ali and I, plus friends of ours, Greg and Christina, stayed with Rory and his girlfriend in a castle which he had rented for the weekend thirty minutes out of Edinburgh. As we pulled up to the old building Rory's girlfriend shivered and remarked how spooky the place was. It was too good a scam to resist. On Sunday Rory went off to a dinner to sing for his supper and Greg and I decided to make the most of the decidedly ghostlike atmosphere. I called Rory on his mobile to find out what time he was returning home.

'Listen, Rory, I'm knackered after the game yesterday. Greg and the girls are also pretty bushed. We're all going to bed and we'll catch up with you in the morning.'

'No problem,' Rory said. 'See you tomorrow.'

Then locking the front door and leaving the key on the inside, we all climbed out of a side window to wait in the bushes for Rory to get back. The wind was howling through the trees and the clouds were scudding across the darkened sky. It was enough to scare me stupid and I knew what we were planning to do.

As Rory and partner walked towards the front door I darted from the shadows and swept across the lawn, dressed in a long black coat, waving my arms. Rory's girlfriend saw me first and screamed, assuming I was some pervert rather than a ghost.

Rory didn't hesitate for a moment. In one beautifully co-ordinated movement he thrust his girlfriend aside and ran for the front door shouting, 'Will, Greg, for God's sake open up and let us in.'

One of the best things about meeting and getting on with well-known figures is the shared understanding of the pitfalls of being public property. There is no compulsion to explain or justify the latest article in the newspapers. These guys have all been the subject of ill-informed or outrageous pieces and they ignore that side of life.

It is an incredible relief just to turn up at a party and be normal. Sadly, about a couple of years ago, I went through a phase when I declined invitations to friends' houses if they were including people I didn't know, simply because I knew that for the first couple of hours I would have to unpick the prejudices these people had built up about me. It got to the point where I dreaded having to knock back one rumour or another and, as I rarely enjoyed the evening, I stopped accepting the invitations. With famous people you don't have to explain things. They don't ask about the press. They don't ask certain questions.

Hugh Laurie, as well as being a fantastic actor, is what I would call a classic Englishman. Everything about him is understated. If I told him he was brilliant in a particular sketch or play he would inevitably turn round and say, 'Now, now, Will. Calm down.' He underplays everything, even though he is immensely talented and proficient in so many areas. He gained an Oxbridge blue for rowing and loves his sport, as well as being one of Britain's most popular actors. He is so unassuming that he wrote a book under a pen-name and sent it off to the publishers just so that it would be considered on its merits.

Hugh and I were lucky enough to be given tickets for another England/Scotland match in 1996, though this time it was the football variety, part of Euro '96. Hugh decided that we should travel to Wembley on his bike for two reasons. He reckoned there would be a better chance of beating the traffic and he wanted me to wear a crash helmet as a disguise to make sure none of the Scottish fans recognised me and included him by association as a target. What a journey! Hugh virtually did a wheelie along the entire route to Wembley because, in typical public-school fashion, I refused to snuggle up close to him and wrap my arms round his waist for stability. Fourteen stone of prime English rugby beef was perched over the back tyre, hanging on for dear life to an exhaust outlet which was getting increasingly hotter by the mile, while Hugh fought to control the bike.

That's the best bit about Hugh. His humour embraces those he is with and is non-threatening. Certain people make jokes at the expense of others, belittling them to get a laugh or they tell jokes in an aggressive manner. Angus Deayton and Clive Anderson were like that when I encountered them. Underneath the banter there were egos trying to make statements, saying I'm cleverer and therefore funnier than you. I never felt comfortable in their company. Whenever I've met them they've been surrounded by a coterie of like-minded individuals. There are loads of in-jokes and that is difficult to break down.

If someone asked me now whether I would swap all that I am today to be the Will Carling of ten years ago I would tell him to go and get lost. There are huge benefits to being well known. It makes life easier getting tables in restaurants, booking holidays, staying at hotels. If I want to go to a concert which is sold out, I can ring up late and invariably get a seat which is rarely followed by an invoice. The perks are obvious. So is the downside. It is difficult to have a private life in public. If ever I go out for a walk in the park or have lunch in a pub or restaurant people will ask for an autograph. Most of the time it is a pleasant experience. People are unobtrusive and polite but you do get the odd bloke who will chastise you for not having a pen to sign his cigarette packet, or the one who gives you a hard time for not carrying round a dozen signed photographs which he can give to his mates.

The really intrusive stuff comes from the media. They are the guys who really get you down because they won't take no for an answer and their continual pestering has an effect on people I care about, not just me. One of the worst experiences occurred when Ali first became pregnant in September 1996. She was due to go into hospital for a first scan. Ordinarily I would have accompanied her to the hospital but we both decided that I shouldn't because we did not want the news to get out. I was up in Newcastle when my mobile phone rang and it was a desperately distraught Ali on the line. The eight-week scan had shown that the little thing's heart had stopped. You can imagine the emotions which tore us both up. I was miles away, sitting in a car, and virtually useless to Ali just at the time she needed me most. When she became pregnant a second time soon after, I attended the scan. Thankfully, everything was all right on this occasion, but the very next day there was a reporter from the *Daily Mirror* on our doorstep demanding quotes as he understood Ali was pregnant. The paper must have had a contact at the hospital, which is common practice in tabloid journalism. That aspect of the media appals me. It gets to the stage where you make decisions, as we did, based on an avoidance of publicity. You start to live your life as a reaction to theirs and I can never forgive the press for that. Never. People say it's the price of fame but they wouldn't have used that argument if they could have heard Ali crying on the end of a phone. Thankfully those experiences do not occur too frequently.

And then there's the business side of things. I am the first to acknowledge that I have milked my name and my stint as England captain. That enabled me to meet people whom I would not have encountered in other circumstances. But once the introduction has been made, it has always been incumbent on me to make a success of the relationship. No one these days does business with an individual or company if they do not deliver the goods. What can be annoying is the automatic assumption that everyone in the public eye is very wealthy. One of the more regular accusations I have had to deal with is that I have made a million out of rugby. David Campese was the first to spark that rumour and it refuses to go away. Well, I'm not a millionaire. My contract with Harlequins was worth £150,000 and I will earn more from Insights, TV and radio work, speaking engagements and this book. It all adds up to a massive amount of money by anyone's standards but, after tax and costs, it does not place me in the millionaire bracket. If I were more careful, in four or five years I could save a considerable sum but I want to enjoy life and not worry too much about the future. Jon Holmes goes berserk with that attitude. He is forever warning me that one day the money will run out and that I should plan with that in mind. Maybe it will, but I will cross that bridge as and when.

It can be difficult to maintain a sense of perspective where money is concerned. Last year, partly as a reaction to the break-up of my marriage and the interest in my friendship with Diana, Ali and I indulged in some retail therapy. We shopped until we dropped. We both needed new wardrobes and went out and spent a fortune on clothes in less than a week. I was flabbergasted when the bills came through and more than a little embarrassed. It was something I had never done before and I felt guilty. Part of me thought that I had behaved ridiculously, but another part of me took the view that you only live once, so give it a lash.

It is a dilemma I have yet to reconcile. If I see someone begging in the street I feel I must do something and give them £20, very much a soft touch, but I would also go out and lavish ridiculous sums on a couple of Armani shirts. On balance I think it is impossible to attribute morality to money. Who's to say whether the City of London fat cats justify their massive salaries? I know the sacrifices I had to make to rise to the top in sport, I know how volatile and ephemeral that career could have been and I know how lucky I have been. So if people want to pay me staggering sums because of who I am and what I've done it is not my problem. That is the way I have come to view it, although the guilt has never totally disappeared.

It was the same with the England team. I'm sure there were players who resented my ability to earn money in what is quintessentially a team sport but those players would have done the same as me, given the opportunity. In this country we too often see success as a burden. They had the same chances as I did but I got lucky and made the most of it. And now I'm a part of the media circus myself, with television commitments and the odd sports chat show for Radio 5 Live. Presenting ITV's coverage of the Five Nations Championship and other England games, which I started when I retired from international rugby, has been a real test. My intention is to steer clear of the critical role adopted by other ex-players in the media.

This is going to sound arrogant, but I am endeavouring to be educational in my approach. I want to put across how England have tried to play, what they got right or wrong, to get inside the team. It is a piece of cake to lambast someone but the more difficult task is to work out why that player is not performing up to the required standard or is off his game. After all, I am still close enough to the game to be very much aware of how personally some players take the brickbats which fly their way. If England play badly then I am prepared to say that, but I don't see it as my job to be brutal with players. I couldn't do what Alan Hansen does with football. That may be gutless of me and my views may change once I am no longer talking about the players I played with, but I do think the viewer or the reader wants to understand why things are happening. Television shows you the how but you still need people to explain the why.

— 29 —
COUNTRY BEFORE CLUB

L AWRENCE DALLAGLIO now knows the score. He knows what
it's like to captain your country and try to fulfil obligations
to your club. It's tough, almost impossible in this day and age
and I did it for eight years. In April, Lawrence appeared on a
television programme I co-host. We were talking before the
show and he said, 'I used to think you were a bastard because
you never used to play for your club. But now I understand.
Now I know why you put country before club. You just can't
keep two balls in the air forever.'

I've always had a difficult relationship with Harlequins, the
club I joined from Durham University on the advice of Mike
Weston, who was Chairman of England's selectors at the time.
Mike told me the club would provide the finishing touches to
my game which would make me a certainty for England's 1987
World Cup squad. He couldn't have been further from the mark.
The England selectors chose Fran Clough instead. Quins remains
the only club I've had, despite other offers. I half-considered
moving to Wasps when relations between myself and Dick Best
and Andy Keast, Quins' directors of rugby, began to break down
in 1997 and 1998, but I decided against it. For all the talk about
me being a disruptive influence at the club I've only ever wanted
to play for Quins.

On occasions that was a difficult stance to maintain. In 1992 I was approached by Leeds Rugby League Club and offered one million pounds over a four-year period to play for them. Leeds were sponsored by Carling Black Label at the time, so there was obvious marketing potential there. It was an offer I seriously considered. In 1992 one million was a staggering sum, especially as my company hadn't taken off and there were no guarantees that I would remain as England captain or even hold on to my place in the side. I contacted Ellery Hanley to seek his advice and his remarks finally persuaded me to stay in Union. Ellery said I would be a hunted man if I ever went north with that price tag on my head. I would need to be forever looking over my shoulder, waiting for the next punch or double tackle, and it would last for two or three seasons until I had proved I could handle myself. That, and the fact that I had played Union since the age of seven, made up my mind. I admire Rugby League and have the utmost respect for the skills of the men who play it, some of whom are truly exceptional, but it wasn't for me. Quins was the choice, for better or worse.

I'll always be grateful for the support and friendship from the players and officials at the club, the sheer normality of the routine, the jokes and the faces, which kept me sane in the middle of the Diana business. During that crisis her name was never mentioned. And this in an environment where any peccadillo, any weakness is fair game, probed and prodded mercilessly. I had none of that at Quins. Players were spoken to by journalists and offered money to pass on what I had said in the showers or in the bar but no one gave them a thing. The most gratifying feature was that I never asked anyone at the club to lay off or protect me. It just happened and it meant a lot.

On one occasion the attention threatened to disrupt events on the pitch. The Saturday Harlequins played West Hartlepool in the league was the day after I had moved out of the house I shared in Putney with Julia. Fifty or so journalists turned up at the game, safe in the knowledge that I would be there and they would be able to pick up stories and follow me to my new address. But, unbeknown to me, a club official had contacted the Metropolitan Police and they had laid on three police vans to maintain order. Before the game the chief inspector in charge of the operation asked where I was going afterwards and how I intended to leave. I told him I had no idea. I needed to get to the new flat in Covent Garden but had not even begun to think of how I could do that without being chased across London by the rat pack. In the end one of the police officers drove my car to a spot a mile from the ground while the game was in progress and afterwards I was bundled into one of the police vans and taken to my car, while the other two vans blocked the entrance to the ground preventing any of the media from following in their vehicles. That weekend was the first media-free couple of days I had enjoyed for months and it was heaven.

Club rugby has never grabbed me in the way that international rugby did. I always dreamed of the high life, the big occasion, Queen and country, the world stage. In the back of my mind I knew that for most people the route to the summit involved plodding through cold, dark December evenings ankle-deep in mud but I was more fortunate than most. My apprenticeship was short. I was catapulted into the international scene with unseemly haste. I captained my country, not my club, and it enabled me to take a different view. I did not carry round the baggage, which most internationals have, of a long club career. I'm sure I missed out on the friendships formed by years of grunt and grind but my ties of loyalty were still stronger than many people realise.

For much of the time the Quins and I got on well together. There were many things about the club which were hugely appealing, the ability of the squad to pull out all the stops for one-off games, the quirkiness, the characters. But I was most comfortable with the club's attitude to rugby. Many of the players worked in the City of London's financial markets in the amateur days and there was more to them than rugby, rugby, rugby. Their jobs and the London social scene ensured that rugby wasn't the centre of their existence. It was recreation, serious recreation, but one of a number of interests which were equally important. When the game went professional the club somehow managed to find the nice guys and it was a pleasure to play with Laurent Cabannes, the *laissez-faire* Frenchman, Massimo Cuttita, an Italian whose pasta was to die for, and Johnny Ngamo, my co-centre from Tonga, whose idea of a drift defence was to rush up and smash his opposite number into the middle of next week.

Richard Langhorn was a classic old-style Harlequin. Richard played at No. 8 or at lock, and he died at a tragically young age following a routine back operation. He was a natural athlete and a fine player, if not in the top bracket. But it was his zest for life which was so attractive. Richard wasn't consumed by rugby. He skied, sailed, played basketball, worked in the City and enjoyed a hectic social life, yet when it came to Saturday afternoon and a league game he was as switched on and focused as any other player in the country. Most of the Quins were like that and I found that environment healthy and stimulating.

After Richard died Peter Winterbottom and others set up the Richard Langhorn Trust to perpetuate his memory and over the years the Trust has raised substantial funds to enable handicapped kids to enjoy sailing and skiing holidays. Many Quins players and members have given time to further that project. The fund-raising events are invariably chaotic with Winters ringing up on a Friday night and asking people to donate shirts for the auction or speak the following day, but they always seem to go down well. That, to me, is the essence of Quins. When something is important the dilettante image goes out of the window and everyone pulls for everyone else.

Hence the successes in the knock-out cup. Quins could just about manage five do-or-die matches, then a final at Twickenham in front of 40,000 people. It was the nine months' slog for a league title which was distinctly unappetising. If I didn't have England it would have got me down, because I don't believe in doing things half-heartedly. I'm the first to acknowledge that to devote myself to a lifestyle existence with England, yet flit in and out of the club scene, is not an entirely consistent position to take but that's a position I was happy to live with.

I couldn't have handled the Bath experience. The Bath players talk about the Bath family, one for all and all for one stuff, and elevate that above all other concerns, including playing for England. I would have found that horribly claustrophobic. I didn't fancy the idea of traipsing down to the club with the girlfriend for social events to see blokes I had been with the previous day at training. Everything revolves around Bath and that to me is plum crazy. I need more space. Ditto with Leicester, Gloucester or Bristol, come to that. They make a virtue out of how committed their players are to their club. At Quins the club was never the social focus of the players' lives. There was too much to do elsewhere. Every now and then eight or nine of us would head off into town after a game but it wasn't compulsory. No one minded if certain individuals didn't tag along. It did not make us a particularly tight team off the pitch but there was enough grit and determination around to make it work on the pitch when it was necessary.

Quins started to go badly wrong for me when rugby went professional. Dick Best was made director of rugby and decided to whip the club into shape. I had known Dick for a long time, ever since I had walked into the club a fresh-faced youth from Durham University. I liked Dick, still do, despite the fact that he has sworn he will never speak to me again as long as he lives. He was a genuinely funny guy. He could be a bit of a verbal bully but, as long as you weren't the intended victim of one of his tongue-lashings, it was top-notch spectator sport watching him lay into a player for dropping a pass in training or cocking up a move.

He was also an excellent coach. Dick had a spell with England, working alongside Geoff Cooke, before he was eased out by Jack Rowell, and his record was outstanding, thirteen wins from seventeen matches. He was more of a forwards' man and many of his charges, including those whose opinions I respect like Brian Moore, Peter Winterbottom and Wade Dooley, rated him highly. He used to absorb information from South Africa and New Zealand, ponder and pummel it, and then regurgitate it in a manner which made it highly accessible and relevant to Harlequins' or England's players. But professionalism seemed to bring the worst out of Dick. Suddenly he was in charge of forty players; maybe it was the power that changed him.

He seemed to equate professionalism with an exaggerated work ethic. We beat Gloucester at the start of the 1996/97 season by a bucketful of points, yet back in the changing room we were bollocked because we had had a fifteen-minute slow patch in the middle of the match. Dick's view was that everything could be remedied by work and more work and he drove the fun out of training and out of the club.

Rugby doesn't work like that. No sport does. Of course you have to devote time and energy to objectives but a professional attitude does not mean no enjoyment. I don't think it was entirely Dick's fault. The club had placed him in a position for which he wasn't equipped, a position he wasn't comfortable in. A fantastic coach, Dick had no man-management experience. He was at his best as a number two, working alongside people-pleasers such as Geoff Cooke. On his own Dick, I thought was a liability. I was vice-captain in that season and I had regular run-ins with him. Jason Leonard, the club captain, approached me as did other senior players. 'Listen, you know Dick well. Talk to him. We've got to sort this out.' And that is exactly what Jason and I tried to do. Together we asked Dick to ease up on people. We explained that we were in for a long hard season and there was no point flogging the boys half to death in the first three months. But Dick was having none of it. He thought that if he took that line the boys would think he was soft and lose respect for him. He believed his job was to crack the whip as long and as hard as possible.

The irony was that he was fine with me. I had a different contract from the other guys at the club. Mine had a clause which enabled me to pursue my other business interests, provided I spent an appropriate amount of time at the club and did not miss too many training sessions. From a purely selfish point of view, life was hunky-dory for me, as it was for Jason, because he was one of Dick's blue-eyed boys and rarely suffered from his barbed tongue. But it became patently obvious that for the rest of the players Dick's attitude was unacceptable. They used to tell Jason and me that unless the situation changed they wanted out and were talking to their agents to see whether their contract contained any exit clauses. Jason and I continued to see Dick to ask him to lighten up but there was no discernible improvement.

Eventually the atmosphere became so poisonous that around twenty of the squad held a meeting with Dick and Andy Keast, Dick's number two, at the Broadgate Club, a well-known London gym. We were there to do some promotional work for a match with Auckland. The discussion lasted for three hours, during which the players got a lot off their chests. Keith Wood, an outstanding hooker on the 1997 Lions tour who was also Ireland's captain, was especially vocal. The idea was to clear the air but Dick and Andy took the comments personally and that was the beginning of the end. From a position where we had won our first seven matches to sit on top of the league, we began to lose games and at that point the club's trustees became involved.

I was called at home one evening by Edwin Glasgow, a barrister and chairman of the trustees, and asked my opinion. I told it as I saw it. I said that if Dick remained in charge the club was heading for relegation. It was an honest opinion. I said that players were on the verge of quitting in droves, that he was an excellent coach but that his man-management was awful. Jason said the same. Maybe the trustees did not believe what they were hearing. Maybe they wanted confirmation from a quorum of their players but another meeting was held at the Petersham Hotel. Roger Looker, Quins' Chairman, was present, along with twenty-six of the squad. The defining moment came when Roger posed a question. 'OK,' he said to the group. 'Take the contracts away. If none of you had any contractual obligations to Harlequins and I told you Dick and Andy were in place to coach for next season, how many of you would want to stay?' No one raised a hand.

That was the moment when the club knew they had to do something and Dick was sidelined. And being the highest profile player, I carried the can as far as Dick was concerned. Dick was stupid to make it personal. He should have looked and listened to what was happening around him. I had tried to tell him on a number of occasions to get off players' backs. So had Jason. But our combined efforts had no effect whatsoever. It shouldn't have come as a surprise to Dick but it obviously did. He's not spoken to me since. It upsets me that I was the focus for his anger but I was acting in the interests of the club. I would have felt far worse if I had thought, 'He's my mate. I'm not affected by his behaviour. I'll ignore the fact that he's ruining the lives of thirty-five players.' The one time I put myself out for the club, I copped it.

— 30 —
AT DEATH'S DOOR

ICK BEST's departure did not end the Harlequins saga.
Andy Keast was promoted into the director of rugby's job
and the problems continued. Many of the players had wanted
Andy out as well. They argued that he had come in on the same
ticket as Dick, had been tainted by the acrimonious mud-
slinging which had gone on, and would not be able to ignore
what had happened and take the club forward. The players
wanted a completely new man at the helm. But I saw it differently. I reasoned that, with Dick out of the way, Andy would
run things much more sensitively. It was not the first time that
I got a judgement call completely arse about face.

Andy went off on the Lions tour to South Africa as their
analyst. He is extraordinarily competent at analysing videos of
games, highlighting individual and team strengths and weaknesses, and the Lions needed his skill in this area. Andy was
also useful to the Lions in that he had coaching experience with
Natal and was tuned into South African rugby. It was in South
Africa that negotiations took place between Harlequins and
Andy to confirm him as Quins' new director of rugby. During
those negotiations I was told that, because of the previous
season, Andy was very wary of me and I decided to fly to
Durban to clear the air. The purpose of the visit was simple: to

see Andy, chat through any areas of disagreement between us, and talk about the forthcoming season. Those were the only reasons I went. The Lions were in the middle of a Test series against the Springboks but I did not take in a game. I just wanted to get together with Andy and resolve our differences, if any existed.

The visit provided a final chapter in the Fran Cotton saga. He saw me walk into the foyer of the team hotel in Durham and asked Jason Leonard what I was doing in South Africa. Jason told him and Fran said, 'I thought he didn't like Lions tours. When you see him, tell him I don't want him hanging around with any of the players. I don't want them put off.' It was an extraordinary remark to make and quite insulting, especially since Dean Richards, Mike Teague and Peter Winterbottom were all in South Africa with various supporters' tour parties and had been out with some of the Lions players without provoking any comment from Fran.

From the moment I arrived Andy did his level best to avoid me. I accept that he had commitments with the Lions, but he found it almost impossible to find a five-minute window where he and I could meet. We scheduled a meeting on the afternoon I was due to fly back to London, but instead of keeping that appointment, I was told that he had gone shopping. In the two days I was in Durban we got together over a cup of coffee twice, for maybe ten minutes, but it was clear he did not want to talk. It was hopeless. I reiterated that I was looking forward to the season, was fully committed to the club and wanted to help in any way that I was able. I found the experience confusing and I flew back more than a little frustrated. In the end, more in hope than anything else, I tried to convince myself that I had over-reacted, that the 1997/98 season would be one where I could really give club rugby a go. The international scene was done and dusted and it would be fun to play for Quins with comparatively little pressure.

The honeymoon period did not last long. Fifteen minutes before we assembled for the team photograph to herald the start of the 1997/98 season, Andy told Jason Leonard that he was no longer club captain and that he had asked Keith Wood to lead the side with Frenchman Thierry Lacroix as his deputy. Andy knew Thierry from his time in Natal and he had got on well with Woody on the Lions trip. It wasn't the thinking behind the decisions which worried me, just the way the decisions were conveyed. Giving Jason fifteen minutes to digest the news without fully explaining the reasons behind the change in personnel, and then telling the rest of the squad publicly, without allowing Jason time to come to terms with the blow, was not the best example of man-management I had witnessed.

That set the tone for the season. The first disagreement between Andy and myself arose over training schedules. Andy knew that my Quins contract stipulated that there would be certain times when I would be unavailable because of other business commitments but he was reluctant to publish long-term training schedules which would allow me to organise those commitments around my rugby. The following week's training was invariably posted on the club notice board on the Friday which made it impossible for me to plan ahead and arrange my working week to fit in. I did not know whether we would be training morning, noon or night or what that training would consist of. His response, when I asked for a structured week, was to say that rugby was now professional and that players should be available wherever and whenever required to fulfil their contractual obligations to the club. It was a no-win situation. I was getting crucified for missing training, yet whenever I asked for advance notice to allow me to put rugby first it was denied. Eventually Malcolm Wall, who had succeeded Roger Looker as club Chairman, interceded and persuaded Andy to work a monthly rota. But even then he would hold mine back as long as possible and I would have to ring him or see him before he would make it available.

Just when I thought I had sorted that issue, I was dropped. No advance warning, no phone call, just a team sheet without my name on it. I rang Keith Wood.

'Woody, what's going on?'

'Mate, you're not dropped. They don't think they're getting the best out of you. They don't think you're fit enough.'

'So dropping me is the best way of getting the best out of me, is it?'

'Will, you're not dropped. You're rested.'

'Woody, don't bullshit me. I'm dropped.'

'Listen, Will, you'll have to talk to Andy. Give him a call.'

So I did. I rang Andy and the conversation followed similar lines.

'I don't think you're fit enough,' Andy said.

'How do you know I'm not fit enough? You haven't tested me. Alan Watson's got my tests. Have you spoken to him?'

'No.'

'Well, how do you know if I'm fit or not?'

I knew I was on safe ground because Alan had been testing my fitness every three months since 1989. I had first gone to see him when a stress fracture of my shin refused to heal. Two Harley Street doctors had relieved me of a lot of money but had failed to pinpoint the problem. Alan discovered that the fracture was caused by a muscular imbalance in my legs which affected my running style and put pressure on the bone. Under his tutelage I built up certain muscle groups, changed my running style and the problem disappeared.

Alan was as scrupulously attentive to matters of fitness as he was with injuries. His preferred method of torture was to sit me on a cybex bike and get me to work to exhaustion in short spells. The first time I trained on the bike my thighs increased one and a half inches in size due to the build-up of lactic acid in the muscles. When the session ended I fell off the machine completely exhausted and lay on the floor in a foetal position for twenty minutes before throwing up. Alan was meticulous in all aspects of my rugby preparation and I knew that if he assured me my fitness was up to standard then that was the case. Andy was just using it as an excuse.

The next day I saw Andy and the other coaches at the club.

'I don't think your heart is in Quins,' Andy said. 'I don't believe you are committed to the club.'

But loyalty is a two-way thing. Those officials who accused me of being disloyal should take a long hard look into their shaving mirrors. Many's the time a New Zealander or a South African wandering through London on some sort of sabbatical was hoiked straight into the Harlequins first team, usually at the expense of some loyal soldier who hadn't missed a club training session for the best part of two years. Quins had no problem with that. They encouraged it in fact, basking in the reflected glory of having eight players from the club (seven Englishmen and Troy Coker, an Australian) in the 1991 World Cup final. So for them to bang the loyalty drum was a touch hypocritical.

Andy started to give me little tests so that I could convince him how loyal I was. If I was left out of the side he would give me the option of a weekend off rather than sitting on the bench to measure my desire. I used to choose the bench. It all seems extremely childish and petty now but at the time it was important. I wanted to play for Quins, to end my career with them in a season unencumbered by international duty. It mattered to me. I wasn't going to be forced out without a fight and I pursued Woody and Andy as ferociously as I could. Nothing they had said or done had made any sense to me. I was singled out for my supposed lack of fitness but I was fitter than Keith Wood. It would have been easier to accept if they thought I wasn't playing well, or if they had someone who was more capable than me, but they never hinted at that.

Ali's illness put the whole sorry situation into perspective. We had accompanied Colin and Sandy Herridge to the United States for a short holiday. It was the middle of the Five Nations Championship and everyone at Quins had been given a week off. The club knew where I was and who I was with. What should have been a relaxing few days amidst the glitter and buzz of America's liveliest city turned into a disaster when Ali contracted a virus and very nearly died. We were in our hotel with Henry our six-week-old son when Ali collapsed with acute stomach pains. I have never been as frightened in my entire life. She was curled up on the floor, unable to speak with the pain. I got hold of a doctor but he said he would be unable to visit for at least a couple of hours. I sensed that Ali would not hold out that long and screamed at the doctor to get here sooner. He told us to grab a taxi and head for the nearest hospital. By this stage Ali was barely able to walk, Henry was his usual demanding self and I was trying to get hold of a cab to take us all to a hospital we knew nothing about.

Emergency departments in American hospitals are unreal. We arrived to find two armed guards on the door and were forced to contact the staff via a speaker-phone before we were allowed in. Even then they would not examine Ali until they had recorded our details, including credit card numbers for payment. Ali was now grey, Henry had not been fed for two hours, we were due to fly home that evening and we had not been able to contact the Herridges.

I could see the doctors starting to panic. I'll never forget that feeling. I was hanging on to Henry in a completely alien environment watching something over which I had no control whatsoever unfold. Ali was beside herself, screaming with agony because the doctors were unable to prescribe any painkillers until they sourced the problem. Suddenly one of them thrust a piece of paper at me. 'Look, we have to operate. We don't know what the hell it is but we're losing her.' And I signed. I didn't know what I was signing. I didn't read the piece of paper or think about the ramifications of the decision I was making. I wasn't in a fit state to do any of those things. All I wanted was for Ali to get better.

They opened her up and discovered a virulent infection. As only the Americans can, the doctors subsequently showed me the pictures they had taken inside Ali with a microscopic camera. There was pus everywhere. She was put on heavy antibiotics which were introduced intravenously via a drip, and remained in hospital for eight days until she was healthy enough to leave.

I was told later that people with her complaint, who hadn't received the appropriate treatment quickly enough, had died. Even after the operation I was frantic with worry. I was convinced she was not going to pull through. The doctors said otherwise, but I refused to believe them. For two days she was unable to eat anything, throwing up all the time. She lost two stone in weight and she was wafer thin before the illness. I would go in and sit with her every day, all day. Apart from the Herridges, I did not speak to anyone for three days. Michelle Lineker and Ali's mother flew out to look after Henry when the Herridges were forced to return, and between us, with Ali in a wheel-chair, we eventually managed to get everyone home safely, though it would be four months before she regained her strength and returned to her old self.

We arrived back in England on the Saturday and the following Monday I reported for training at Harlequins. Colin Herridge had rung the club to tell them what had happened and to keep them informed of developments. I hadn't called because, stuck in a New York hospital for eight days, rugby wasn't exactly top of my agenda. The coaches never said a word when I turned up at the club. All the players were asking after Ali but Andy Keast never once referred to it. Instead I found a letter from him explaining that he had a problem with me, that he wanted a motivated squad, that he was concerned with the team not individuals, and that he intended to impose fines for missed training sessions. To be fair to Andy, the letter was written before I went to New York but there was still no phone call to say, 'Listen, I know what happened to Ali, come in and we'll talk about the note.'

I went ballistic on reading the letter and called Malcolm Wall, the Quins Chairman, in an attempt to straighten everything out. He must have spoken to Andy. The next day I walked into Andy's office.

'Have you got a problem with me? You've spoken to the chairman.'

'Keasty, let me explain what happened in New York.' Which

I did. 'I'm still fairly emotional about the last ten days and my state of mind was not improved when I arrived back to find your letter. If I over-reacted I'm sorry, but understand it from my point of view. It wasn't exactly the best couple of weeks of my life.'

His reply staggered me. 'I don't think you handled yourself in a professional way,' he said. 'You didn't ring us from New York.'

'Andy, for God's sake. Colin Herridge rang. He used to be a director of the club. You knew what was going on. I wasn't in the mood to talk to anyone.'

But Andy was adamant. 'I don't think it was very professional,' he reiterated. I couldn't believe what I was hearing. 'Look,' Andy went on. 'You're not in the side for the weekend because you didn't train. If you don't train, you don't play. It's a professional sport, Will. You've got to come to terms with that.'

'Andy, you don't seem to understand. Ali nearly died in New York and you're talking about missing training sessions.'

It was then that I knew that Harlequins and rugby were over for me. I turned on my heel and left the room.

Malcolm Wall tried to persuade me to change my mind but it was made up. I wasn't in love with the sport and in any case I was too long in the tooth to seek out a new club and start all over again.

The saddest thing for me is that Andy Keast is one of the most disappointing men I have ever met in rugby. I had loved rugby from the age of seven and his one achievement was to extinguish my enthusiasm and tarnish some of the memories. He did that in six months. I had hoped it would be different after Dick Best left, but Andy is not in the same league as Dick as a coach, and his man-management is far worse. Harlequins eventually concurred because three months after I quit Andy left by mutual agreement.

I don't miss rugby and I don't regret the decision to quit. I was disappointed with the circumstances which caused me to walk away but I never intended to ride out of rugby on a white charger accompanied by banners and trumpets. Life doesn't work like that. My last game for Quins was against London Irish. I was substituted halfway through but it's not the leaving which I remember, more the feeling when I ran onto the pitch at the start of the game. I stood in the middle of the arena and I didn't feel anything. Nothing, not the slightest shiver of anticipation for the battle ahead. There was no sense of excitement. Whatever level of rugby I've played, I've always left the changing room intending to achieve something but the desire wasn't there against the Irish. Aged thirty-two, I had finally been weaned off rugby.

I don't feel bitter towards Quins because, to me, the club has always been the players and I'm still in touch with them. But the club has got to get its act together or it will not do justice to its proud heritage. I hope Malcolm Wall and Edwin Glasgow come to their senses and build a professional team to work in a professional structure. You can't run a rugby club on a part-time basis with individuals who are ill-equipped to hold down their present positions.

At least the episode with Andy Keast helped me grow up. During this time it had been becoming clear that Ali and I were not getting on as well as we had done. The bond which had drawn us so tightly together when we shared the Covent Garden flat had loosened and the mutual understanding and affection we had for each other then was not so apparent. There were no volcanic eruptions, no moments of insight to make us realise that a life together wouldn't be fulfilling and rewarding. The process was far more gradual than that. But, slowly, I came to understand that we had too little in common; that to hang on to each other, even for Henry's sake, would be to live a lie which would, ultimately, be damaging for all three of us.

I know people will accuse me of callousness of toying with the lives of others. Many will say that Michelle Lineker was dead right when she warned Ali not to get involved with me. I can't do anything about that. All I know is that I lived with the growing knowledge that Ali and I weren't made for each other for a year after Henry's birth, and it tore me apart. The easy option would have been to stick together, to pretend that everything was all right, but I'm not like that.

Heaven knows what the future may bring, but whatever happens I will remain committed to Ali and Henry. We have agreed to live apart but close to each other so that we can spend time together; in this way I can try and give all the help and encouragement I can to Henry in his life because, like all fathers, I believe he is a very special little man. It is not an ideal situation, and certainly not one of which I am in the least bit proud.

— 31 —

GOING FORWARD LOOKING BACK

R ICHARD BRANSON offered the possibility of a final chapter
to my career. He wrote and asked if I would consider joining the London Broncos, a Rugby League club which he owned.
Part of me was flattered and up for a new challenge but deep
down I knew I wouldn't be in it for the long haul. Home matches
would be OK. The Broncos ground-shared with Harlequins but
it was the away games to places like Hull I didn't fancy. I was
too old to learn the techniques and disciplines of a new sport
and bed down with a fresh set of team-mates.

Instead I would remember the Union good times, and they
had been many: my first match as captain and the victory against
Australia; the World Cup quarter-final in 1991 against France,
the most physically demanding game I've ever played in; beating New Zealand in 1993 with the Twickenham crowd at its
most fervent; the First Test in Pretoria in 1994 when we smashed
the Springboks; the three Grand Slams. Those are memories
I will take to the grave, evidence of England's rise from the
under-achievers of European rugby to credibility on the world
stage.

Yet that credibility remains paper thin. Defeat by Australia in
the World Cup final of 1991 and the humiliation inflicted by
Jonah Lomu and his fellow All Blacks in South Africa four years

later have shown that England have much to do before they can share the same peer group with the southern hemisphere countries. That was always my benchmark as player and captain, and I did not achieve it. At the time, those defeats were achingly important. They still smart, but the moment you leave the side the hurt fades and now it is the players who provide the strongest memories. Seeing that great French full-back Serge Blanco bidding farewell to some of his English mates in the Parc des Princes changing room after the 1991 World Cup quarter-final was especially poignant. We should have marked his departure with an organised tribute of some sort but all he received was a few cursory pats on the back from some exhausted England players. But that was what it was like. You lived for the moment. Tomorrow would take care of itself and the past was irrelevant even when that involved Blanco, a man I admired enormously.

Likewise with David Campese. At odds for much of our respective careers, I was never able to tell him how much I enjoyed his talent. His awareness of space was exemplary and he had the balls to try things which ordinary mortals could not even conceptualise. With Nick Farr-Jones and Michael Lynagh, it was their intelligence which set them apart. Individually they were special, together they were unbeatable. Nothing escaped them, and they were able to play within themselves, yet, in so doing, set standards of excellence which were impossible to match. Sean Fitzpatrick offered an unrivalled intensity. He was simply the most focused, driven individual I have ever come across on a rugby pitch. François Pienaar was different again. His greatness lay in the way he could extract performances from his team. He was not the finest flanker in the world but he was a special leader. Before the World Cup he took the Springboks round Robben Island to see the prison where Nelson Mandela was incarcerated for so many years. That in itself was remarkable. The Springboks were the symbol of what Mandela had been struggling against all his life and Pienaar was confronting his team with a monument to their injustice and using it as a springboard for them to unite the country by winning the tournament. I did not agree with Pienaar and his players using the World Cup final as a glorified prayer mat when the referee blew for full time. I've always thought God has more important events to worry about than the outcome of a rugby match, but there was no denying the Springboks' unity and strength of purpose and Pienaar's charismatic leadership.

Can England produce players of that stature? They can and they have. Dean Richards, Peter Winterbottom, Wade Dooley, Rory Underwood, Jeremy Guscott, Lawrence Dallaglio, Martin Johnson and Rob Andrew were all good enough to make and grace the sides which Pienaar, Farr-Jones, Lynagh and Fitz-patrick played in. The reasons for England under-achieving have been structural. English rugby has never evolved a level of com-petition to match the Super 12 tournament in the southern hemi-sphere. In those countries everything is geared to producing the best possible international team, to the extent where players are moved to different provinces if there is a surplus in a particular position. Every effort is made to assist the national coaches in producing successful outfits. In England, Geoff Cooke, Jack Rowell and especially Clive Woodward have been constantly frustrated in their attempts to raise standards.

Fran Cotton is right when he claims that club rugby is no preparation for the international scene, but he is off-beam when he suggests that the way forward is to establish regional sides to include England's top sixty players. Regional sides have been tried before and they were shelved because the players did not want to play for them and the fans did not want to watch them. The culture of rugby in this country is based on the clubs, not some amorphous geographic lumps which are impossible to identify with.

The way forward is to develop a dozen or so super-clubs across Europe and get the best players playing each other in that competition. Chuck in the best referees and coaches and standards would shoot up. It won't happen because existing clubs would be put out of business as a result, but until someone takes steps to restructure English rugby along those lines we will always be playing catch-up to Australia, New Zealand and South Africa.

Yet there is more to sport than trophy-gathering and the quest for supremacy. I've always wanted to get as much out of myself as possible, whatever I'm doing. I'm anxious to develop emotionally, psychologically, to learn more the whole time. That's always been important to me. I'm intrigued to know how much I can do, how much I can take, what my breaking point is. I just want to find out what my limits are and, once I've discovered them, push them that little bit further. International rugby offered me the opportunity for self-discovery and I stepped away when it stopped presenting the same intensity of challenge. After ten years I had experienced it often enough to be familiar with it. I didn't retire because I had beaten it. Even to think that would be ridiculously arrogant, but I had sucked it dry and it was time to move on to something else.

I don't necessarily want to achieve a great deal more in life but I want to learn more. It's not to do with money or status. It's more to do with self-awareness, self-discovery. Part of me thinks that at sixty I want to sit down and be one of those people that eighteen-year-olds consider a wise old man, very calm, very together. Occasionally you come across old guys who seem really at peace with themselves, very knowledgeable. They might not say much but when you talk to them they will offer advice which is really pertinent. That's where I want to be, someone who has worked a few things out. I don't think I'll ever get there. I can't see myself as a calm person, but that's the ambition.

Over the past couple of years I have been making some tentative steps in this direction thanks to the help and therapy I've received from Alice, John Cleese's wife. I had met John first at some function and then, during the World Cup in 1995, he wrote me a letter telling me that he had read a book which he thought I might be interested in. He was aware that my company offered seminars in motivation and leadership and asked if I wanted to have dinner when I returned from South Africa. I gave him a ring when I got back, went out for a meal, and got to know him from there. Then, when all the Diana stuff blew up, he called me again and said: 'Listen, if you ever want to talk matters through with anyone, I can recommend Alice. That's what she does.' We met and immediately I knew it was going to work out. I felt safe opening up to her because she was married to a very famous person and could understand something of what I was going through. I wouldn't have trusted anyone else.

Alice was especially sensitive and our discussions were genuinely interesting as well as enabling me to make sense of a whole host of issues. Alice has a mews house which she uses as an office near where she lives. I used to meet her there and just chat one-to-one. I was staggered at how much came from my relationship with my parents. Talking with Alice helped me to articulate my views on women, how I saw myself, retirement and the associated emotions. I discovered that I behaved in certain ways in certain situations and eventually I began to understand why I behaved like that.

Take my relationship with friends. If they did something which upset me, I wouldn't tell them. I would just black mark them. It sounds crazy but when they reached ten black marks that would be it. I wouldn't speak to them and they wouldn't know why because I never talked it through with them. This may have come from the way my mother behaved with me. She rarely explained why she was angry or upset and I suppose that was the behaviour I became used to and grew up with. I was never able to say to someone, 'Look, you've upset me here,' without getting worked up.

My diffidence in forming close friendships surfaced in other ways. If I had a mate and hadn't spoken to him for six months I'd feel guilty. I would ignore the fact that he hadn't rung me for six months. If he did call I would be a bit embarrassed, stand-offish even, instead of thinking that he, like me, had probably been furiously busy and just hadn't found the time to keep in touch. That would have been the rational position to take but I rarely took it. I have always felt guilty for anything that has happened, another consequence of my childhood. A lot of the time I get criticised for being aloof. The truth is that I'm actually insecure and that's why I keep myself to myself.

Alice helped me to come to terms with that and people who know me say I'm now much more relaxed. We've stopped the regular meetings but I still see her when there's stuff I want to work at. She clarifies things all the time and helped in the early days with Ali. 'For eight years you were captain of England,' Alice said. 'You were used to all the fuss and attention which went with the job. You thought it was all perfectly normal. Then you met Ali and took her to these functions. It must have been very hard for her. That's a life very few people understand.' Put like that, it explained why Ali was initially quite shy in certain situations, but I had never even thought about it in those terms.

Alice and I also explored the whole rugby phenomenon when I was giving up the captaincy and contemplating retirement. I was concerned that I might feel bitter, might even dislike the guy who would take over from me. It was very useful to talk it all through with her and get a sense of what it would be like. I had to understand the future before I made the decision. She told me to think of it in terms of moving on. I had finished that part of my life, learnt what I could from it, and it was time to set new goals.

Once you've accepted that bitterness and regret are inevitable, part of the process, the decision becomes easier to take and live with. Not going on the 1997 Lions tour to South Africa was a similar experience. The Lions ended up beating the Springboks 2–1 in the Tests, a magnificent achievement, and part of me thought, 'Bugger it. I should have been there.' I felt like meeting these new young Lions off the plane and roaring and saying I can still do this but, once you've dealt with the macho sporting nonsense and considered the other aspects of touring, the decision to stay at home made perfect sense. I would have had to spend two and a half months in a hotel on the Lions tour which was precisely why I gave up – all those interminable team meetings and training sessions, all those boring hours spent killing time because you couldn't go out and do anything which would sap your energy. You forget about those moments when you represent your country or the British Isles but they are as much a part of the whole business as running out into a packed and passionate Twickenham stadium.

Getting older and mellowing out has also helped. In the last two years with Alice's help I've learned to acknowledge and accept my faults. My instinct had been to deny or ignore any failings but I know now that I'm vain. I've got an ego. Coming to terms with my own pet hates has been very therapeutic, too. I can't stand lateness. Punctuality is a big thing with me and I abhor people who dither, who don't know where they're going. I'm very practical. If there's a problem I will think it all through, very deliberately – worst case/best case scenario. Once I've rationalised it in those terms, it's just a question of making the decision and following it through. I'm not one for second thoughts. And if the decision or course of action looks iffy, my escape clause is to put the issue into context. If it all goes belly-up, if England lose, or I don't get picked for a team, or if my business suddenly folds, it isn't the end of the world. No one's dead.

Having said that, there are certain areas in my life which are sacrosanct and will always be so. Not very many people are dear to me, but those who are I try to look after as best I can. I hate interference of any kind. Recently, I suppose, I've watered down my views and become happier to listen to others. I never used to take advice in my private life because I honestly believed I knew better and could sort out problems for myself.

And now it's over. Rugby, the pride of representing my country, the honour of playing with my heroes. All gone. Geoff Cooke got it about right when he talked about the impact of his resignation. 'It's like taking your hand out of a bucket of water,' he said. 'You'd like to see a hole, some evidence that something has been removed, but in seconds the surface has reformed and no one has noticed the difference.'

Clever man, Geoff Cooke.

CAREER RECORD

The facts and figures of Will Carling's career
have been compiled by John Griffiths

WILL CARLING'S SENIOR INTERNATIONAL CAREER

LOST 9–10 v FRANCE, 16th January 1988, Parc des Princes, Paris
Makes debut as a Durham University student in the first England XV managed by Geoff Cooke. Underdogs England give France a fright in Paris. Carling makes a clever first-half break to send Kevin Simms to within an inch of the French line.
England: J M Webb; M E Harrison (*captain*), W D C Carling,
K G Simms, R Underwood; L Cusworth, N D Melville;
P A G Rendall, B C Moore, J A Probyn, J Orwin, W A Dooley,
M G Skinner, D Richards, P J Winterbottom
England scorers: *Penalty goals:* Webb 2   *Dropped goal:* Cusworth

LOST 3–11 v WALES, 6th February 1988, Twickenham
Twickenham Test debut. Six years pass before he plays in another Five Nations defeat at home.
England: J M Webb; M E Harrison (*captain*), W D C Carling,
K G Simms, R Underwood; L Cusworth, N D Melville;
P A G Rendall, B C Moore, J A Probyn, J Orwin, W A Dooley,
M G Skinner, D Richards, P J Winterbottom
England scorer: *Penalty goal:* Webb

WON 9–6 v SCOTLAND, 5th March 1988, Murrayfield, Edinburgh
In a dour match devoid of tries, Carling makes telling defensive contribution to England's first away victory in the Five Nations for six seasons.
England: J M Webb; R Underwood, S J Halliday, W D C Carling,
C Oti; C R Andrew, N D Melville (captain); P A G Rendall,
B C Moore, J A Probyn, J Orwin, W A Dooley, M G Skinner,
D Richards, P J Winterbottom (rep G W Rees)
England scorers: *Penalty goals:* Webb 2   *Dropped goal:* Andrew

WON 35–3 v IRELAND, 19th March 1988, Twickenham
England register a then record victory over Ireland. The team scores six second-half tries, Carling and the midfield setting up five for the wings. Swing Low, Sweet Chariot, later to become the anthem of the Carling era, heard at Twickenham for the first time. England finish third in the Five Nations.
England: J M Webb; R Underwood, S J Halliday, W D C Carling,
C Oti; C R Andrew, N D Melville (captain) (rep R M Harding);

P A G Rendall, B C Moore, J A Probyn, J Orwin, W A Dooley,
M G Skinner, D Richards, G W Rees
England scorers: *Tries:* Oti 3, Underwood 2, Rees   *Conversions:*
Andrew 3, Webb   *Penalty goal:* Webb

WON 21–10 v IRELAND, 23rd April 1988, Lansdowne Road, Dublin

*In the special Dublin Millennium match, Carling turns in another solid
performance to confirm his place in the England side for the summer tour to
Australia. Roger Uttley predicts that the side could become as successful as
the 1980 Grand Slam team.*
England: J M Webb; J Bentley, S J Halliday, W D C Carling,
R Underwood; C R Andrew, R M Harding; P A G Rendall (rep
G J Chilcott), B C Moore, J A Probyn, J Orwin (*captain*),
W A Dooley, M G Skinner, D W Egerton, G W Rees
England scorers: *Tries:* Underwood, Harding   *Conversions:* Webb 2
Penalty goal: Webb 3

LOST 8–28 v AUSTRALIA, 12th June 1988, Concord Oval, Sydney

*Returns to the England side having missed the Brisbane Test owing to final
examinations for his Durham University course in psychology.*
England: J M Webb; B J Evans, B Barley, W D C Carling,
R Underwood; C R Andrew, R M Harding; P A G Rendall,
B C Moore, J A Probyn, J Orwin (*captain*), W A Dooley, G W Rees,
D Richards, R A Robinson
England scorers: *Tries:* Underwood, Richards

WON 25–12 v FIJI, 16th June 1988, National Stadium, Suva

*Last England Test as an ordinary foot soldier. More than eight years pass before
he again wears an England shirt without the added burdens of the captaincy.*
England: C R Andrew; B J Evans, B Barley, W D C Carling,
R Underwood; S Barnes, R M Harding (*captain*); G S Pearce,
B C Moore, G J Chilcott, N C Redman, W A Dooley, G W Rees (rep
D W Egerton), D Richards, R A Robinson
England scorers: *Tries:* Underwood 2, Barley   *Conversions:* Barnes 2
Penalty goal: Barnes 3

WON 28–19 v AUSTRALIA, 5th November 1988, Twickenham

*Leads England for the first time as the youngest member of the team and, at
22, the youngest man to skipper England since Peter Howard in 1931. Leading
from the front, he makes the break that leads to Simon Halliday's decisive*

late try as England rattle up their highest-ever score against the Aussies. Reluctantly leaves the field in injury time with concussion. One leading critic reports, 'He [Carling] may have ushered his team into a new era.'
England: J M Webb; A T Harriman, W D C Carling (*captain*) (rep J R D Buckton), S J Halliday, R Underwood; C R Andrew, C D Morris; P A G Rendall, B C Moore, J A Probyn, W A Dooley, P J Ackford, R A Robinson, D Richards, D W Egerton
England scorers: *Tries:* Underwood 2, Morris, Halliday   *Conversions:* Webb 3   *Penalty goals:* Webb 2

DRAWN 12–12 v SCOTLAND, 4th February 1989, Twickenham
First Five Nations match as captain. England disappoint their followers by failing to make the most of their countless attacking opportunities.
England: J M Webb; R Underwood, W D C Carling (*captain*), S J Halliday, C Oti; C R Andrew, C D Morris; P A G Rendall, B C Moore, J A Probyn, W A Dooley, P J Ackford, M C Teague, D Richards, R A Robinson
England scorers: *Penalty goals:* Andrew 2, Webb 2

WON 16–3 v IRELAND, 18th February 1989, Lansdowne Road, Dublin
First Five Nations success as captain. His growing confidence as a captain is reflected in a second-half decision to eschew a kickable penalty and go, instead, for a tap-penalty. The forwards maul to the line for a try which is claimed by both Dewi Morris and Brian Moore.
England: J M Webb; R Underwood, W D C Carling (*captain*), S J Halliday, C Oti; C R Andrew, C D Morris; P A G Rendall, B C Moore, J A Probyn (rep G J Chilcott), W A Dooley, P J Ackford, M C Teague, D Richards, R A Robinson
England scorers: *Tries:* Richards, Moore   *Conversion:* Andrew
Penalty goals: Andrew 2

WON 11–0 v FRANCE, 4th March 1989, Twickenham
Scores first England try as his side records its first win against France since 1982. His unbeaten team are installed as favourites to win the Five Nations title.
England: J M Webb; R Underwood, W D C Carling (*captain*), S J Halliday, C Oti; C R Andrew, C D Morris; P A G Rendall, B C Moore, G J Chilcott, W A Dooley, P J Ackford, M C Teague, D Richards, R A Robinson

England scorers: *Tries:* Carling, Robinson   *Penalty goal:* Andrew

LOST 9–12 v WALES, 18th March 1989, Cardiff Arms Park
Not even a resurgent England side can break the Arms Park bogey. A lack of tactical flexibility and a Welsh try awarded in error leave England to lick their wounds after losing their first match of the season. Carling's first Five Nations in charge finishes with his side runners-up to France.
England: J M Webb; R Underwood, W D C Carling (*captain*), S J Halliday, C Oti; C R Andrew, C D Morris; P A G Rendall, B C Moore, G J Chilcott, W A Dooley, P J Ackford, M C Teague (rep G W Rees), D Richards, R A Robinson
England scorer: *Penalty goals:* Andrew 2   *Dropped goal:* Andrew

WON 58–23 v FIJI, 4th November 1989, Twickenham
After missing England's game with Romania and a Lions tour of Australia through injury, Carling bounces back to launch a world record centre partner-ship (45 pairings including a Test for the Lions) with Jeremy Guscott. The skipper's straight running is a revelation in England's ten-try romp.
England: S D Hodgkinson; R Underwood, W D C Carling (*captain*), J C Guscott, M D Bailey (rep S J Halliday); C R Andrew, R J Hill; M S Linnett, B C Moore, A R Mullins, W A Dooley, P J Ackford, M G Skinner, D W Egerton, P J Winterbottom (rep G W Rees)
England scorers: *Tries:* Underwood 5, Skinner, Bailey, Linnett, Ackford, Guscott   *Conversions:* Hodgkinson 5, Andrew   *Penalty goals:* Hodgkinson 2

WON 23–0 v IRELAND, 20th January 1990, Twickenham
England give notice of their potential, especially through the sumptuous running of the captain and the rest of the midfield backs. Ireland are demol-ished by a brilliant English performance in the last quarter of the game.
England: S D Hodgkinson; R Underwood, W D C Carling (*captain*), J C Guscott, M D Bailey; C R Andrew, R J Hill; P A G Rendall, B C Moore, J A Probyn, W A Dooley, P J Ackford, M G Skinner, D W Egerton, P J Winterbottom
England scorers: *Tries:* Underwood, Probyn, Egerton, Guscott   *Conversions:* Hodgkinson 2   *Penalty goals:* Hodgkinson

WON 26–7 v FRANCE, 3rd February 1990, Parc des Princes, Paris
England's biggest post-war winning margin in Paris is sealed with Carling's late score – his second try in consecutive appearances against the French. England, moreover, achieve a stylish win through playing fifteen-man rugby.

England: S D Hodgkinson; R Underwood, W D C Carling (*captain*),
J C Guscott, M D Bailey; C R Andrew, R J Hill; P A G Rendall,
B C Moore, J A Probyn, W A Dooley, P J Ackford, M G Skinner,
M C Teague, P J Winterbottom
England scorers: *Tries:* Underwood, Guscott, Carling *Conversion:*
Hodgkinson *Penalty goals:* Hodgkinson 4

WON 34–6 v WALES, 17th February 1990, Twickenham
England carry on from where they left off against the French, posting a record winning margin against the Welsh. The captain scores the first of England's four tries with a determined effort in the corner.
England: S D Hodgkinson; S J Halliday, W D C Carling (*captain*),
J C Guscott, R Underwood; C R Andrew, R J Hill; P A G Rendall,
B C Moore, J A Probyn, W A Dooley, P J Ackford, M G Skinner,
M C Teague, P J Winterbottom
England scorers: *Tries:* Underwood 2, Carling, Hill *Conversions:*
Hodgkinson 3 *Penalty goals:* Hodgkinson 4

LOST 7–13 v SCOTLAND, 17th March 1990, Murrayfield, Edinburgh
In a head-on collision for the Grand Slam, England's chariot is overturned by a resolute Scottish XV. Carling makes the clean break that leads to Jerry Guscott's try, but the captain is unable to inspire an over-confident side and England, once again, finish as runners-up in the Five Nations.
England: S D Hodgkinson; S J Halliday, W D C Carling (*captain*),
J C Guscott (rep M D Bailey), R Underwood; C R Andrew, R J Hill;
P A G Rendall, B C Moore, J A Probyn, P J Ackford, W A Dooley,
M G Skinner, M C Teague, P J Winterbottom
England scorers: *Try:* Guscott *Penalty goal:* Hodgkinson

WON 25–12 v ARGENTINA, 28th July 1990, Vélez Sarsfield, Buenos Aires
After losing three of their first four tour matches, England show that they can adapt their tactics to match the occasion when appropriate. Carling adopts aggressive defence and forward dominance to pave the way to an important victory. He also sets up the decisive score of the match: a corner try by Chris Oti.
England: S D Hodgkinson; N J Heslop, W D C Carling (*captain*),
J R D Buckton, C Oti; D Pears, R J Hill; J Leonard, B C Moore,
J A Probyn, N C Redman, W A Dooley, M G Skinner, D Ryan,
P J Winterbottom

England scorers: *Tries:* Ryan, Oti   *Conversion:* Hodgkinson   *Penalty goals:* Hodgkinson 5

LOST 13–15 v ARGENTINA, 4th August 1990, Vélez Sarsfield, Buenos Aires

England discover how hard it is to win a series in Argentina. Playing a more expansive game than the week before, they lose by five penalties despite scoring two tries. Carling has a hand in the first try and makes a 50-metre dash late in the match that leads to a missed penalty attempt by Simon Hodgkinson.
England: S D Hodgkinson; N J Heslop, W D C Carling (*captain*), J R D Buckton, C Oti; D Pears, R J Hill; J Leonard, B C Moore, J A Probyn, N C Redman, W A Dooley (rep D W Egerton), M G Skinner, D Ryan, P J Winterbottom
England scorers: *Tries:* Hodgkinson, Heslop   *Conversion:* Hodgkinson   *Penalty goal:* Hodgkinson

WON 51–0 v ARGENTINA, 3rd November 1990, Twickenham

Forwards and backs combine effectively to rattle up England's highest score without reply at Test level.
England: S D Hodgkinson; N J Heslop, W D C Carling (*captain*), J C Guscott, R Underwood; C R Andrew, R J Hill; J Leonard, C J Olver, J A Probyn, P J Ackford (rep G W Rees), W A Dooley, J P Hall, D Richards, P J Winterbottom
England scorers: *Tries:* Underwood 3, Guscott 2, Hill, Hall *Conversions:* Hodgkinson 7   *Penalty goals:* Hodgkinson 3

WON 25–6 v WALES, 19th January 1991, Cardiff Arms Park

England's then biggest Cardiff win is their first in the Welsh capital since 1963. Carling becomes the first captain to lead England to successive wins against Wales since Ronald Cove-Smith in 1928 and 1929.
England: S D Hodgkinson; N J Heslop, W D C Carling (*captain*), J C Guscott, R Underwood; C R Andrew, R J Hill; J Leonard, B C Moore, J A Probyn, P J Ackford, W A Dooley, M C Teague, D Richards, P J Winterbottom
England scorers: *Try:* Teague   *Penalty goals:* Hodgkinson 7

WON 21–12 v SCOTLAND, 16th February 1991, Twickenham

England's 11th victory under Carling matches the national record established by Bill Beaumont who was successful 11 times in 21 games as skipper.
England: S D Hodgkinson; N J Heslop, W D C Carling (*captain*), J C Guscott, R Underwood; C R Andrew, R J Hill; J Leonard,

B C Moore, J A Probyn, P J Ackford, W A Dooley, M C Teague,
D Richards, P J Winterbottom
England scorers: *Try:* Heslop   *Conversion:* Hodgkinson   *Penalty goals:* Hodgkinson 5

WON 16–7 v IRELAND, 2nd March 1991, Lansdowne Road, Dublin

England's first recognised award under Carling's captaincy is the Triple Crown won in Dublin. Carling becomes the most successful England captain of all time, notching up his 12th victory.
England: S D Hodgkinson; N J Heslop, W D C Carling (*captain*),
J C Guscott, R Underwood; C R Andrew, R J Hill; J Leonard,
B C Moore, J A Probyn, P J Ackford, W A Dooley, M C Teague,
D Richards, P J Winterbottom
England scorers: *Tries:* Underwood, Teague   *Conversion:* Hodgkinson   *Penalty goals:* Hodgkinson 2

WON 21–19 v FRANCE, 16th March 1991, Twickenham

The Grand Slam is England's for the first time since 1980. Carling is the first man to captain an unchanged England XV to the Five Nations title.
England: S D Hodgkinson; N J Heslop, W D C Carling (*captain*),
J C Guscott, R Underwood; C R Andrew, R J Hill; J Leonard,
B C Moore, J A Probyn, P J Ackford, W A Dooley, M C Teague,
D Richards, P J Winterbottom
England scorers: *Try:* Underwood   *Conversion:* Hodgkinson
Penalty goals: Hodgkinson 4   *Dropped goal:* Andrew

WON 28–12 v FIJI, 20th July 1991, National Stadium, Suva

England make an unimpressive start to their World Cup warm-up tour of Fiji and Australia. Carling's searing break midway through the second spell leads to a Rory Underwood try that is the catalyst for a late scoring surge. England's sixth successive Test win marks their best international run since 1929.
England: J M Webb; R Underwood, W D C Carling (*captain*),
J C Guscott, C Oti; C R Andrew, R J Hill; J Leonard, B C Moore,
J A Probyn, N C Redman, M C Bayfield, M C Teague (rep
M G Skinner), D Richards, G W Rees
England scorers: *Tries:* Probyn, Underwood, Andrew   *Conversions:* Webb 2   *Penalty goals:* Webb 2   *Dropped goals:* Andrew 2

LOST 15–40 v AUSTRALIA, 27th July 1991, Sydney Football Stadium

England realise the enormity of the World Cup task ahead as Australia become only the second side in history to reach 40 points in a Test against them. Only consolation for the captain is that his clean break early in the match leads to a score for Jerry Guscott.

England: J M Webb; R Underwood, W D C Carling (*captain*), J C Guscott, C Oti; C R Andrew, R J Hill; J Leonard, B C Moore, J A Probyn, P J Ackford, M C Bayfield, M C Teague, D Richards, P J Winterbottom

England scorers: *Try:* Guscott   *Conversion:* Webb   *Penalty goals:* Webb 3

LOST 12–18 v NEW ZEALAND, 3rd October 1991, Twickenham

World Cup campaign opens with a solid England performance against the defending World Champions. Carling loses consecutive Tests as captain for the first time.

England: J M Webb; R Underwood, W D C Carling (*captain*), J C Guscott, C Oti; C R Andrew, R J Hill; J Leonard, B C Moore, J A Probyn, P J Ackford, W A Dooley, M C Teague, D Richards, P J Winterbottom

England scorers: *Penalty goals:* Webb 3   *Dropped goal:* Andrew

WON 36–6 v ITALY, 8th October 1991, Twickenham

Carling leads England for the 21st time in this World Cup pool match, equalling the national captaincy record set by Bill Beaumont between 1978 and 1982.

England: J M Webb; C Oti, W D C Carling (*captain*), J C Guscott, R Underwood; C R Andrew, R J Hill; J Leonard, B C Moore, J A Probyn (rep P A G Rendall), P J Ackford, N C Redman, M C Teague, D Richards, P J Winterbottom

England scorers: *Tries:* Guscott 2, Underwood, Webb   *Conversions:* Webb 4   *Penalty goals:* Webb 4

WON 37–9 v UNITED STATES, 11th October 1991, Twickenham

England complete their World Cup pool matches by coasting to victory against the US Eagles. Carling sets a new England captaincy record, leading the side for the 22nd time in a Test. Celebrates by scoring his fourth try for his country.

England: S D Hodgkinson; N J Heslop, W D C Carling (*captain*), S J Halliday, R Underwood; C R Andrew, R J Hill; J Leonard,

C J Olver, G S Pearce, N C Redman, W A Dooley, M G Skinner,
D Richards, G W Rees
England scorers: *Tries:* Underwood 2, Heslop, Skinner, Carling
Conversions: Hodgkinson 4   *Penalty goals:* Hodgkinson 3

WON 19–10 v FRANCE, 19th October 1991, Parc des Princes, Paris

Carling becomes the first England captain to lead the side to four consecutive wins against France. His injury time try sets the seal on this World Cup quarter-final.
England: J M Webb; N J Heslop, W D C Carling (*captain*),
J C Guscott, R Underwood; C R Andrew, R J Hill; J Leonard,
B C Moore, J A Probyn, P J Ackford, W A Dooley, M G Skinner,
M C Teague, P J Winterbottom
England scorers: *Tries:* Underwood , Carling   *Conversion:* Webb
Penalty goals: Webb 3

WON 9–6 v SCOTLAND, 26th October 1991, Murrayfield, Edinburgh

Murrayfield 1990 is avenged as Carling becomes the only Home Unions captain to date to lead his country to a World Cup final.
England: J M Webb; S J Halliday, W D C Carling (*captain*),
J C Guscott, R Underwood; C R Andrew, R J Hill; J Leonard,
B C Moore, J A Probyn, P J Ackford, W A Dooley, M G Skinner,
M C Teague, P J Winterbottom
England scorers: *Penalty goals:* Webb 2   *Dropped goal:* Andrew

LOST 6–12 v AUSTRALIA, 2nd November 1991, Twickenham

The World Cup final proves a match too far for England, who are unable to tighten the tactical screw on a first-rate Australian XV. Carling, in his 32nd Test, equals Paul Dodge's record for most appearances in the England centre.
England: J M Webb; S J Halliday, W D C Carling (*captain*),
J C Guscott, R Underwood; C R Andrew, R J Hill; J Leonard,
B C Moore, J A Probyn, P J Ackford, W A Dooley, M G Skinner,
M C Teague, P J Winterbottom
England scorer: *Penalty goals:* Webb 2

WON 25–7 v SCOTLAND, 18th January 1992, Murrayfield, Edinburgh

England's margin of victory is their then highest at Murrayfield. Carling becomes England's most-capped centre.
England: J M Webb; S J Halliday, W D C Carling (*captain*),

J C Guscott, R Underwood; C R Andrew, C D Morris; J Leonard,
B C Moore, J A Probyn, M C Bayfield, W A Dooley, M G Skinner,
T A K Rodber (rep D Richards), P J Winterbottom
England scorers: *Tries:* Underwood, Morris   *Conversion:* Webb
Penalty goals: Webb 4   *Dropped goal:* Guscott

WON 38–9 v IRELAND, 1st February 1992, Twickenham
*Running the ball at every opportunity, England record their highest score in
a Five Nations match since 1914 as Carling tucks his 20th win as England
captain under his belt.*
England: J M Webb; S J Halliday, W D C Carling (*captain*), J C Guscott,
R Underwood; C R Andrew, C D Morris; J Leonard, B C Moore,
J A Probyn, M C Bayfield, W A Dooley, M G Skinner, T A K Rodber,
P J Winterbottom
England scorers: *Tries:* Webb 2, Halliday, Underwood, Morris,
Guscott   *Conversions:* Webb 4   *Penalty goals:* Webb 2

WON 31–13 v FRANCE, 15th February 1992, Parc des Princes
*Another exhilarating display. England's score is their highest at the modern
Parc des Princes and takes their total for the season to 94 in only three
matches, passing their previous championship record of 90 in four games in
1990. Two-thirds of the French front-row is sent off in the last ten minutes.*
England: J M Webb; S J Halliday, W D C Carling (*captain*),
J C Guscott, R Underwood; C R Andrew (rep D Pears), C D Morris;
J Leonard, B C Moore, J A Probyn, M C Bayfield, W A Dooley,
M G Skinner, D Richards, P J Winterbottom
England scorers: *Tries:* Webb, Underwood, Morris, penalty try
Conversions: Webb 3   *Penalty goals:* Webb 3

WON 24–0 v WALES, 7th March 1992, Twickenham
*Carling scores in the first minute to send England on the way to back-to-back
Grand Slams for the first time since 1924, when Wavell Wakefield (a Sedbergh
product like Carling) was captain. England finish with 118 points for the
season, a new Five Nations record.*
England: J M Webb; S J Halliday, W D C Carling (*captain*) (rep
N J Heslop), J C Guscott, R Underwood; C R Andrew, C D Morris;
J Leonard, B C Moore, J A Probyn, M C Bayfield, W A Dooley,
M G Skinner, D Richards, P J Winterbottom
England scorers: *Tries:* Carling, Skinner, Dooley   *Conversions:* Webb 3
Penalty goals: Webb 2

WON 26–13 v CANADA, 17th October 1992, Wembley Stadium
The captain sets a new world record, passing Wilson Whineray (New Zealand) by leading his side to a 23rd victory in this first full rugby union international staged at Wembley Stadium.
England: J M Webb; I Hunter, W D C Carling (*captain*), J C Guscott, T Underwood; C R Andrew, C D Morris; J Leonard, C J Olver, V E Ubogu, M C Bayfield, W A Dooley, D Ryan, D Richards, P J Winterbottom
England scorers: *Tries:* Hunter 2, Winterbottom, Guscott *Penalty goals:* Webb 2

WON 33–16 v SOUTH AFRICA, 14th November 1992, Twickenham
In their first post-apartheid match with the Springboks, England establish their highest score for a Test against South Africa and become the first nation to pass 30 points against them.
England: J M Webb; T Underwood (rep P R de Glanville), W D C Carling (*captain*), J C Guscott, R Underwood; C R Andrew, C D Morris; J Leonard, B C Moore, V E Ubogu, M C Bayfield, W A Dooley, M C Teague, B B Clarke, P J Winterbottom
England scorers: *Tries:* T Underwood, Guscott, Morris, Carling *Conversions:* Webb 2 *Penalty goals:* Webb 3

WON 16–15 v FRANCE, 16th January 1993, Twickenham
England's ninth successive Five Nations win under Carling, one match shy of the England record set in the early 1920s. This is also their sixth victory in a row against France
England: J M Webb; I Hunter, W D C Carling (*captain*), J C Guscott, R Underwood; C R Andrew, C D Morris; J Leonard, B C Moore, J A Probyn, M C Bayfield, M O Johnson, M C Teague, B B Clarke, P J Winterbottom
England scorers: *Try:* Hunter *Conversion:* Webb *Penalty goals:* Webb 3

LOST 9–10 v WALES, 6th February 1993, Cardiff Arms Park
The unbeaten run stretching back to 1990 in the Five Nations ends in a one-point defeat. England appear dull and tired, and are unable to exercise any tactical grip on a buoyant Welsh XV. The new five-point try affects the outcome of an international match for the first time: under the points values of the previous season the result would have been 9-all.

England: J M Webb; I Hunter (rep P R de Glanville), W D C Carling (*captain*), J C Guscott, R Underwood; C R Andrew, C D Morris; J Leonard, B C Moore, J A Probyn, M C Bayfield, W A Dooley, M C Teague, B B Clarke, P J Winterbottom
England scorers: *Penalty goals:* Webb 2   *Dropped goal:* Guscott

WON 26–12 v SCOTLAND, 6th March 1993, Twickenham

England keep alive hopes of retaining the Five Nations title with a positive performance. The introduction of Stuart Barnes at 10 enables Carling and a renascent Jerry Guscott to show their abundant attacking skills. England's threequarters score all three tries.

England: J M Webb; T Underwood, W D C Carling (*captain*), J C Guscott, R Underwood; S Barnes, C D Morris; J Leonard, B C Moore, J A Probyn, M C Bayfield, W A Dooley, M C Teague, B B Clarke, P J Winterbottom
England scorers: *Tries:* Guscott, T Underwood, R Underwood *Conversion:* Webb   *Penalty goals:* Webb 3

LOST 3–17 v IRELAND, 20th March 1993, Lansdowne Road, Dublin

England slump to their heaviest Five Nations defeat of the Carling years. The side finishes third in the championship and several critics describe the match as marking the end of an era.

England: J M Webb; T Underwood, W D C Carling (*captain*), J C Guscott, R Underwood; S Barnes, C D Morris; J Leonard, B C Moore, J A Probyn, M C Bayfield, W A Dooley, M C Teague, B B Clarke, P J Winterbottom
England scorer: *Penalty goal:* Webb

LOST 18–20 v NEW ZEALAND, 12th June 1993, Lancaster Park, Christchurch

In the only Lions Test appearance of his career, Carling is paired with Jerry Guscott in the centre of a team led by Scotland's Gavin Hastings. The Lions lose this first Test by a last-minute penalty goal, but Carling's tour form is unimpressive and he is replaced by Wales's Scott Gibbs for the remainder of the series.

Lions: A G Hastings (*captain*); I C Evans, W D C Carling, J C Guscott, R Underwood; C R Andrew, C D Morris; N J Popplewell, K S Milne, A P Burnell, M C Bayfield, A I Reed, B B Clarke, D Richards, P J Winterbottom

292

Lions scorer: *Penalty goals:* Hastings 6

WON 15–9 v NEW ZEALAND, 27th November 1993, Twickenham
A famous win completes Carling's collection of victories as captain against all seven of the other senior International Board countries. Australia's Nick Farr-Jones is the only other captain who has achieved the feat.
England: J E B Callard; T Underwood, W D C Carling (*captain*), P R de Glanville, R Underwood; C R Andrew, K P P Bracken; J Leonard, B C Moore, V E Ubogu, M O Johnson, N C Redman, T A K Rodber, D Richards, B B Clarke
England scorers: *Penalty goals:* Callard 4   *Dropped goal:* Andrew

WON 15–14 v SCOTLAND, 5th February 1994, Murrayfield, Edinburgh
Carling breaks the world record set by Nick Farr-Jones of Australia for most major internationals as captain. He leads his country for the 37th time and registers his 28th win: an ongoing world record.
England: J E B Callard; T Underwood, W D C Carling (*captain*), P R de Glanville, R Underwood; C R Andrew, K P P Bracken; J Leonard, B C Moore, V E Ubogu, M O Johnson, M C Bayfield, J P Hall, B B Clarke, N A Back
England scorer: *Penalty goals:* Callard 5

LOST 12–13 v IRELAND, 19th February 1994, Twickenham
England lack purpose and disappoint their supporters who see the side lose at Twickenham in the Five Nations for the first time since 1988. Thus ends the national side's best home run in the championship since the 1920s.
England: J E B Callard; T Underwood, W D C Carling (*captain*), P R de Glanville, R Underwood; C R Andrew, K P P Bracken; J Leonard, B C Moore, V E Ubogu, M O Johnson, M C Bayfield, T A K Rodber, S O Ojomoh, N A Back
England scorer: *Penalty goals:* Callard 4

WON 18–14 v FRANCE, 5th March 1994, Parc des Princes, Paris
England grind out a morale-raising victory that means that they need to beat Wales by 15 points in the final match of the season to win the Five Nations trophy.
England: D Pears; I Hunter, W D C Carling (*captain*), P R de Glanville, R Underwood; C R Andrew, C D Morris; J Leonard, B C Moore, V E Ubogu, M O Johnson, N C Redman, T A K Rodber, S O Ojomoh, B B Clarke

England scorer: *Penalty goals:* Andrew 5   *Dropped goal:* Andrew

WON 15–8 v WALES, 19th March 1994, Twickenham

Geoff Cooke retires as England manager and sees Carling, in his 40th match as captain, lead the side to a victory that denies Wales the Grand Slam. England fail, however, to win by a margin that is big enough to overhaul Wales's points difference and thus finish the Five Nations as runners-up. England's tenth-minute try is their first in six Tests.

England: I Hunter; T Underwood, W D C Carling (*captain*), P R de Glanville, R Underwood; C R Andrew (rep M J Catt), C D Morris; J Leonard, B C Moore, V E Ubogu, M O Johnson, N C Redman, T A K Rodber, D Richards, B B Clarke

England scorers: *Tries:* R Underwood, Rodber   *Conversion:* Andrew   *Penalty goal:* Andrew

WON 32–15 v SOUTH AFRICA, 4th June 1994, Loftus Versfeld, Pretoria

Carling gets the vote of confidence from new manager Jack Rowell to carry on as captain. England respond by posting their best-ever away performance in a Test against the southern hemisphere's super powers. 'We have peaked too early in my managerial career,' jokes Rowell afterwards.

England: P A Hull; T Underwood, W D C Carling (*captain*), P R de Glanville, R Underwood; C R Andrew, C D Morris; J Leonard, B C Moore, V E Ubogu, M C Bayfield, N C Redman, T A K Rodber, D Richards (rep S O Ojomoh), B B Clarke

England scorers: *Tries:* Clarke, Andrew   *Conversions:* Andrew 2   *Penalty goals:* Andrew 5   *Dropped goal:* Andrew

LOST 9–27 v SOUTH AFRICA, 11th June 1994, Newlands, Cape Town

A week later (and a year away from the third World Cup) England crash to their heaviest defeat for three years, losing by 18 points to a rejuvenated Springbok XV that records its first home Test win against a major nation for ten years. Carling plays his 37th consecutive England Test since 1989, overtaking the previous England record set by John Pullin.

England: P A Hull; T Underwood, W D C Carling (*captain*), P R de Glanville, R Underwood; C R Andrew, C D Morris; J Leonard, B C Moore, V E Ubogu, M C Bayfield, N C Redman, T A K Rodber, B B Clarke, S O Ojomoh

England scorer: *Penalty goals:* Andrew 3

WON 54–3 v ROMANIA, 12th November 1994, Twickenham
His 50th cap for England. This early season romp against Romania finds Carling and Jerry Guscott (back in the side after recuperating from injury) paired for the 29th time in Tests, a new world record for a centre partnership.
England: P A Hull; T Underwood, W D C Carling (*captain*),
J C Guscott, R Underwood; C R Andrew, C D Morris; J Leonard,
B C Moore, V E Ubogu, M O Johnson, M C Bayfield, T A K Rodber,
B B Clarke, S O Ojomoh
England scorers: *Tries:* T Underwood 2, R Underwood, Rodber,
Carling, penalty try   *Conversions:* Andrew 6   *Penalty goals:* Andrew 4

WON 60–19 v CANADA, 10th December 1994, Twickenham
England equal their highest ever score in a cap match.
England: P A Hull (rep M J Catt); T Underwood (rep P R de
Glanville), W D C Carling (*captain*), J C Guscott, R Underwood;
C R Andrew, K P P Bracken; J Leonard, B C Moore, V E Ubogu,
M O Johnson, M C Bayfield, T A K Rodber, D Richards, B B Clarke
England scorers: *Tries:* R Underwood 2, Catt 2, T Underwood,
Bracken   *Conversions:* Andrew 6   *Penalty goals:* Andrew 6

WON 20–8 v IRELAND, 21st January 1995, Lansdowne Road, Dublin
Carling begins his seventh Five Nations campaign as captain and shows that he retains all his old edge by scoring the opening try and making a steaming run to set up the ruck from which Tony Underwood scores a try.
England: M J Catt; T Underwood, W D C Carling (*captain*),
J C Guscott, R Underwood; C R Andrew, K P P Bracken; J Leonard,
B C Moore, V E Ubogu, M O Johnson, M C Bayfield, T A K Rodber,
D Richards, B B Clarke
England scorers: *Tries:* Carling, T Underwood, Clarke   *Conversion:*
Andrew   *Penalty goal:* Andrew

WON 31–10 v FRANCE, 4th February 1995, Twickenham
England's eighth successive win against France and their best winning margin against them since 1914.
England: M J Catt; T Underwood, W D C Carling (*captain*),
J C Guscott, R Underwood; C R Andrew, K P P Bracken; J Leonard,
B C Moore, V E Ubogu, M O Johnson, M C Bayfield, T A K Rodber,
D Richards, B B Clarke

England scorers: *Tries:* T Underwood 2, Guscott   *Conversions:*
Andrew 2   *Penalty goals:* Andrew 4

WON 23–9 v WALES, 18th February 1995, Cardiff Arms Park

Carling becomes the first England captain to lead a second winning side at
Cardiff.
England: M J Catt; T Underwood, W D C Carling (*captain*),
J C Guscott, R Underwood; C R Andrew, K P P Bracken; J Leonard,
B C Moore, V E Ubogu, M O Johnson, M C Bayfield, T A K Rodber,
D Richards, B B Clarke
England scorers: *Tries:* R Underwood 2, Ubogu   *Conversion:*
Andrew   *Penalty goals:* Andrew 2

WON 24–12 v SCOTLAND, 18th March 1995, Twickenham

Carling sets a unique record by captaining a third Grand Slam side. For only
the third time in history England start each match of a Five Nations season
with the same 15 players.
England: M J Catt; T Underwood, W D C Carling (*captain*),
J C Guscott, R Underwood; C R Andrew, K P P Bracken (temp rep
C D Morris); J Leonard (temp rep G C Rowntree), B C Moore,
V E Ubogu, M O Johnson, M C Bayfield, T A K Rodber, D Richards
(rep S O Ojomoh), B B Clarke
England scorer: *Penalty goals:* Andrew 7   *Dropped goal:* Andrew

WON 24–18 v ARGENTINA, 27th May 1995, King's Park, Durban

In the first match after the Old Farts crisis Carling is injured late in a drab
game that opens England's World Cup campaign. Knee and ankle injuries
mean that he is rested for the next pool match (another undistinguished
performance: a 27–20 win against Italy in which Rob Andrew deputises for
the captain).
England: M J Catt; T Underwood, W D C Carling (*captain*) (rep
P R de Glanville), J C Guscott, R Underwood; C R Andrew,
C D Morris; J Leonard, B C Moore, V E Ubogu, M O Johnson,
M C Bayfield, T A K Rodber, S O Ojomoh (temp rep N A Back),
B B Clarke
England scorer: *Penalty goals:* Andrew 6   *Dropped goals:* Andrew 2

WON 44–22 v WESTERN SAMOA, 4th June 1995, King's Park, Durban

Carling's 50th Test as England captain. He returns to lead England to a
much improved performance in a gruelling match against the hard-tackling

Samoans. For the first time, England complete their World Cup preliminaries with three wins in three pool matches.
England: J E B Callard; I Hunter, W D C Carling (*captain*) (rep
D P Hopley), P R de Glanville, R Underwood; M J Catt, C D Morris;
G C Rowntree (rep J Mallett), R G R Dawe, V E Ubogu,
M O Johnson, R J West, S O Ojomoh, D Richards (rep B C Moore),
N A Back (rep T A K Rodber who was temp rep by K P P Bracken)
England scorers: *Tries:* R Underwood 2, penalty try, Back
Conversions: Callard 3   *Penalty goals:* Callard 5   *Dropped goal:* Catt

WON 25–22 v AUSTRALIA, 11th June 1995, Newlands, Cape Town
Last-minute win takes England into their second successive World Cup semi-final. It is England's tenth consecutive Test win, equalling the national record set between 1882 and 1886.
England: M J Catt; T Underwood, W D C Carling (*captain*),
J C Guscott, R Underwood; C R Andrew, C D Morris; J Leonard,
B C Moore, V E Ubogu, M O Johnson, M C Bayfield, T A K Rodber,
D Richards (temp rep S O Ojomoh), B B Clarke
England scorers: *Try:* T Underwood   *Conversion:* Andrew   *Penalty goals:* Andrew 5   *Dropped goal:* Andrew

LOST 29–45 v NEW ZEALAND, 18th June 1995, Newlands, Cape Town
End of the World Cup road for England as the All Blacks register a then record highest score for a Test team against England. Carling scores two consolation tries to take his tally for England into double figures.
England: M J Catt; T Underwood, W D C Carling (*captain*),
J C Guscott, R Underwood; C R Andrew, C D Morris; J Leonard,
B C Moore, V E Ubogu, M O Johnson, M C Bayfield, T A K Rodber,
D Richards, B B Clarke
England scorers: *Tries:* R Underwood 2, Carling 2   *Conversions:*
Andrew 3   *Penalty goal:* Andrew

LOST 9–19 v FRANCE, 22nd June 1995, Loftus Versfeld, Pretoria
England lose to France for the first time since 1988 in this third/fourth place play-off. Defeat means that England will have to play qualifying matches before reaching the final stages of the 1999 competition.
England: M J Catt; I Hunter, W D C Carling (*captain*), J C Guscott,
R Underwood; C R Andrew, C D Morris; J Leonard, B C Moore,

V E Ubogu, M O Johnson, M C Bayfield, T A K Rodber,
S O Ojomoh, B B Clarke
England scorer: *Penalty goals:* Andrew 3

LOST 14–24 v SOUTH AFRICA, 18th November 1995, Twickenham
England's first Test of the professional era. They lose their third match in a row for the only time during Carling's Test career. The captain is carried off in the closing minutes suffering from concussion.
England: J E B Callard; D P Hopley, W D C Carling (*captain*) (rep P R de Glanville), J C Guscott, R Underwood; M J Catt, K P P Bracken; J Leonard, M P Regan, V E Ubogu, M O Johnson, M C Bayfield, T A K Rodber (rep L B N Dallaglio), B B Clarke, R A Robinson
England scorers: *Try:* de Glanville   *Penalty goals:* Callard 3

WON 27–9 v WESTERN SAMOA, 16th December 1995, Twickenham
Although England win comfortably, few of the home XV distinguish them-selves in a dull match which prompts many among the 78,000 capacity crowd to produce a barrage of catcalls.
England: M J Catt; D P Hopley, W D C Carling (*captain*), J C Guscott, R Underwood; P J Grayson, M J S Dawson; G C Rowntree, M P Regan, J Leonard, M O Johnson, M C Bayfield, T A K Rodber, B B Clarke, L B N Dallaglio
England scorers: *Tries:* Dallaglio, Underwood   *Conversion:* Grayson   *Penalty goals:* Grayson 5

LOST 12–15 v FRANCE, 20th January 1996, Parc des Princes, Paris
England lose their opening Five Nations match for the first time since Carling entered the side in 1988.
England: M J Catt; J M Sleightholme, W D C Carling (*captain*), J C Guscott, R Underwood; P J Grayson, M J S Dawson; G C Rowntree, M P Regan, J Leonard, M O Johnson, M C Bayfield, S O Ojomoh, B B Clarke (temp rep D Richards), L B N Dallaglio
England scorer: *Penalty goals:* Grayson 2   *Dropped goals:* Grayson 2

WON 21–15 v WALES, 3rd February 1996, Twickenham
England win an indifferent match against a lively Welsh side. Despite giving his all the captain is unable to lift his side to the heights of the previous

Grand Slam season, though his influence is clearly missed after he leaves the field injured in the 53rd minute.
England: M J Catt; J M Sleightholme, W D C Carling (*captain*) (rep P R de Glanville), J C Guscott, R Underwood; P J Grayson, M J S Dawson; G C Rowntree, M P Regan, J Leonard, M O Johnson, M C Bayfield, T A K Rodber, B B Clarke, L B N Dallaglio
England scorers: *Tries:* Underwood, Guscott   *Conversion:* Grayson *Penalty goals:* Grayson 3

WON 18–9 v SCOTLAND, 2nd March 1996, Murrayfield, Edinburgh

England deny Scotland the Grand Slam and keep alive their own chances of retaining the Five Nations title. A grinding win is England's seventh in succession against the Scots, but does little to silence extensive criticism of England's narrow tactical approach.
England: M J Catt; J M Sleightholme, W D C Carling (*captain*), J C Guscott, R Underwood; P J Grayson, M J S Dawson; G C Rowntree, M P Regan, J Leonard, M O Johnson, G S Archer, B B Clarke, D Richards (rep T A K Rodber), L B N Dallaglio
England scorer: *Penalty goals:* Grayson 6

WON 28–15 v IRELAND, 16th March 1996, Twickenham

Carling stands down as captain after leading the side in 32 Five Nations matches of which 25 were won, one drawn and six lost. A freak first-half injury forces him to watch out the game from the stands. England win the Triple Crown for the fourth time under his captaincy and pick up the Five Nations title also for the fourth time in his reign.
England: M J Catt; J M Sleightholme, W D C Carling (*captain*) (rep P R de Glanville), J C Guscott, R Underwood; P J Grayson, M J S Dawson; G C Rowntree, M P Regan, J Leonard, M O Johnson, G S Archer, B B Clarke, D Richards, L B N Dallaglio (temp rep T A K Rodber)
England scorers: *Try:* Sleightholme   *Conversion:* Grayson   *Penalty goals:* Grayson 6   *Dropped goal:* Grayson

WON 54–21 v ITALY, 23rd November 1996, Twickenham

Carling's continued availability for Test duty coupled with his impressive club form for Harlequins make him an automatic choice for the side captained by co-centre Phil de Glanville. His forceful play shows that he has lost none of his appetite for Test rugby.

England: T R G Stimpson; J M Sleightholme, W D C Carling, P R de Glanville (*captain*), A A Adebayo; M J Catt, A C T Gomarsall (rep K P P Bracken); G C Rowntree, M P Regan (rep P B T Greening), J Leonard (rep R J K Hardwick), M O Johnson, S D Shaw, T A K Rodber, C M A Sheasby, L B N Dallaglio
England scorers: *Tries:* Gomarsall 2, Sleightholme, Johnson, Dallaglio, Rodber, Sheasby   *Conversions:* Catt 5   *Penalty goals:* Catt 3

WON 20–18 v ARGENTINA, 14th December 1996, Twickenham
With de Glanville sidelined through injury, Jason Leonard becomes makeshift captain. Carling and his faithful consort Jerry Guscott are the only members of the home XV who shine in a disappointing England performance.
England: N D Beal; J M Sleightholme, W D C Carling, J C Guscott, T Underwood; M J Catt, A C T Gomarsall; G C Rowntree, M P Regan, J Leonard (*captain*), M O Johnson, S D Shaw, T A K Rodber, C M A Sheasby (rep B B Clarke), L B N Dallaglio
England scorers: *Try:* Leonard   *Penalty goals:* Catt 5

WON 41–13 v SCOTLAND, 1st February 1997, Twickenham
Carling fires the backs to a record England score for a Five Nations match. The former captain also becomes only the fourth Englishman to reach a dozen tries in Tests when he crosses late in the second half.
England: T R G Stimpson; J M Sleightholme, W D C Carling, P R de Glanville (*captain*), T Underwood; P J Grayson, A C T Gomarsall; G C Rowntree, M P Regan, J Leonard, M O Johnson, S D Shaw, L B N Dallaglio, T A K Rodber, R A Hill
England scorers: *Tries:* penalty try, Gomarsall, Carling, de Glanville   *Conversions:* Grayson 3   *Penalty goals:* Grayson 5

WON 46–6 v IRELAND, 15th February 1997, Lansdowne Road, Dublin
In his 70th England Test Carling has another sound game in a side that registers a then biggest winning margin for any Five Nations match.
England: T R G Stimpson; J M Sleightholme, W D C Carling (rep J C Guscott), P R de Glanville (*captain*), T Underwood; P J Grayson, A C T Gomarsall (rep A S Healey); G C Rowntree, M P Regan, J Leonard, M O Johnson, S D Shaw, L B N Dallaglio, T A K Rodber, R A Hill
England scorers: *Tries:* Sleightholme 2, Underwood 2, Hill, Gomarsall   *Conversions:* Grayson 2   *Penalty goals:* Grayson 4

LOST 20–23 v FRANCE, 1st March 1997, Twickenham
This is only the third home Five Nations defeat suffered during Carling's England career. In his last Twickenham international he is part of a side that plays brilliantly to run up a seemingly unassailable 20–6 lead. France, however, are allowed to score 17 points in the last quarter to win a remarkable match.
England: T R G Stimpson; J M Sleightholme, W D C Carling, P R de Glanville (*captain*), T Underwood; P J Grayson, A C T Gomarsall; G C Rowntree, M P Regan, J Leonard, M O Johnson, S D Shaw, L B N Dallaglio, T A K Rodber, R A Hill
England scorers: *Try:* Dallaglio   *Penalty goals:* Grayson 4   *Dropped goal:* Grayson

WON 34–13 v WALES, 15th March 1997, Cardiff Arms Park
His 72nd and last England Test is also the last staged on the old Arms Park. This is England's best ever win at Cardiff and Carling, together with Jason Leonard, Jerry Guscott and Rob Andrew, plays in his third winning Test at the ground. England finish runners-up in the Five Nations, but win their third successive Triple Crown.
England: T R G Stimpson; J M Sleightholme (rep J C Guscott), W D C Carling, P R de Glanville (*captain*), T Underwood; M J Catt (rep C R Andrew), A S Healey; G C Rowntree (rep D J Garforth), M P Regan (rep P B T Greening), J Leonard, M O Johnson, S D Shaw, B B Clarke (rep C M A Sheasby), T A K Rodber, R A Hill
England scorers: *Tries:* Stimpson, Underwood, Hill, de Glanville *Conversions:* Catt 4   *Penalty goals:* Catt 2

WILL CARLING'S PLACE IN WORLD TEST RECORDS

(to the end of northern hemisphere season 1998)

MOST CAPPED PLAYERS
(figures in brackets denote Tests for the Lions)

Caps	Player	Career span
111	P Sella (France)	1982 to 1995
101	D I Campese (Australia)	1982 to 1996
93	S Blanco (France)	1980 to 1991
92	S B T Fitzpatrick (N Zealand)	1986 to 1997
91 (6)	R Underwood (England/Lions)	1984 to 1996
81 (12)	C M H Gibson (Ireland/Lions)	1964 to 1979
80 (17)	W J McBride (Ireland/Lions)	1962 to 1975
79 (7)	I C Evans (Wales/Lions)	1987 to 1998
76 (5)	C R Andrew (England/Lions)	1985 to 1997
73 (1)	**W D C Carling (England/Lions)**	**1988 to 1997**

MOST TESTS AS CAPTAIN

Tests	Captain	Span
59	**W D C Carling (England)**	**1988 to 1996**
51	S B T Fitzpatrick (N Zealand)	1992 to 1997
36	N C Farr-Jones (Australia)	1988 to 1992
34	J-P Rives (France)	1978 to 1984
34	P Saint-André (France)	1994 to 1997
30	W J Whineray (N Zealand)	1958 to 1965
29	J F Pienaar (S Africa)	1993 to 1996

MOST TESTS AS A CENTRE

Tests	Player	Span
104	P Sella (France)	1982 to 1995
73 (1)	**W D C Carling (England/Lions)**	**1988 to 1997**

WILL CARLING'S PLACE IN ENGLAND'S TEST RECORDS

(to the end of northern hemisphere season 1998 and including team records set during his captaincy)

TEAM RECORDS

MOST CONSECUTIVE TEST WINS
10   1882 v *W*, 1883 v *I,S*, 1884 v *W,I,S*, 1885 v *W,I*, 1886 v *W,I*
10   1994 v R,C, 1995 v I,F,W,S,Arg,It,WS,A

MOST CONSECUTIVE TESTS WITHOUT DEFEAT

Matches	Wins	Draws	Period
12	10	2	1882 to 1887
11	10	1	1922 to 1924
10	6	4	1878 to 1882
10	**10**	**0**	**1994 to 1995**

MOST POINTS IN A MATCH

Pts	Opponents	Venue	Year
60	Japan	Sydney	1987
60	**Canada**	**Twickenham**	**1994**
60	Wales	Twickenham	1998
58	Romania*	Bucharest	1989
58	**Fiji**	**Twickenham**	**1989**
54	**Romania**	**Twickenham**	**1994**
54	**Italy**	**Twickenham**	**1996**

* denotes that Carling was unavailable through injury

MOST TRIES IN A MATCH

Tries	Opponents	Venue	Year
13	Wales	Blackheath	1881
10	Japan	Sydney	1987
10	**Fiji**	**Twickenham**	**1989**

CAREER RECORDS

MOST CAPPED PLAYERS

Caps	Player	Career span
85	R Underwood	1984 to 1996
72	**W D C Carling**	**1988 to 1997**
71	C R Andrew	1985 to 1997
64	B C Moore	1987 to 1995
63	J Leonard	1990 to 1998

MOST CONSECUTIVE TESTS

Tests	Player	Span
44	**W D C Carling**	**1989 to 1995**
40	J Leonard	1990 to 1995
36	J V Pullin	1968 to 1975
33	W B Beaumont	1975 to 1982
30	R Underwood	1992 to 1996

MOST TESTS AS CAPTAIN

Tests	Captain	Span
59	**W D C Carling**	**1988 to 1996**
21	W B Beaumont	1978 to 1982
13	W W Wakefield	1924 to 1926
13	N M Hall	1949 to 1955
13	R E G Jeeps	1960 to 1962
13	J V Pullin	1972 to 1975

CAPTAINCY SUMMARY

Opponents	Played	Won	Drawn	Lost
Argentina	4	3	0	1
Australia	4	2	0	2
Canada	2	2	0	0
Fiji	2	2	0	0

table continues

CAPTAINCY SUMMARY [continued]

Opponents	Played	Won	Drawn	Lost
France	10	8	0	2
Ireland	8	6	0	2
Italy	1	1	0	0
New Zealand	3	1	0	2
Romania	1	1	0	0
Scotland	9	7	1	1
South Africa	4	2	0	2
United States	1	1	0	0
Wales	8	6	0	2
Western Samoa	2	2	0	0
OVERALL RECORD	**59**	**44**	**1**	**14**

YOUNGEST CAPTAINS

Name	Debut as captain	Age
J Daniell	v Ireland 1900	21 yrs, 1 month
L A N Slocock	v Scotland 1908	21 yrs, 2 months
P D Howard	v Ireland 1931	22 yrs, 1 month
W D C Carling	**v Australia 1988**	**22 yrs, 10 months**

MOST TESTS IN INDIVIDUAL POSITIONS

Position	Player	Tests	Span
Full-back	J M Webb	33	1987 to 1993
Wing	R Underwood	85	1984 to 1996
Centre	**W D C Carling**	**72**	**1988 to 1997**
Fly-half	C R Andrew	70	1985 to 1997
Scrum-half	R J Hill	29	1984 to 1991
Prop	J Leonard	63	1990 to 1998
Hooker	B C Moore	63*	1987 to 1995
Lock	W A Dooley	55	1985 to 1993
Flanker	P J Winterbottom	58	1982 to 1993
No. 8	D Richards	47*	1986 to 1996

excludes an appearance as a temporary replacement

MOST TRIES IN TESTS

Tries	Player	Tests	Career
49	R Underwood	85	1984 to 1996
18	C N Lowe	25	1913 to 1923
18	J C Guscott	52	1989 to 1998
13	T Underwood	25	1992 to 1997
12	**W D C Carling**	**72**	**1988 to 1997**

WILL CARLING'S HARLEQUINS CAREER: 1987–1997

League   Made 97 Division One appearances, scoring 162 points including 20 tries.

Cup Finals   Made four appearances as follows:

WON 28–22 v BRISTOL, 30th April 1988, Twickenham
Carling's two tries set up Quins' win in their first appearance in a Cup final. The victory breaks Bath's four-year stranglehold on the Cup and is a fitting reward for the club's inventive approach on the field. One critic describes the game as, 'the best of the 17 finals so far'.
Harlequins: S E Thresher; A T Harriman, J L B Salmon, W D C Carling, E G Davis; A L Thompson, R H Q B Moon; P S Curtis, C J Olver (*captain*), A R Mullins, N G B Edwards, P J Ackford, M G Skinner, R S Langhorn, T P Bell
Harlequins scorers: *Tries:* Carling 2, Harriman   *Conversions:* Thresher, Salmon   *Penalty goals:* Salmon 3, Thresher

WON 25–13 v NORTHAMPTON, 4th May 1991, Twickenham
Carling stars in a lively backline that scores three of the Quins' four tries in an exciting final that goes into extra time.
Harlequins: S E Thresher; A T Harriman, W D C Carling, S J Halliday, E G Davis; D Pears, R J Glenister; J Leonard, B C Moore, A R Mullins, T Coker, P J Ackford, M G Skinner, R S Langhorn, P J Winterbottom (*captain*)
Harlequins scorers: *Tries:* Langhorn, Harriman, Halliday, Glenister   *Conversions:* Pears 3   *Penalty goal:* Pears

LOST 12–15 v BATH, 2nd May 1992, Twickenham
Quins are beaten in the final minute of extra time by a long-range drop-goal kicked by Stuart Barnes. In his third final, Carling wins praise for the strength of his kicking game in attack.
Harlequins: D Pears; M A Wedderburn, W D C Carling, S J Halliday, E G Davis; A P Challinor, T C Luxton; M J Hobley, B C Moore, A R Mullins, N G B Edwards, P J Ackford, M P Russell, C M A Sheasby, P J Winterbottom (*captain*)
Harlequins scorers: *Try:* Winterbottom   *Conversion:* Pears   *Penalty goals:* Pears 2

LOST 16–23 v LEICESTER, 1st May 1993, Twickenham
Carling becomes one of only two Quins (Andy Mullins is the other) to play in all four of the club's Twickenham finals.
Harlequins: K A Bray; C S Madderson, W D C Carling,
G J Thompson, J R Alexander; A P Challinor, R J Glenister;
J Leonard, N Killick, A R Mullins, A C W Snow, R S Langhorn,
M P Russell, C M A Sheasby, P J Winterbottom (*captain*)
Harlequins scorers: *Try:* Glenister   *Conversion:* Challinor   *Penalty goals:* Challinor 3

INDEX